D0652468

Making
Words Dance

Making Words Dance

Reflections on Red Smith, Journalism, and Writing

EDITED AND WITH AN INTRODUCTION
BY ROBERT SCHMUHL

PROLOGUE BY TERENCE SMITH

**Andrews McMeel
Publishing, LLC**

Kansas City • Sydney • London

Making Words Dance copyright © 2010 by the University of Notre Dame. Prologue copyright © 2010 by Terence Smith. Articles by Red Smith copyright © 2010 by the Estate of Walter W. Smith.. All rights reserved. Printed in the United States of America. No part of this book may be used or reproduced in any manner whatsoever without written permission except in the case of reprints in the context of reviews. For information, write Andrews McMeel Publishing, LLC, an Andrews McMeel Universal company, 1130 Walnut Street, Kansas City, Missouri 64106.

10 11 12 13 14 RR4 10 9 8 7 6 5 4 3 2 1

ISBN-13: 978-0-7407-9009-6
ISBN-10: 0-7407-9009-9

Library of Congress Control Number: 2009939476

www.andrewsmcmeel.com

ATTENTION: SCHOOLS AND BUSINESSES

Andrews McMeel books are available at quantity discounts with bulk purchase for educational, business, or sales promotional use. For information, please write to: Special Sales Department, Andrews McMeel Publishing, LLC, 1130 Walnut Street, Kansas City, Missouri 64106.

For Rev. Theodore M. Hesburgh, C.S.C.,
Notre Dame's second founder
and consummate *homme engagé*,
with admiration and gratitude

Contents

PREFACE

This book provides a quarter-century chorus of tribute for a newspaper columnist with an enduring legacy and appeal. When Red Smith died in 1982, the University of Notre Dame decided to honor a revered alumnus in journalism by creating a lecture series in his name. Whether examining the state of news in America, celebrating stylish writing, or both, the Red Smith Lecture in Journalism is a continuing reminder of the value and values of the craft Smith practiced for fifty-five years.

In the pages that follow, some of this country's most respected journalists and writers focus on subjects that are simultaneously timely and timeless. From James Reston's lecture in 1983 through Tim Russert's in 2008, the reader can trace the revolutionary change that's been taking place throughout the news media and the media in general over the past twenty-five years. But continuity abides, too, especially the magic of engaging prose, with words that dance, in telling the public what's happening, who might be involved, and why it's significant.

To a certain extent, these lectures provide a running historical account of American journalism in the late twentieth and early twenty-first centuries. Because news people naturally tend to gravitate to contemporary affairs, a reference here or there might elude a younger reader. A brief Google search will solve the mystery—and, truth be told, the larger point of the lecture is more important. The prologue and introduction focus directly on Smith, the man and the writer, and these sections appear in this volume for the first time.

Since its beginning, the Smith Lecture series has sought to foster good writing. Each invited speaker is asked to come to Notre Dame to deliver the talk, with the understanding that a revised text of the remarks will be published. These booklets are then distributed to journalists and educators, with multiple copies often used in newsrooms and classrooms to discuss issues raised in the lecture.

The presentation of the lectures on the Notre Dame campus and their later publication have never followed a strict, repeating pattern or format. Terence Smith (Red's son, a Notre Dame alumnus and a noted print and broadcast journalist) has frequently participated in activities by talking about his father or introducing the speaker. After Murray Kempton and

Dave Kindred delivered their lectures, formal responses to the remarks by well-known commentators visiting the university followed, and they are reprinted in this book. Some speakers have engaged in postlecture discussions with the public; others have declined to do so. Some statements from question-and-answer periods appear here, particularly those that contribute perceptions distinct from the lecture or that amplify points mentioned in the prepared remarks.

Because most lectures recognize Smith's literary skills, representative examples—from meticulously reported columns to truth-stretching personal tales, from the traditional column to the more comprehensive magazine feature—appear throughout the volume and separate each talk. Young readers, in particular, will have the chance to see (and even study) how journalism, often composed on deadline, can aspire to be literature.

Two Smith Lecturers, Art Buchwald (in 1988) and Robert Maynard (in 1989), delivered their talks, but neither submitted a final version for publication. Buchwald visited Notre Dame the day the Red Smith Collection was dedicated at the university's Theodore M. Hesburgh Library. All of Smith's papers, books, writing tools, and sports memorabilia were donated to his alma mater in September 1987 and opened to the public on March 23, 1988.

Buchwald donated his honorarium to the Red Smith Writing Scholarship at Notre Dame, which had been created by Smith's family and friends shortly after his death. Buchwald had previously been the principal speaker at a luncheon in Washington, D.C., on behalf of the scholarship fund. Rather than a formal disquisition on journalism, the satiric columnist's performance on campus ("While the Gipper Slept") was vintage Buchwald, with quips and one-liners convulsing the assembled crowd.

As the editor and owner of the *Oakland Tribune* and a columnist for Universal Press Syndicate, Maynard was always confronting daily deadlines to meet professional obligations, and then in 1988 he began an extended battle with cancer. Unfortunately, he was never able to complete to his satisfaction a written version of his manuscript, "Red Smith's America and Mine," before his untimely death in 1993.

Throughout his decades as a columnist, Smith saw his writing enjoy second and third lives in books and other publications. One of the funniest columns he ever composed—describing the fire-and-ice ritual akin to "human sacrifice" he endured during a sauna in Finland—was published in the *New York Herald Tribune* on July 29, 1952, with a later appearance in Smith's collection *Views of Sport* (1954). *Reader's Digest* featured this "joust with the mother tongue" in its August 1968 editions, which were circulated in English and several other languages worldwide.

Similarly, several Smith Lectures have found their way into anthologies, newspapers, and magazines. Charles Kuralt's words in "The View from the Road" are the most traveled, including stops in journalism textbooks and, yes, *Reader's Digest*.

In the biography *Sportswriter: The Life and Times of Grantland Rice*, published by Oxford University Press in 1993, Charles Fountain looks beyond his principal subject and Rice's achievements to observe, "Anyone who has read an American sports page in the second half of the twentieth century has felt the influence of Red Smith. No American newspaper writer—hell, no American writer period—ever took greater pride in the craft than did Walter Wellesley Smith of Green Bay, Wisconsin."

The Red Smith Lecture in Journalism at Notre Dame continues to take pride in its namesake and the craft he honored with his memorable prose. Part celebration of one life, part tutorial in the writer's art, and part examination of the state of American journalism, the ensuing pages give permanence to that enduring pride.

— **ROBERT SCHMUHL**
NOTRE DAME, INDIANA

Rare Red Smith

BY ROBERT SCHMUHL

I f you look closely at the photograph of Red Smith on the cover of his collection of newspaper columns, *To Absent Friends*, you will see volumes of poetry chockablock with sports encyclopedias in the bookcase behind him. For readers of Smith's writing, the shelving is neither incongruous nor haphazard. In his work, literary accomplishment went hand in hand with athletic competition, verse alongside versus.

Throughout nearly four decades of his fifty-five-year career in journalism, Smith piled up recognition like cordwood. A 1958 *Newsweek* cover story called him "Star of the Press Box," and a 1981 *60 Minutes* profile on CBS went further: "America's foremost newspaperman." The Pulitzer Prize he won for commentary in 1976 noted, "In an area heavy with tradition and routine, Mr. Smith is unique in the erudition, the literary quality, the vitality and freshness of viewpoint he brings to his work and in the sustained quality of his columns."

Acclaim didn't end with his death in 1982. At the close of the twentieth century, *Editor & Publisher* impaneled a journalistic jury to select the twenty-five most influential newspaper professionals of the past hundred years. Smith was there—along with H. L. Mencken and Walter Lippmann—and the only sportswriter on the honor roll.

Achieving the stature of superlatives and a lasting legacy is a story of competition comparable to the careers of many sports figures Smith chronicled. Arriving at journalism's equivalent to the big leagues came only after an extended apprenticeship, and later years featured a comeback tale worthy of a veteran athlete determined to stay on top.

Born Walter Wellesley Smith on September 25, 1905, he didn't adopt the distance-reducing byline "Red Smith" until 1936, when he started writing sports for the *Philadelphia Record*. Stints at the *Milwaukee Sentinel* and the *St. Louis Star* (and, later, *Star-Times*) followed graduation from the University of Notre Dame in 1927, and he handled general news assignments along with sports in St. Louis.

"I never had any soaring ambition to be a sportswriter, per se," Smith said in an oral autobiography for the book *No Cheering in the Press Box.* "I wanted to be a newspaperman, and came to realize I didn't really care which side of the paper I worked on."

Arriving in Philadelphia, Smith was unaware whether he'd be working for the city desk or in sports. What mattered—besides a larger paycheck—was that he was moving to an East Coast newspaper nearer the capital of American communications, New York City. Journalism was his passion rather than sports, a viewpoint that never changed.

"The guy I admire most in the world is a good reporter," he said in *No Cheering in the Press Box.* "I respect a good reporter, and I'd like to be called that. I'd like to be considered good and honest and reasonably accurate. The reporter has one of the toughest jobs in the world—getting as near the truth as possible is a terribly tough job."

With strong reporting his lodestar, Smith began in Philadelphia and was assigned to the sports beat. First as a staff writer and later as a seven-day-a-week columnist also filing event stories, Smith became a literate, witty, and unavoidable presence on the *Record* for nine years.

Smith's work caught the eye of Stanley Woodward, sports editor of the *New York Herald Tribune.* As Woodward tells it in *Sports Page* (1949), Smith was composing "probably 500,000 words a year" in Philadelphia. The *Herald Tribune* wanted "a first-class man" to fill out the sports department after World War II, and Smith moved to New York in the fall of 1945. The new hire "only needed to write one story a day"—an estimated two hundred thousand words per year—and Woodward could see the quality rise with the decline in quantity: "In my judgment he has become the greatest of all sports writers, by which I mean that he is better than all the ancients as well as the moderns."

Smith joined the *Herald Tribune* well into his writing prime—his first article was published September 24, 1945, one day before his fortieth birthday, with his inaugural column appearing December 5 of that year—and he immediately enhanced its reputation as "the newspaperman's newspaper," devoted to inventive rather than pedestrian prose. That commendable approach didn't survive the New York newspaper wars of the 1960s, however, and the *Herald Tribune* folded in 1966, with its ill-fated successor, the *World Journal Tribune*, lasting just another eight months until its demise in 1967.

But Smith's twenty-one years at the *Herald Tribune* kept proving

Woodward's judgment in *Sports Page*. When Grantland Rice died in 1954, Smith lost a close friend and roistering sidekick. Despite personal sorrow, movingly evoked in several columns, Smith was enlisted to fill the void left by Rice's death. As Ira Berkow explains in the biography *Red*, Smith became "the most widely syndicated sports columnist in the nation, with about 70 papers and some 20 million readers."

Besides his six columns a week, Smith also contributed articles to an array of national magazines (*The Saturday Evening Post, Collier's, Outdoor Life, Liberty, Holiday*), and he was the subject of flattering features in *Newsweek, Esquire, Time, Harper's*, and *Life*. In 1959, a few months after the *Newsweek* cover treatment, Smith and his wife, Catherine (Kay), invited viewers of Edward R. Murrow's popular CBS program *Person to Person* to their home in Stamford, Connecticut, television's certification of national reputation and celebrity.

Books appeared regularly. Collections of columns came out in 1950 (*Out of the Red*), 1954 (*Views of Sport*), 1961 (*Red Smith's Annual, 1961*), and 1963 (*The Best of Red Smith* and *Red Smith on Fishing*). In addition, Prentice Hall launched *The Red Smith Sports Series*, with such figures as Vince Lombardi and Bob Cousy collaborating with noted writers on personal narratives about their athletic lives.

For nearly two decades, Red Smith's name on his syndicated column, magazine pieces, and books created what in today's marketing parlance would be called a brand, the most readily identifiable and reliable mark of distinctive work. Except for *Views of Sport*, his name was a prominent feature on each book, and the phrase "Views of Sport" was the title of his well-known column.

Smith's work won a wide following, especially among those championing stylish, original prose. Ernest Hemingway devoted a scene in his novel *Across the River and into the Trees* (1950) to a character reading—and liking—Smith. In 1963, author Irwin Shaw sent Smith a letter, saying "how much I like your stuff." Shaw then told a story:

> A few years ago Hemingway was asked to name the three best books he had read that year and the cold, brilliant brute (who by that time was feuding with me as he feuded with a lot of his old friends) named books by Faulkner, you and me for his list. I couldn't have been more pleased or more in agreement with the man.

Shortly after this letter arrived, Smith sat down with the *Chicago Sun-Times* for a profile, published next to one of his syndicated columns. "I flinch whenever I see the word literature used in the same sentence with my name," he admitted. "I'm just a bum trying to make a living running a typewriter."

During the *Herald Tribune* years, Smith received awards (what Woodward sarcastically called "bottle caps") frequently but not the one he coveted most. When Arthur Daley, a sports columnist for the *New York Times*, won a Pulitzer Prize in 1956, consensus among the journalistic cognoscenti was that the first Pulitzer that went to a sports columnist had gone to the wrong recipient. As Smith's son, Terence, a print and broadcast journalist of distinction in his own right, told Berkow in *Red*, "My father was a fierce competitor who drove himself, who wanted and sought the kind of recognition that the prize represented. And he felt plainly and simply that if anyone was going to get the award, he should be the one."

Smith's principal competitor was himself. He engaged in an unending "joust with the mother tongue," as he phrased his wrestling matches with typewriters. But the period after the demise of the *Herald Tribune* was more professionally troubling than not winning a certain "bottle cap." Based in New York but without a major metropolitan New York newspaper to call home, he had to rely on syndication of his column (in, among other papers, the *Washington Post*, the *Boston Globe*, the *Los Angeles Times*, and the *Chicago Sun-Times*) to maintain his national reputation.

Then, late in 1971, when Smith was sixty-six, nearly five years of wandering in the sports wilderness ended when he signed to write a column for the *New York Times*, which he'd previously viewed as an institution akin to a cathedral. Smith's work went to five hundred more papers in America and abroad via the New York Times News Service, and, more importantly for him, he again had a marquee outlet in Manhattan. He wrote four columns a week for the *Times* during a decade there, with his final one appearing just four days before his death on January 10, 1982.

The years with the *Times* were among Smith's most significant and productive. The Pulitzer committee finally honored him (at age seventy), and magazine essays appeared in *Saturday Review, Esquire, American Heritage*, and *The New York Times Magazine*. In 1974, he became outdoor editor of *Argosy* with a regular feature "Red All Over," and the same year a new collection, *Strawberries in the Wintertime*, was published. Another he assembled, *To Absent Friends*, came out not long after his death. He also edited and introduced *Press Box: Red Smith's Favorite Sports Stories* (1976).

The *Times* coverage of Smith's death included a page one, two-column headline over a lengthy obituary: "Red Smith, Sports Columnist Who Won Pulitzer, Dies at 76." His perambulations on the sports beat concluded as he wished to be remembered—as a columnist *and* as a Pulitzer Prize recipient.

Competitive as Smith was in trying to write well, he presented himself as he rendered most subjects. "The natural habitat of the tongue is the left cheek," he often said, and that slant produced smiles or snickers. Early in his New York days, he submitted a sketch of himself to a periodical:

> Red Smith, christened Walter Wellesley Smith on a cold day in 1905 in Green Bay, Wis., has been bleeding out a daily column for the *Herald Tribune* for about three years. Previous conditions of servitude have included 10 years at hard labor on the *Philadelphia Record*, eight years on the *St. Louis Star-Times* and a year with the *Milwaukee Sentinel*. He admires sports for others and might have been a great athlete himself except that he is small, puny, slow, inept, uncoordinated, myopic and yellow. He is the proprietor of two small children, one large mortgage.

Frugal with the first-person pronoun, he referred to himself in columns as "the tenant in this literary flophouse," "a newspaper stiff," "a greenhorn," and even "a rube." Some self-references extended beyond a word or phrase. Describing himself after a colloquy he conducted in 1958 with Ford Frick, the commissioner of major league baseball, Smith wrote, "Mr. Frick's inquisitor was a seedy amateur with watery eyes behind glittering glasses, a retiring chin, a hole in his frowzy haircut, and a good deal of dandruff on the shoulders."

Although he poked fun at himself, his "turquoise and amethyst prose," and his sporting journalism cohort (typically "the sweaty literati," "typewriter jockeys," or "the flower of American letters"), Smith took his craft seriously. Late in his life during an interview, he recalled being "dragooned to speak to the advertising salesmen of the *Herald Tribune*. I got up and told a couple of stories and said, 'You fellas probably think I've got the softest job in the world. And as a matter of fact, I have. All you do is sit down and open a vein and bleed it out drop by drop.'" During another session with a reporter, he recalled a vow he made when he moved to New York: "I made up my mind that every time I sat down to a typewriter I would slash my veins and bleed and that I'd try to make each word dance."

For Smith, sanguinary metaphors and the writing process were inseparable. In 1949, he told *Esquire,* "I bleed." That same year *Newsweek* headlined a feature about him: "Smith, the Bleeder." Subsequent profiles unfailingly repeated the image, now interred in countless compilations of literary quotations, and in announcing his Pulitzer, the *New York Times* reported that he "confessed that writing a column is 'the easiest job in the world—all you have to do is open a vein and bleed it out, drop by drop.'"

The same man with the sponge-like photographic memory that could summon a precise detail about a sporting figure or event from a bygone era talked about the ordeal of composition with almost word-for-word consistency for decades.

Searching for the *mot juste,* firecracker phrase, or arresting image meant that a column could take six hours to write and produce a wastebasket full of crumpled copy paper. Smith was often the last person to leave a press box, and his home office (according to Berkow in *Red*) was designated "The Sweat Shop" or "Torture Chamber." The painstaking prose never seemed labored, however. As he liked to say, "You sweat blood to make it sound so smooth, so natural, it reads as though you knocked it off while running for a bus."

Despite learning literary moves and tricks from (in another Smith metaphor) "blacksmithing out" thousands of articles and millions of words, he told his biographer that age and experience never reduced the anguish: "Writing well always has been and always will be one of the most difficult of human endeavors. And it never gets easier."

The blank page became Smith's chief opponent, creating a lifelong love–hate relationship. "I hate to get to that typewriter," he said in a television interview not long after receiving the Pulitzer. "I love everything about my job, except the pain of writing, and that is the price I have to pay for this lovely job." He kept playing against himself in private so his exacting, winning prose would keep the public reading.

Literary connoisseurs understood Smith's self-competition and reacted to it. Introducing *The Best American Sports Writing 1997,* George Plimpton wore the double-billed cap of literary critic and creator of notable books on sporting subjects, such as *Out of My League* (1961) and *Paper Lion* (1966).

He recalled covering Secretariat's last horse race and watching "Red Smith at the press desk down the line, slamming away with two fingers at a little portable typewriter, absorbed in a cocoon of concentration. We were both on the same assignment . . . and seeing Red Smith at work tempted one to snap the top back on one's pen and hope for an assignment the next time that didn't involve him." Other writers harbored similar thoughts as they competed against themselves and against Smith.

Just as he had definite demands for his own work, Smith maintained fixed opinions about sports columns. In the main, he saw himself as an entertainer. "I've always had the notion," he said in *No Cheering in the Press Box*, "that people go to spectator sports to have fun and then they grab the paper to read about it and have fun again."

Similarly, in a sentiment he expressed almost as often as the one about the bloodletting involved in writing, he noted, "These are just little games that little boys can play, and it really isn't important to the future of civilization whether the Athletics or the Browns win. If you can accept it as entertainment, then I think that's what spectator sports are meant to be."

This playing-field-as-playful-place perspective kept Smith from inflating athletic contests to Armageddon battles or sports figures to Shakespearean heroes. Yet it never restricted his field of vision or panoramic view. "It can be stated as a law," he once wrote, "that the sportswriter whose horizons are no wider than the outfield fences is a bad sportswriter, because he has no sense of proportion and no awareness of the real world around him."

Unlike such journalists as Heywood Broun, Westbrook Pegler, and James Reston, who started in sports and subsequently shifted to political writing, Smith stuck with sports, except for the occasional assignment to cover national political conventions as the sporty, competitive spectacles they used to be. The "real world," though, kept intruding on Smith's writing.

The lead of a column in May 1958 put world affairs in perspective at the same time when Stan Musial of the St. Louis Cardinals was sweating to get his three-thousandth hit in the major leagues:

> France and Algeria heaved in ferment, South Americans chucked rocks at the goodwill ambassador from the United States, Sputnik III thrust its nose into the pathless realms of space—and the attention of some millions of baseball fans was concentrated on a grown man in flannel rompers swinging a stick on a Chicago playground called Wrigley Field.

Especially in his later years, Smith was willing to probe areas beyond the fun-and-games of sports. When he urged the United States to boycott the 1980 Olympic Games in Moscow to make a foursquare stand against the Soviet Union's invasion of Afghanistan, President Jimmy Carter and other public officials paid attention and ultimately decided not to have America compete. Smith saw his stand, controversial initially, as "common decency," telling a reporter, "How can you go over and play games with these people when they're committing a naked act of aggression against a neighboring country?"

Increasingly, big-time sports were more than larkish games of youth, and on occasion Smith was willing to assume the role of sports conscience. As Jane Leavy pointed out in a 1978 *Village Voice* profile, Smith's literary quality was just one factor in the Pulitzer Prize for commentary he won two years earlier. "Seven of the 10 columns submitted to the Pulitzer jury," she reported, "concerned the political implications and litigations surrounding our national pastimes."

Similar to Mark Twain's writing as he got older, Smith's addressed worldly problems more frequently and openly. Both writers came to realize that certain subjects demanded something more than the provocation of laughter. In Smith's precinct, the serpentine connections among sports, money, and politics clamored for analysis and appraisal, and with his advancing years, clouds kept popping up to darken the once sunny athletic fields.

Maintaining perspective and recognizing complexity were hallmarks of Smith's approach from his first days as a columnist; it's just that his later work, responding to the more tangled times of mammon's dubious influence, tended to spotlight more serious concerns. Back in 1955, he began one of his obituary columns ("A Fan Named Bob Sherwood") with a career-defending generalization before praising Sherwood's literary and political accomplishments:

> Some intellectuals deem an interest in games evidence of
> arrested development. . . . Theirs is a foolish snobbery that
> exposes their own inability to see a whole, round world in
> which games have a part along with politics and science
> and industry and art.

In other words, Smith and Sherwood shared the "sense of proportion" Smith saw as fundamental, with sporting life one pursuit among many. Others might possess greater significance, but you needed to see the complete picture.

A few months later, another elegiac column tried to come to terms with the many sides of Connie Mack, the baseball player, manager, and owner who participated in major league baseball for seven decades of his ninety-three years. The first two paragraphs introduce a person worthy of a Herman Melville novel:

> It is not for mortals anywhere to suggest that another has lived too long, yet for those who knew and, necessarily, loved him it is difficult to regard Connie Mack's last years as part and parcel of a life that was a beacon in our time. Toward the end he was old and sick and saddened, a figure of forlorn dignity bewildered by the bickering around him as the baseball monument that he had built crumbled away.
>
> That wasn't Connie Mack. Neither was the bloodless saint so often painted, a sanctimonious old Puritan patting babies on the skull and mumbling minced oaths and platitudes. As long as he was Connie Mack he was tough and human and clever. He was tough and warm and wonderful, kind and stubborn and courtly and unreasonable and generous and calculating and naïve and gentle and proud and humorous and demanding and unpredictable.

The repeated word *and*, along with the succession of descriptive adjectives, suggests the contradictions and dimensions of someone Smith had observed closely since his time in Philadelphia in the 1930s and 1940s. Later, recalling "the small foibles of his great humanity," Smith mentions Mack's "unfailing gift for getting names wrong."

In this case and others, Smith dramatized the departed in ways that brought them back to life for readers, making the collection *To Absent Friends* his most vibrant, comprehensive, and engaging book. The mini-biographies and personal remembrances provide orienting background that sprightly pieces describing a particular game, prizefight, or horse race tend to lack.

Even then, with Smith elbow to elbow with other reporters on the scene, the words still danced, after the bloody struggle of composition. More diamond cutter than blacksmith, he tried to make phrases sparkle and all facets of a column look finished. For Smith, a new gymnasium became "a center of the perspiring arts" and Ted Williams's spitting at baseball hecklers "a moist expression of contempt." A famous auto race was a "twelve-hour orgy of noise and grime" one day and "the great grease festival" the next. Bucking broncos were "four-legged outlaws" and a former boxer "a dressy little walking-stick of a man." A sports executive "smiled with the warmth of a brave man having splinters thrust under his fingernails," and an outfielder jumping to make a catch "stayed aloft so long he looked like an empty uniform hanging in its locker."

Smith made clichés turn cartwheels and perform backflips to mock the trite, tired prose then more prevalent than today in print journalism. The two words "teapot tempests" sounded fresher than their well-worn elders. The adage that today's newspaper wraps tomorrow's fish came out of Smith's typewriter as "these pages become a shroud for some obsolete haddock."

He playfully dismissed the sports section as a newspaper's "toy department," but Smith never wrote down to any suggested grade-school level for readers. He gave his copy a literate lift. Fishing to him was "piscicide," "basscicide," and "perchicide." A football tailback looked like a "frumious bandersnatch." For Horse of the Year honors in 1970, Personality was named "boss hoss," in a decision to which there was dissent. "Pooh," Smith exclaimed. "The perspicacious Mike Casale, the perceptive Dave Alexander . . . and the pertinacious Red Smith say Ta Wee."

Word-pictures derived from close observation. Knute Rockne's nose "had been remodeled by a baseball bat," and he "gave the impression that instead of dressing he just stood in a room and let clothes drop on him." In retirement Babe Ruth continued to travel at the center of a big-league entourage, with "a squad of cops fending off the autograph hounds and a horde of junior executives chuffing and scurrying like tugboats around a liner." For a miserable day at Santa Anita Turf Club, "the crowned heads of Hollywood turtled down into their minks and sables and probably saw nothing." A judge at the Westminster Kennel Club show "was imperious; he was painstakingly studious; he was profoundly authoritative of mien. He had splendid conformation—broad shoulders, white hair and an erect carriage—and was beautifully turned out in an ensemble of rich brown."

The clever phrasing and striking sketches—Smith thought the dog show dandy should have awarded first place to himself—decorated fully rounded essays that relied on traditional techniques of storytelling: a specific scene, discrete action, vivid characters, and delectable dialogue. In the annual anthology of *Best Sports Stories*, which began competition that included book publication in 1944 and continued until 1990, Smith was a frequent winner or runner-up in the news feature category. For stories written under deadline and usually as an immediate response to an event, the designation is appropriate, revealing Smith's skill as a reporter *and* writer.

Those anthologies and his own collections gave permanence to words that, in others' hands, often had the longevity of a mayfly. Red Smith was a rarity. To him, news features of daily journalism could aspire to become enduring. Indeed, six methodically selected book-length volumes reprinted Smith's work during his life, and three more have appeared posthumously: *To Absent Friends* and *The Red Smith Reader* in 1982 and *Red Smith on Baseball* in 2000.

Smith credited his journalism teacher at Notre Dame, John Michael Cooney, with classifying writers as either sprinters or milers. A column or magazine piece attracted the sprinter, and a book seemed more natural to someone preferring distance. Although personally bookish—he edited and provided forewords to nearly a dozen more volumes and read omnivorously himself—Smith rejected publishers' overtures to write his memoirs or treatises on sports-related subjects. "Thanks for the suggestion," he responded to one proposal, "but I'd rather commit adultery than do a book."

Smith's column, "that spelling lesson six days a week," in a phrase he repeated for two decades, became his vocation and abiding preoccupation. As early as 1949, he had rewritten "The Lord's Prayer" to request, "Give me my daily plinth," or a stone column's base. He started writing a column in Philadelphia in September 1939 and continued through January 1982. Over those four decades, his weekly output varied from seven to three, with the longest stretch at the *Herald Tribune* featuring six.

Despite his aversion to authorship and the regularity of a column deadline, Smith contributed longer articles to magazines at an astonishing rate for a notoriously slow writer. His byline ornamented big-circulation publications, but he also composed pieces for more obscure journals. In what today seems a faith-based rather than soiled-lucre commitment, he served as "contributing editor for sports" at *The Sign*, a Catholic monthly, from January 1954 through March 1966. Ten to twelve times a year Smith provided a less time-sensitive feature, periodically focusing on himself and his experiences with droll self-deprecation.

More than five-finger exercises of a two-fingered typist, these "essays" (the designation Smith preferred for such confections) match the prose standards of his syndicated column. A reminiscence in *The Sign* about

St. Louis Cardinal standout and Gas House Gang prankster Pepper Martin begins this way:

> Jostling crowds eddied and elbowed in the lobby of Philadelphia's Benjamin Franklin Hotel. In the eye of the storm stood a rawboned young man bearing the indelible stamp of rural America. His lank, brown hair was not quite tidy. On his extraordinary shoulders, his jacket fitted as though he had left the hanger in. He wore a smile that wouldn't come off, a wide, joyous smile that could have made him good-looking except for a great, curved beak in the middle of it.
>
> "Mr. Martin," a paunchy stranger asked, "where did you learn to run the way you do?"
>
> "Well, sir, I grew up in Oklahoma, and out there, once you start runnin' there ain't nothin' to stop you."
>
> "Pepper, how do you account for the way you're going?"
>
> "I dunno. I'm just takin' my natural swing, and the ball keeps hittin' the fat part of the bat."

Amusing paragraph after amusing paragraph, Pepper's portrait takes shape and comes to life. Martin's head-first base-stealing prowess ended "in a great bellywhopping slide, that hawk beak's plowing up dust like a yacht's prow splitting the waves" that made him "come up coated like a chocolate bar."

Curiously (and unfortunately), almost none of Smith's longer articles found their way into his book-length collections. Two fishing stories for *Sports Afield* appear in *Strawberries in the Wintertime*, but other volumes stick to columns—and to the sports he liked to follow. In *Views of Sport*, there are seven sections: "Flannel Rompers" (baseball), "The Cavalry" (horse racing), "Leather Goods" (boxing), "Points North" (the Olympics), "In Our Set" (personal and offbeat), "Long After Walton" (fishing), and "The Undergraduates" (college athletics, primarily football). Twenty years later, in *Strawberries in the Wintertime*, he provided nine witty headings, adding golf and outdoor adventures distinct from fishing to the roster.

To a certain extent (and to paraphrase Peter DeVries), winter—and winter sports—left Smith cold, worthy of dismissal in one column as "the empty months of basketball and bowling." Basketball and hockey, fan favorites of team competition during that season, didn't conform to narrative demands he imposed on his column. "What makes hockey and basketball difficult to write is the fact that they are running games," Smith told an interviewer shortly before he died. "The flow of the game goes up and down. They shoot at the goal and either score or miss. That's all there is to it."

Criticizing basketball served as a running joke in Smith's writing. In a 1951 essay for *Collier's*, "Anyone for Basketball?" he didn't hold back:

> The trouble with basketball is, it has made demigods out of carnival freaks. It has become a refuge for acromegalic accidents whom nature never meant for public exhibition in chemise and step-ins. It is the only sport in the world which places a bigger premium on a hyperpituitary condition than on muscles, speed, agility or combativeness.

Seventeen additional paragraphs extend this critique, including this summary judgment: "If it isn't the silliest game yet devised, it is administered by the silliest people outside the booby hatch."

Even with his hardwood reservations set in stone, Smith found basketball (or, in his frequent rendering, "bounceball") irresistible. A large trout he caught in the Chilean Andes "looked as long as a dishonest basketball player." One player guarding an opponent "adopts the techniques of a lovelorn octopus," and another "moves more like an institution than a man, with agonizing deliberation and great grinding of gears."

Yet, recalling a victory by St. John's University in the National Invitational Tournament, Smith confessed to being moved by the celebration engulfing his friend Joe Lapchick, the St. John's coach, and "tears stood in all four of these eyes." A touching response could supersede a comic crotchet this one time.

By definition, a column offers individual opinion, and late in life Smith formulated a generalization as revealing as the animus he directed at up-and-down sports: "I have known rogues and reformers and generally preferred the rogues."

Rogues were better copy, more completely human—and always pregnant with comic potential. Boxing and horse racing attracted (and abounded in) earthlings not usually associated with routine dailiness of American life. "There are more good stories and colorful people to be met on the backstretch of a racetrack than anywhere else," Smith said. "Now, I don't mean the rich owners. I am more interested in the trainers, grooms, hot-walkers, exercise boys and jockeys. There is hardly one of them who doesn't have a rags-to-riches or riches-to-rags story, or both."

The people of sports, characters of an absorbing human drama (and comedy), were Smith's principal concern, another reason *To Absent Friends* holds up so well as a compendium of prose portraits. Yes, you find the occasional sentimental lapse: "How can you say in a newspaper that a man had a beautiful soul?" But, in the main, warts still obtrude, providing flesh-and-blood roundness to the sketch. One football coach "was the toughest nice guy or the nicest tough guy I ever knew." Walter O'Malley, the major league owner who moved the Dodgers from Brooklyn to Los Angeles, possessed "financial acumen" that "ultimately made him the most powerful figure in baseball, where no other quality is held in such reverence as the ability to make one and one equal three." A jockey with barely a double-digit inseam becomes furious when mounts keep throwing him: "You wouldn't believe a man his size could contain so much rage."

Quoting Red Smith is dangerous. A phrase, sentence, or whole paragraph of literary grace leads invariably to another phrase, sentence, or paragraph of comparable merit. In his last column, "Writing Less—and Better?" he worried that cutting back from four to three per week would provide him less chance to be good or to recover from what he judged an unsatisfactory effort. At age seventy-six and with more than ten thousand columns to his name, Smith remained hopeful of improvement and still competitive. Consummate craftsman, he always believed future words might dance with new kicks and previously untried gyrations.

Three decades before his own death, Smith remarked about tennis champion Bill Tilden, "He would have been great in any age; he lived in the age that was exactly right for him." The same judgment could be made about the composer of that sentence. Stylish, memorable prose will find an audience regardless of how it's delivered: on newsprint or slick paper, between covers of a book, or via a computer screen. At a time when sports journalism often seems embalmed with clichés or empurpled with prose closer to parody than poetry, Smith continues to serve as an original and an exemplar.

But Smith thrived when newspapers still enjoyed their heyday and syndication of sports columns meant national stature for a New York–based writer. Today, with more and more newspapers struggling and greater emphasis on staff-written columns, the influence Smith achieved would be impossible. The success of ESPN as a multimedia enterprise helps sportswriters in major cities gain broad visibility, but the different means of distributing their views create a different kind of impact.

The spoken word, notably brash and quickly formulated, competes against the written one, with local columnists often becoming more well known for what they chatter about than what they compose more deliberately for their print outlets. It's not necessarily inferior—we're still talking about games little boys and girls can play—but it's clearly distinct from Smith's earlier era of a print-dominant culture.

The new media environment notwithstanding, Smith's shadow remains long. Besides the nine book-length collections, his writing still often finds its way into anthologies and other volumes. In *The Best American Sports Writing of the Century* (1999), editor David Halberstam selected five Smith columns, the most of any contributor, commenting that he "was far and away the best sports columnist of his time, and he stayed at the top of his game for more than thirty years: his columns at their best were like miniature short stories." The same year Halberstam's comprehensive collection came out, the Red Smith School was dedicated in Smith's hometown of Green Bay.

Shortly before his death, the Associated Press Sports Editors named its annual lifetime achievement award for Smith, and since 1983 the Red Smith Kentucky Derby Writing Contest has honored the best coverage of America's most celebrated race by invoking Smith's name. The Red Smith Handicap has been run at New York's Aqueduct Race Track the past quarter century, and the press box at Pimlico Race Course, home of the Preakness, was named for Smith in 1981.

At his alma mater, Notre Dame, both a scholarship in writing and a lecture series in journalism and writing have recognized Smith's life and career since 1983. Earlier, in 1968, the university awarded him one of several honorary degrees he received. As Smith was battling to make his New York comeback and eight years before Pulitzer distinction, the citation praised his "solid place in American letters" and positioned him on "the high plateau" of writers about sports. The scholarly scroll traced his work "back to Hazlitt and to Walton, perhaps to Homer, certainly to Ben Jonson; for, as Wolcott Gibbs said, there are only two great writers who have used their nicknames: Ben Jonson and Rare Red Smith."

Rare, indeed.

Remembering Red

BY TERENCE SMITH

I n its first quarter century, the Red Smith Lecture series has attracted some of the most thoughtful, literate, and entertaining journalistic voices of our times. All of them speak generously, even extravagantly, in these pages of my father as a journalist, sportswriter, columnist, and commentator on the American scene. He was all of those things.

But you might also want to know a little about him as a man, husband, father, mentor, career counselor, newspaperman, cartoonist, fisherman, outdoorsman, two-fingered typist, and notoriously inept handyman. He was all of those things, too.

To hear him tell it, his life and career just fell into place by happy happenstance. He grew up in Green Bay, Wisconsin, enjoying a classic *Boy's Life* sort of childhood, tramping through the woods, fishing in streams, playing baseball and football in backyards and empty lots. Vince Engel, the older brother of a friend, who taught him fly fishing, was something of a hero. Vince was going to Notre Dame and studying journalism. So Pop would do the same. Simple as that.

He did go to Notre Dame and study journalism and go on to a career in newspapers, but I doubt it was all that simple. Life rarely is. I suspect Notre Dame and newspapers constituted a means to fulfill the quiet ambition he developed to escape the confines of small-town life in Green Bay. In any event, he pursued it with the same steady determination he displayed later when he was writing seven columns a week, hustling freelance assignments on the side, and dreaming of going to New York. His career didn't just happen; he made it happen by hard work. The Smith family fortunes were modest, to say the least, so he worked for a year between high school and college and borrowed from a cousin to get the money to go to Notre Dame. Once there, he waited tables and edited the yearbook to get through the four years.

Graduating from Notre Dame in 1927, he was ready to leap into the world of big-time journalism. He told me he wrote fifty letters to papers around the country announcing his availability. He got one response, from the *New York Times*, which was "No."

Instead, he went to the *Milwaukee Sentinel* as a cub reporter for twenty-four dollars a week. He moved on to the *St. Louis Star*, where he met and married my mother and during which time my sister, Kit, was born. The next stop was Philadelphia, where I came along. Pop covered sports and wrote columns for ten years for the long-departed *Philadelphia Record* (always working for the second or lesser paper in town, my father claimed he killed every paper he ever wrote for, and with the exception of the *Sentinel* and, later, the *New York Times*, that was true).

There was a method to this itinerant madness: He was heading in crab-wise fashion toward New York, which was the epicenter of the newspaper world and his lifelong goal. To him, writing for a big paper in New York was akin to playing the Palace.

The initial palace proved to be the *New York Herald Tribune*, a "writer's paper." Those two decades, from 1946 to 1966, under the guiding hand of the great sports editor Stanley Woodward, were the period in which he flourished as a writer and a columnist with his own distinctive, witty, wry voice.

As a personality, Pop was often described as shy, diffident, modest about his own accomplishments—and he was. But he was also disciplined, ambitious, quietly competitive, and, in his understated way, proud of the recognition that came along in those years. He loved it—who wouldn't?—when Ernest Hemingway mentioned his writing approvingly in one of his novels and when Toots Shor ushered him straight to the highly visible table No. 1 in his famous saloon. When Grantland Rice died in 1954, Pop became the most widely syndicated sports columnist in the country. In 1958, he was a national figure, celebrated on the cover of *Newsweek* under the headline "Red Smith, Star of the Press Box." People recognized him on the street and at sports events, and although he adopted an "aw shucks" manner, I know he was grateful. He felt he had worked for it.

His competitive streak surfaced when not he, but Arthur Daley, his rival and opposite number on the *New York Times*, became the first sports columnist to win the Pulitzer Prize. For years afterward, Pop dismissed the Pulitzer as a hollow, self-indulgent token handed out by the journalistic old-boy network to its favorites. When he finally won *his* Pulitzer for distinguished commentary in 1976, I was the *Times'* correspondent in Israel. I called him from Jerusalem and got him on the phone in the *Times'* city room, where the champagne corks were popping.

"You'll refuse it, of course," I teased, deadpan. There was a pause and then he whispered conspiratorially into the phone: "Not on your life!"

People often marveled at his ear for dialogue: With only a few notes, he could re-create a pitch-perfect account of a locker room interview or running conversation and build most of an eight-hundred-word column around long blocks of unbroken dialogue. In part, it was childhood conditioning; for fun, he played memory games at home. Showing a flair for the flowery, he memorized the hundred-plus verses of the *Rubaiyat of Omar Khayyám*. Years later, growing up, I tested him by plucking a verse out of the middle of the *Rubaiyat*. He could pick it up and recite it forward or, frighteningly, backward. He could see the entire work on the printed page in his mind's eye. For fun, he entertained Kit and me by reciting Alfred Noyes's melodramatic epic *The Highwayman*, another poem stuck in his head from childhood, along with scores of verses from Shakespeare. Of course, now *The Highwayman* is stuck in my head as well.

But his legendary memory for sports statistics—he was invited onto television quiz shows as an expert—actually came from the reference books that lined the shelves of his study. "People think I can remember how many men were on base or what the count was in this game or that," he chuckled. "Of course I can, if I look it up."

He also treated us as kids with cartoons drawn on cocktail napkins and the back of envelopes. Every birthday or Christmas brought a hand-drawn card with a wonderful image lampooning some event of the past year. He was good and quick, capturing a profile with just a few strokes of a pen or pencil. And he greatly admired illustrators such as Willard Mullin, James Thurber, and Marc Simont. But although he flirted with the idea of making his living that way, in the end he decided he was better with words than pictures. In either case, he argued, it was better than lifting things.

The sports beat governed our life as a family: spring training in Florida, baseball's opening day, the Masters, racing's Triple Crown, opening day on the trout streams, the All-Star games, the U.S. Open at Forest Hills, fight camps in the Catskills before championship bouts, August racing at Saratoga, college football in the fall, the World Series, the Super Bowl, and the Olympics. It was the Smith family liturgical calendar, with a wonderful, predictable quality to it. If it was the first Saturday in May, it was Kentucky Derby day, and my parents were at Churchill Downs. My sister and I tagged along when school and other commitments allowed.

As a kid, I loved getting up before dawn and driving with Pop to the track at Belmont or Aqueduct to see the morning works and, if we were lucky, have breakfast in the barns cooked by the great thoroughbred trainer Sunny Jim Fitzsimmons. Or he and I and his great pal W. C. Heinz would spend a day or two at a fight camp in the Catskills, watching Rocky Marciano or Floyd Patterson train for a big bout.

I went along whenever I could, but sometimes it made for long days. Pop was a slow, careful writer, and I can remember more than once sitting in a cold, deserted football stadium as darkness descended. I'd look up and see him sitting in the brightly lit press box, the last man typing, wondering when we could go home.

In my memory, he was *always* writing a column. At home, on the road, in a press box, even driving out to summer vacations in Wisconsin, typing on his portable on his knees in the passenger seat while my mother drove and my sister and I wrestled in the back seat. Once, when we were moving into a new house in Connecticut, the furniture was being hauled out of the van. At noon, my father had the moving men set up a table and chair under a tree next to the driveway. Out came the portable, and a couple of hours later, out came a column.

Not surprisingly, it occurred to me as I grew up that this was not a bad way to make a living. After my freshman year at Notre Dame, I told my father that I wanted to become a newspaperman. I suspect that he was privately delighted, but he didn't let it show right away. Instead, he talked about how much he enjoyed it, how it gave him a front-row seat in life, how it had been good to him. But, he warned, it was not easy.

"You'll never make any money at it," he said, "and it can be a tough business. But if you work hard, you'll know soon enough whether you are cut out for it. And if you are, and get a few lucky breaks, it can be a terrific life."

I followed up on that advice by applying at the *Stamford Advocate*, which was then an afternoon paper published in Stamford, Connecticut, where we lived. The editor, Ed McCullough, was straight out of central casting: gruff, white-haired, suspenders over a white shirt, a big cigar in the corner of his mouth. "If you're half as good as your old man," he growled, giving me a summer reporting job, "you'll be fine. And with what I'm going to pay you, it's not much of a gamble." After the forty-four years of daily journalism in print and television that followed that first summer job, I'd say that both my father and Ed McCullough were right.

After a couple of summers covering sports in Stamford and a stint in the Army, I moved on to New York, where I covered politics and general news. I enjoyed sports but was drawn to politics, and at that point my father was doing his column, my uncle Art was writing the *Tribune*'s rod-and-gun column, and my cousin Pat was in the sports department. Somebody in the family had to break the mold.

Sports remained the focus of my father's writing for his fifty-five-year career, and although he was occasionally defensive about it, he never regretted it. He admitted that when there was a war on page one or other huge news, he sometimes felt irrelevant writing, as he said, "about the intricacies of the infield fly rule." He and I once both appeared on the *Times'* front page, when he was in Munich writing about the massacre of Israeli athletes in the 1972 Olympics and I was in Jerusalem covering the reaction.

But he believed that even in the midst of big news, sports were relevant as morale boosters that were part of the fabric of people's lives. To him, sports were a way of writing about the American scene and, ultimately, about people. Besides, they were fun and entertaining, and he tried to be entertaining covering them. That never struck him as a waste of time or beneath his skills.

The daily column suited him as well. He enjoyed the format, the length, and the challenge of conveying the essence of an event or personality in eight hundred words. And he liked being read on a daily basis by the people he saw on the beat or in the evening at Shor's. That's why the "dark period"—between 1966, when the *Herald Tribune* folded, and 1971, when the *Times* hired him—was so dispiriting for him. He continued writing his column for the syndicate, which placed it in papers around the country, but he had no outlet in New York. Producing every day but not having feedback from the people he ran into was, he said, the equivalent of "writing the column and flushing it down the toilet."

The late, great Murray Kempton theorizes in these pages that the dark period, the experience of being shut out of New York when the *Herald Tribune* and its brief, hapless offspring, the *World Journal Tribune*, were closed down, confirmed my father as the champion of the working stiff over wealthy owners. "Red Smith had found out that the world falls into two classes," Kempton says in his lecture, "those who own property and those who work for a living . . . and that they have nothing in common."

Perhaps, but Pop's consistent support of ballplayers over team owners, for example, predated the dark period. He struggled through the Depression, after all, and was a New Deal Democrat who scrambled financially until he reached New York just before he turned forty. Only then, when he developed a national reputation and his column went into syndication, could he afford to take his family along on trips or pick up the tab for his table at Shor's. "I don't recall seeing any of the Vanderbilts or the Whitneys or baseball owners on the bread lines," he told me.

Even the star athletes were worth the big salaries they earned, in his view, because they brought in the gate receipts and their careers were often short. I have no way of knowing whether he would still stick up for the ballplayers today, when the journeymen make a million a year and the stars tens of millions, but I suspect he would. To him, they were the hired help and could be laid off at any moment. He saw himself in the same light. He always worried whether his contract would be renewed by the publisher, even after his Pulitzer and when the *Times* hired him at age sixty-six. "The public is fickle," he used to tell my sister, Kit, "next year they may be tired of me." He never lost that Depression-era mentality.

Beyond his newspaper column, Pop wrote scores of longer magazine pieces and happily had his columns collected in hardcover, but he resisted repeated suggestions that he tackle a book on sports, or anything else for that matter. He knew he was good at the column, and he stuck with it. Similarly, he resisted having books written about him. "Being written about," he said to me once, when he had declined to cooperate with a proposed biography, "is the same thing as being written off."

An autobiography seemed even less appetizing to him. "Who cares?" he asked when publishers invited him to write about his life. He had little sense of his place in American letters and showed it by discarding his original typewritten columns once he had filed or phoned them in, tossing much of his correspondence after he had answered it, and breaking up the wooden backs of dozens of awards for kindling. It wasn't false modesty or purposeful destruction; he didn't believe his papers or records would be of much interest to anyone.

He knew he was good at what he did, even very good, and he took satisfaction in that. He worked hard but never took himself all that seriously. Instead, he often quoted and endorsed the sardonic sentiment expressed by the great city editor Stanley Walker, who wrote,

What makes a good newspaperman? The answer is easy. He knows everything. He is aware not only of what goes on in the world today, but his brain is a repository of the accumulated wisdom of the ages. He is not only handsome, but he has the physical strength which enables him to perform great feats of energy. He can go for nights on end without sleep. He dresses well and talks with charm. Men admire him; women adore him; tycoons and statesmen are willing to share their secrets with him. He hates lies and meanness and sham, but keeps his temper. He is loyal to his paper and to what he looks upon as the profession; whether it is a profession or merely a craft, he resents attempts to debase it. When he dies, a lot of people are sorry, and some of them remember him for several days.

He would be astonished—gratified, but astonished—to know that two or three decades after his death people are still talking about him in lectures at Notre Dame or reading about him or, better yet, reading him. Posterity was not something he expected to be part of.

If he was good at writing his column, he was singularly inept at other things. Home repairs confounded him. Beyond changing a light bulb, he was inclined to call a repairman. I shared his mechanical aptitude, so our joint projects—mercifully few—were usually disasters. One exception, our triumph, was a garbage bin behind the house in Stamford.

Raccoons had been toppling the cans and scattering the contents around the back. This time, the men of the house sprang into action. Down to the hardware store, home with two-by-fours, sheets of plywood, metal hinges, a can of paint, brushes, turpentine. The architectural drawings were sketched in pencil on—where else?—the back of yellow copy paper from that day's column. The design was deceptively simple: three sides, waist-high, nailed to the back of the house, with a sloping cover hinged to the back wall. Enough room inside for three garbage cans. A handsome latch on the front was designed to defeat the most determined raccoon.

Saws sawed, hammers hammered, nails were driven, screws turned, paint applied, and the two master craftsmen stepped back to admire their handiwork. A thing of beauty, for sure. But would it serve its purpose? Only that night would tell. We would watch and wait.

The next morning: Success! The three garbage cans in the bin were undisturbed, covers on, waiting for the twice-weekly pickup. The hungry, frustrated raccoons had waddled off to terrorize another house. Exploding with pride, my father dubbed it the "garbage-o-rama" and began talking of patents and fortunes to be made. Every house would need one. Except, of course, there was no time for mass production. There was another column to be written.

Much was made during his lifetime of the fact that this sportswriter was no athlete himself. How could he really understand what he was writing about? Pop rejected the logic of this argument, countering famously that if first-hand experience was essential, "only dead men could write obits."

In fact, he had briefly run track in college, played tennis and golf, sailed, and was a strong swimmer and skilled diver. His passion was fishing, specifically dry-fly fishing, which he pursued in every leisure moment from the streams and river near our house in Connecticut to Montana to freshwater lakes high in the Andes. Every summer, we devoted much of July to the calculated murder of smallmouth bass in Sturgeon Bay, Wisconsin. Most of these adventures ended up as columns, of course, and they were among his most witty, literate, and creative. Eventually they were collected in a separate volume, *Red Smith on Fishing*.

Toward the end of his life, after seventy-three years of excellent health, he survived a bout with cancer and was burdened with congestive heart failure. Even a brief walk down a country lane near his house in New Canaan, Connecticut, would leave him short of breath. Gradually, he got discouraged about regaining his vitality. "I want to get better," he told me a month before he died, "I hope I'll get better, but if I don't, I can't complain. I've had a great run."

To prolong that run, I kept urging him to cut back on his workload. He had once written seven columns a week, then six, now he was down to four. Finally, I got him to agree to write three a week, which seemed to me a full diet for a seventy-six-year-old.

He saw it differently. He had never wanted to retire entirely. The column was his contract with life. To stop writing, in his view, was to stop living. Seven a week was almost easier than three a week because it was four more chances to be good. He agreed to reduce to three reluctantly, and you could read that reluctance between the lines of his last column, in which he announced his new schedule to his readers. "We shall have to wait and see if the quality improves," he wrote. Even then, with his strength fading, he wanted to improve.

He recalled in that final column an encounter with the publisher, John S. Knight, at a bar in the Arlington Park racetrack.

> "Nobody can write six good columns a week," he said. "Why don't you write three? Want me to fix it up?"
>
> "Look, Mr. Knight," I said. "Suppose I wrote three stinkers. I wouldn't have the rest of the week to recover." One of the beauties of this job is that there is always tomorrow. Tomorrow, things will be better.

That last column apparently didn't want to be filed. In his fatigue, Pop managed to lose the last third of it in the computer when he pushed the button to send it to the *Times*. Frustrated and angry with himself, unable to retrieve the deleted copy, he had to rewrite the last portion and send it again. Just as he finished, I called from the West Coast, where I was on assignment. I commiserated with his tale of technological woe and asked, "Are you okay now?"

"I'm two vodka-tonics away from being fine," he said.

The next day, things were not better. The day after that, he was taken to the hospital. He held on for about thirty-six hours and died on January 15, 1982.

Much too soon for me. But, as he said, he had "a great run."

Making Words Dance

JAMES RESTON A two-time Pulitzer Prize winner, James Reston

began his career in journalism as a sportswriter. In 1939, he joined

the *New York Times*, an association that continued for nearly five

decades. Besides serving as a foreign correspondent, Washington

reporter, and columnist, he was Washington bureau chief, associ-

ate editor, executive editor, and vice president in charge of news

production. Considered the most influential Washington journalist

of his time, Reston wrote several books: *Prelude to Victory* (1942),

Sketches in the Sand (1967), *The Artillery of the Press* (1967), and

the memoir *Deadline* (1991). He died in 1995. Reston delivered

this lecture on April 20, 1983.

JAMES RESTON

Sports and Politics

Father Hesburgh, Mr. Chairman, Ladies and Gentlemen:
What we have just heard from Terry Smith tells us a lot about his father and his mother, who didn't get a Pulitzer Prize but got Terry and Terry's sister, Kit, who are with us this evening. Red once delivered a brief eulogy at the funeral of a colleague. "Dying is no big deal," he said. "The least of us can manage it. Living is the trick." He knew the trick. And the proof lies at the end, when your children become your friends, and sons can talk about their fathers as Terry talked about Red.

I'm fairly sure Red Smith didn't like lectures. They are the calisthenics most young reporters have to endure during the spring practice of their youth, but later on we tend to doze off during lectures and wonder who is that old geezer reading this paper, and who do you suppose wrote it for him, and how long will he go on?

I didn't really know Red very well. I broke into this business thinking of him as a *Herald Tribune* man—one of those cheeky poets on 40th Street in New York who got together at Bleeck's Pub after work and wondered why the *Times* was so stuffy.

There were only three blocks between the *Times* on 43rd Street and the *Herald Tribune*, but that was quite a distance. We concentrated on the solemn aspects of life, and always boasted that our circulation was larger than theirs, maybe because a lot of obscure professors were always dying on the obit pages of the *Times*, whereas their departure never seemed to be noticed in the *Herald Tribune*. On 40th Street, they had more fun, though the saddest obit we ever ran in the *Times* was about the death of the *Herald Tribune*, and we didn't know how much we needed it until it was gone.

I envied Red. He stuck to sports reporting all his life and knew at the end of each day who won, whereas I drifted into the reporting of foreign affairs, where you have to wait twenty-five years to know how it all came out, and maybe not even then.

Our paths crossed from time to time, occasionally at the end of his life on Martha's Vineyard, but we had different tastes in sports. He loved fishing,

3

which I thought was a sucker's game, because I never caught anything. I loved basketball, which I still think, next to ice skating, is the nearest thing in sports to ballet. But Red mocked it as "round-ball," with a lot of giants running up and down a shiny floor in their underwear.

Fortunately, my prejudices weren't shared by Jim Roach, the sports editor of the *Times*, who thought Red was better than Grantland Rice or Westbrook Pegler or any of the other illustrious sportswriters who had gone before him, because he worked harder and wrote better than any of them. Somebody once asked Red whether it was "easy" to write. "Sure," he said, "all I do is cut open a vein and bleed." Anyway, Roach happily brought Red over to the *Times* in 1971, and that closed the gap between 40th and 43rd streets.

My guess is that Red would have preferred it if Notre Dame had not invested in the Department of American Studies but in the sports department and concentrated on getting another good quarterback. Maybe he will forgive me, however, if I talked, not too long, about sports, and politics, and newspapers, which were among the many American studies that amused him.

Sports play a more important part in our lives than we realize, because they are about the only thing left to us these days that are definite. They are played by rules that most folks understand. They have umpires and referees who settle disputes with a whistle and a wave of the hand. (I wish we could do that in Washington.) They have a beginning, a halftime for reflection, and a definite conclusion.

Also, they demand precision under stress. It is said that diplomacy requires the same. But anybody who watched Joe Theismann of Notre Dame passing the Washington Redskins to victory in the Super Bowl last year, with a charging line before him, and with inches between the receiver and the defender, and between victory and defeat, knows the difference.

H. G. Wells, who was no athlete, and probably never heard of Knute Rockne, made a point I think Red Smith would have liked. Despite all his success as a novelist and a prophet, Wells wrote, "I am a journalist all the time, and what I write goes now and will presently die."

Of course, Wells was wrong about Red Smith, who is still alive in this room today, but Wells said something about the difference between the physical and intellectual worlds that is worth remembering.

"Are there no men of politics," he asked, "to think as earnestly as one climbs a mountain, and to write with the uttermost pride? Are there no men (in politics) to face the truth as those boys at Mons faced shrapnel, and to stick for the honor of the mind and for truth and beauty as those lads stuck to their trenches?" He would have liked Red.

Maybe this is a poor analogy, for it's a little easier to coach a team than to direct a foreign policy in a turbulent world without rules. But the physical struggle for excellence is not irrelevant to the political world of ideas.

Anybody who works in the nation's capital is constantly reminded of the difference between sports and politics. Coaches recruit the best talent available, and insist on performance. Presidents all too often settle for a pickup team of friends and loyalists and tolerate incompetence. If a coach keeps losing more games than he wins, the head of the athletic department doesn't keep him on with the excuse that he's a nice guy who didn't mean to lose. He gets rid of him. Parliamentary governments do the same, but not under our system in Washington. There, recruiting and hiring are remarkably casual, and resigning, even among incompetents, almost unheard of.

When Argentina invaded the Falkland Islands, to the surprise and embarrassment of the British government, Lord Carrington, the foreign secretary, resigned at once, but after the fiasco of the Bay of Pigs, the tragedy of Vietnam, and the aborted military raid in the desert of Iran, nobody quit and nobody was fired, with the exception of Cyrus Vance in the Iran affair. The administration of sports may be harsh and sometimes cruel, but in many ways it is preferable to our administration of government.

I believe in sports, with some reservations I will come to later, and I think Red Smith did too. For a time, I was in charge of sports publicity at Ohio State University in 1933. The next year, I was traveling secretary for the Cincinnati Reds and helped Larry MacPhail introduce night baseball into our national life. I'm not boasting, for in those two years, with my brilliant advice, Ohio State's football team had about the worst season in its history, and the Reds ended up in the National League cellar.

But I learned something in the process, though I remind you that I'm a Scotch Calvinist, and nothing makes us happier than misery. What I learned in Columbus, or so I believe, is something about the relationship between sports and academic opportunity in a university.

For the people and legislature of the State of Ohio paid more attention to its teams than to the university's Department of Liberal Arts and Sciences. They wanted a university equal to the best in the Big Ten or anywhere else, not only in sports but in everything else. And the legislature, populated mainly by Ohio State's graduates, voted the funds to keep the university in the forefront of American education.

One other point about the importance of sports to American studies: Some years ago, the late Paul Douglas, the senator from Illinois, was invited by the Touchdown Club of Washington, D.C., to address the All-American high school, college, and professional football players, all arrayed uncomfortably in their starched shirts and black ties.

"You have done a wonderful thing for this country," he said. "You have brought back pageantry. When America revolted against the British Crown, it rejected the pageantry of the monarchy. But pageantry is important, and you have restored it on the playing fields of America. In your conflicts, you have made clear the pride of the States. You have given us heroes, now in short supply. But what will happen to the heroes after it's all over?" he asked. This was a question that troubled Red Smith until the very end.

Sports reporting is by far the best discipline and school of journalism. It has an audience that has seen the game and instant replay on television on disputed points.

The political reporter may get an argument if he's wrong, but the sports reporter may get a punch in the nose. This encourages accuracy.

I don't want to get into the middle here between the English department and the sports department, but I think they have more things in common than they realize. I have had the privilege of knowing, for many years, William Saltonstall, who was principal of one of our most distinguished academies at Exeter for two decades—a superb athlete and teacher, whom I admire as much as any person I have ever met.

Just before he retired, he said he was proud of the academy's record in the teaching of mathematics and science, and he hoped in honest dealing, but he was disappointed in the record of teaching young people how to write. There was something wrong, he thought, at least for the rising generation, in the process of teaching kids to write through parsing sentences and juggling subjects, adverbs, and verbs. Was there another way? Could journalism help?

We never got around to testing that question, but I believe the simple arts of reporting may have something to contribute if, for example, the teacher invites somebody to come into the classroom, who says something, does something, and departs. And the question is put, "What happened? What did this character look like, and say and do?" And then let the students write their answers, and challenge one another's reports—making the practical point that whatever they do in future life, as doctors, lawyers, or garage superintendents, they must know how to make their thought clear, especially when they are writing love letters, which I hope has not gone out of style.

Parenthetically, I wonder if it would not be useful to offer such a course in sports reporting at Notre Dame, with Red Smith's columns as a textbook. One of the things that trouble universities is how to prepare their athletes for a career after their playing days are over. They are attracted to the world of communications, but most of them have little training for it.

As another subject for American studies I would argue that sports in my generation have probably done as much to remove the stain of racial prejudice as anything else. I am just old enough to have known Branch Rickey and remember the fuss when he brought Jackie Robinson as the first black into the big leagues. And now to see the basketball playoffs for the national championship dominated by black players is a transformation in our time that could scarcely have been imagined a generation ago.

I don't want to get too silly or too romantic about this. I'll get to the bad news later, but meanwhile a few words about sports and politics. Red didn't write much about politics, but he was very good when he did and usually very funny. Once, by accident, when the Philadelphia Athletics were training in Mexico, he wrote about an interview with Leon Trotsky, then banished by Stalin to the suburbs outside Mexico City, and headlined, "Red Trotsky Talks to Red Smith." It's a good example of Red's gifts of observation, description, and humor. You ought to look it up.

In 1956 he went to the Democratic Presidential Nominating Convention in Chicago and described in sporting terms Harry Truman's entrance into the hall. This was after Mr. Truman had retired, if he ever did.

"The old champ," Red wrote, "came striding down the aisle with outriders in front of him and cops behind, and memory recaptured the classic lines which once described Jack Dempsey's entrance in a ring:

"'Hail! The conquering hero comes,

Surrounded by a bunch of bums.'"

There are some similarities between sports and politics in America. They are both very hard and even cruel in their temptations on the players and the families. I have come to believe that the ideal life should be a gradual ascending journey stretching across the decades until at last you reach the top with the respect of your colleagues, as Father Hesburgh has done in this university and as Red Smith did in journalism.

But that's not what normally happens in sports or politics. It is not a gradual ascending journey over the years even for the stars; not a marathon but a hundred-yard dash, marked by spectacular victories and defeats, often measured by inches and accidents. There is very little room at the top, and even for those who make it, the glory road is all too short and the rest of it "a treadmill to oblivion."

Some, of course, clear the hurdles from sports to politics and continue the journey, for example, Jack Kemp, the former pro quarterback from Buffalo on the Republican side, and Bill Bradley of the New York Knicks and New Jersey on the Democratic side—both among the most effective members of the Congress.

But in general, life for most of the big shots in both fields is almost too dramatic at the beginning and too lonely at the end. This was not true of Dwight Eisenhower, an indifferent football player who went from his triumph in the last World War to the White House, or of Jerry Ford, who went from center on Fielding Yost's Michigan football team to the Congress and the presidency. And it is certainly not true of that old sports announcer out of Illinois, Ronald Reagan, who went from the football bench to Hollywood, on to be governor of California and preside over the White House.

Even so, when you look at the political record as a whole, there is a different story. Since 1960, we have had six presidents. Kennedy, who came so fast, so early, was murdered. Johnson, who succeeded him, gave up in despair. Nixon, who did so many good things, made one terrible fumble and trick play at Watergate, and was run out of town.

And Jimmy Carter, the triumphant underdog, had the misfortune to run into Iran, as Johnson ran into Vietnam, and is now, like Nixon, living with his memories and his regrets.

I won't bore you by recounting the sad stories of the many sports heroes, from Lou Gehrig, who was struck down by illness, to so many of his successors, who thought they could prolong their successes with drugs, or relieve their defeats with booze. All I'm saying is that successes in sports and politics have one thing in common: It's a sometime thing, giving them more praise than they deserve and, often later, more pain than they can bear.

This is one of the many things that impressed me about Red Smith. He had a sense of pity for the sports heroes who were gone. He lived long enough to know them when they were rookies, described their skill at the height of their careers, but never forgot them when their knees gave out.

He gathered together on Martha's Vineyard, at the urging of some publisher and his son, Terry, a collection of his columns, *To Absent Friends*. It is a beautiful book and typical of Red. For it was a series of memories of the forgotten sports heroes, many of them written before the old boys died so that they would know that somebody remembered.

Yet there are differences between sports and politics in America, I think, that have affected public opinion, and not always in a good way.

We are coming down now to George Orwell's *1984*, and his fear that the corruption of politics began with the corruption of language. He thought that if we couldn't describe in words where we were going, we'd never get there. The English department here would probably agree.

The language of sports is vivid. It deals with dramatic limited events, as on a stage. And in Red Smith's generation and mine, which has stretched from the days of our national isolation to the deepest involvement in the politics of the world, politicians and the political reporters have come to use the language of sports to describe the conflicts of politics at home and abroad.

We talk incessantly on the sports pages about who's number one and who's ahead. Of ancient rivalries and trick plays, and runs, hits, and errors, of pennant races and throwing the bomb on the football field—all natural terms in describing games.

We have come to use the same terms in our discussion of domestic and world politics. We are engaged in a momentous debate now about who's number one in the nuclear arms race, whether the offense or the defense is ahead in the development of these apocalyptic weapons. We measure who's ahead in the presidential race by statistics, like box scores—all in keeping with Frank Kent's book entitled *The Great Game of Politics*.

This box score approach to politics expresses, I think, a national attitude, a way of looking at a complicated world in simplistic sports terms, which is easy but not very helpful. For world politics today is no game, if it ever was. It's not like sports, where the clear object is to win, tear down the goalposts, and go home. For there is seldom ever an end to conflict in world affairs, and often you dare not win, for the only home you can go home to is the world, which is increasingly demanding cooperation rather than confrontation.

Also in a changing world, there are no unavoidable, unchangeable rivalries. At the beginning of this century, there seemed no greater menace to peace than the rivalry between France and Great Britain, but within a little more than a decade, they had signed the Entente Cordiale and a few years later were allies together in the terrible First World War. The enemies in the Second World War, Germany and Japan, are now allies, and the Soviet Union, our ally in World War II, is now our most serious adversary. And I remind you of the paradox and unpredictability of history, for both world wars were supposed to have been fought to defend the freedom of Poland and the other Eastern European states that are now the satellites of the Soviet Empire.

All this talk of who's ahead and who's behind reminds me of one of Adlai Stevenson's favorite stories from the last world war, when he was at the Pentagon in charge of shipping arms to the Russians in the early days of the struggle against Hitler and the Nazis. The Soviet minister in Washington complained to him that Washington was behind in delivering its weapons to Moscow. Stevenson said this was probably so because Moscow was behind in defining precisely what weapons were needed. "Look," the Soviet minister said, "I'm not here to discuss my behind but your behind."

But now *I'm* getting behind, so to go on. The English department, I think, is going to have to help us speak across the barriers of this complicated world in something other than the simplistic clichés of the sports press box.

Sports clichés are too simple, too combative, too dramatic, whereas the work of politics in the largest sense is to work away patiently until some honorable compromise is reached. The religious wars went on for hundreds of years partly because of the unyielding language on both sides and did not end until the spirit of toleration rescued both those who believed in the Cross and those who believed in the Crescent.

I hasten to add, this criticism didn't apply to Red. For he had the gift of writing serious things in an amiable way without clichés and without rancor. Maybe he acquired it here at Notre Dame, but my guess is that he had it in him, because his writing was essentially a reflection of his character. He mastered the art of criticism without hurting people—or leaving so much as a drop of poison in his wake. Maybe this is because he suffered himself along the way.

Finally, it pleases me, Father Hesburgh, to think that Notre Dame is remembering him in this way, for I know he loved this university, and if occasionally even a few students look through his writings and remember that living is the trick, that would please Smith—such a common name for so uncommon a man.

When he died, nobody of his generation in our profession was celebrated with more respect from his colleagues—which he prized the most—except perhaps Walter Lippmann, so I'll close with a remark Lippmann made to his own university colleagues many years ago.

"We have come back here, along with those we love," he said, "to see one another again. And being together, we shall remember that we are part of a great company; we shall remember that we are not mere individuals isolated in a tempest, but that we are members of a community—that what we have to do, we shall do together, with friends beside us. And their friendliness will quiet our anxieties, and ours will quiet theirs."

I thank you, Father Hesburgh and the university, for giving me the opportunity to say a few words in honor of so fine a human being.

When I Was an Athlete

RED SMITH
THE SIGN
FEBRUARY 1964

Also, in order to pass gymnasium (and you had to pass it to graduate), you had to learn to swim if you didn't know how. I didn't like the swimming pool, I didn't like swimming, and I didn't like the swimming instructor, and after all these years, I still don't. I never swam, but I passed my gym work anyway, by having another student give my gymnasium number (978) and swim across the pool in my place."

I don't know how many times I read this passage in James Thurber's account of his hard times at Ohio State before I related it to my own trials as a freshman at Notre Dame.

We, too, had to pass gym in order to graduate, and I didn't like my gym instructor, and after all these years, I still don't.

He was a senior, a member of the track team—a quarter-miler, I seem to remember—and when he led us in calisthenics, he wore his blue sweater with the ND monogram in gold chenille. He hollered at us after the manner of Sergeant Quirt (the movie *What Price Glory?* was big in those days).

Although the class met only one hour a week, I took all the cuts the rules allowed. Then, faced with the intolerable prospect of resuming my place in the formation and, on command, rising on my toes and flapping my arms like a buzzard trying to take off, I read the fine print in the college catalogue.

It said that a student who went out for the team in any recognized sport was exempted from gym during the season of his sport. It was now early winter, and I presented myself to Knute Rockne as a candidate for freshman indoor track—specialty: one mile.

In those prehistoric days, Rock coached football and track; functioned as athletic director, whose approval was required when Jack Hicok, the hockey captain, scheduled an Eastern tour for the Christmas holidays; kept the financial accounts for the athletic department; made speaking tours on the side; had a syndicated column in the papers; and either wrote books or had them written under his name.

When the trackmen moved outdoors, he'd have runners on the cinders of Cartier Field, jumpers and vaulters in the pits, and the football players taking spring practice on the infield, and he seemed able to see what everybody was doing every moment.

He accepted me as an incipient miler with a calm which, in retrospect, seems almost divine. (I happened to know that I couldn't beat a fat professor of Romance languages from Walsh to Sorin Hall, but I didn't mention that.)

"Just reporting, aah?" he said. "Well, take about three wind-sprints and then just jog six laps."

Each afternoon for maybe two weeks, I followed instructions like these. My practice time was limited, because I had to knock off early to catch a trolley into South Bend, where I was employed during the lunch and dinner hours as a waiter in the College Inn, not a very good restaurant. For this I got two meals a day and a dollar a week for carfare.

A Saturday dawned, the day of the freshman–varsity handicap meet, the annual opening of indoor competition. That noon I worked as usual at the College Inn and, as usual, ate my salary. Peter Caras, the restaurateur, wasn't a bad guy, but I loathed his brother the chef, a sneering Greek contemptuous of college punks. The only way I could get even

for his insults was to make him cook a full meal for me twice a day.

For lunch I had pork chops with applesauce, mashed potatoes, green peas, salad, several glasses of milk, and pie à la mode. Then I hustled out to the gym.

Paul Kennedy, captain of the varsity, was a miler. He and a freshman named Joe Nulty were the scratch runners. The rest of us were given head starts, depending on our demonstrated ability. I was with the largest group, who started 145 yards ahead of scratch.

When the gun barked, my pack started off as though they were going 220 yards. "Dopes," I thought, "they're not going to trap me." I settled into a jog.

For a while I was alone. Then the short-handicap runners moved up, ran with me briefly, and went on. Pretty soon Kennedy and Nulty passed, and I was alone again. But not for long. Here came the eager ones pouring past, with a full lap on me.

Now my breath rasped noisily. I tasted pork chops, I tasted applesauce. Cheering reached me, but there was a kind of a sort of a note in those cheers.

Perhaps I should explain that, as a freshman, I lived in Brownson Hall, which wasn't a separate hall but only a wing of the administration building, the one with the golden dome. We had no private rooms. We slept in a great big dormitory where beds stood row on row, separated one from another by white sheeting hung from plain pipe racks.

In Brownson, you experienced Togetherness. If somebody coughed or snored, you knew it. One morning when I had no early classes and decided to sleep in, ducking chapel, dear but unseen friends dumped my bed upside down, heaved another bed on top, and left me quivering at the bottom of the ruin.

When I crawled out, Brother Alphonsus, the rector, campused me for a month for disturbing the peace of the dormitory. It was, of course, my peace that had been disturbed by parties unknown, but the penalty stuck, except for the night when we all rushed downtown to beat up on the Ku Klux Klan, who were holding a convention in South Bend.

The point is, we freshmen in Brownson were a close-knit group. And now, as I panted around that banked dirt track in the old gym, twelve laps to the mile, I heard this curious sort of cheering. It came from a little triangle of bleachers in a corner, occupied by my buddies from Brownson. I was now far behind the field, and each time I padded past this corner, my friends cheered, and it seemed to take forever to get by them, because by now I was running straight up and down.

I think I was finishing the tenth lap when Rock, in the infield close to the track, suggested that I withdraw. He spoke kind, consoling words, and I gulped and went to the dressing room and was sick. I heard later that Kennedy beat Nulty by a stride in 4:21, excellent time on that track.

Retiring from competition, I did not return to the gym class. I expected to be flunked, but that creepy instructor didn't keep proper records. I was still in good standing on his rolls in the spring, when the swimming tests came along.

I'd been swimming since I was six or seven. When I was a kid in Green Bay, Wisconsin, it was a point of pride to be the first chump in the water in any year. I never achieved that distinction, but we'd all make it into the Muds, a favorite hole in the Fox River near Woodlawn Cemetery, before the ice was out of the bay two or three miles downstream.

I had a friend at Notre Dame named Mark Nevils, from Louisville, Kentucky. He couldn't swim. The guy superintending the swimming test didn't know either of us, so I showed up early, gave my name as Mark Nevils, plunged in, and swam two lengths of the pool with zest. The man marked Nevils a passing grade.

When almost everyone else had taken his test, I stepped up for the second time, meaning to swim in my own name. The man looked at me. "You've already passed?" "Yes sir," I said.

So there I was. I had ducked out of gym class, I had failed as a runner, and I had not passed the swimming test in my own name. I had no right whatever to a gym credit, but I got it because that instructor simply turned in all the names on his roster and everybody passed. I don't know why I should still hate him. But I do.

MURRAY KEMPTON After an apprenticeship working as a copyboy for H. L. Mencken at the *Baltimore Evening Sun*, Murray Kempton wrote for the *New York Post* and *Newsday*, developing into (in the judgment of George Will) "the best columnist the United States has ever produced." Recipient of the Pulitzer Prize for commentary in 1985, he contributed longer essays to *The New York Review of Books*, *Harper's*, *The New Republic*, and *Esquire*. His books include *Part of Our Time* (1955), *America Comes of Middle Age* (1963), *The Briar Patch* (1973), which won a National Book Award, and *Rebellions, Perversities, and Main Events* (1994). He died in 1997. He delivered this lecture on April 25, 1984.

MAX LERNER, the inaugural W. Harold and Martha Welch Chair of American Studies at Notre Dame, responded to the lecture. A newspaper columnist for nearly fifty years, Lerner was the author of numerous books, including *The Mind and Faith of Justice Holmes* (1943), *America as a Civilization* (1957), *The Age of Overkill* (1962), and *Wrestling with the Angel* (1990). He died in 1992.

MURRAY KEMPTON

Finding an Authentic Voice

T he prevailing custom on commemorative occasions like this one is for the speaker to tarry a moment with a feeling but fleeting testament to an honored memory and then hasten to his own obsessions, which turn out only too frequently to be with the self.

But I should like to linger awhile with Red Smith, because his life seems to me such an exemplary one, not just for the way it was lived but for the lessons we can all learn from it.

I cannot talk about him with the authority of intimacy. My own rounds do not carry me to stadiums and gymnasiums often enough to suit my taste for unmixedly pleasurable indulgences; but I am called there now and then when the contagion of some bright particular hour in a team's season commences to infect my city—a phenomenon that has lately been about as common in New York as a total eclipse.

Still, in more glorious times, I essayed the sports beat often enough to pass by if not quite to touch Red Smith. He was about as awesome a presence as anyone that self-effacing could ever be, and he was singular among great men for an entire absence of those affectations we come to think of as the great man's act. All the same, to be younger and smaller in one's dimensions was to feel a bit the distance. Red Smith had gone about longer than the rest of us, and the players he had known earliest were managers, field or general, by now, and at such ceremonies as we shared, we would watch him gravitate, with the fraternity of ancient acquaintance, to the grandest paladin on the premises. Owners courted him while the rest of us prayed not to be snubbed by whatever transient favorite of the gods had been above himself long enough to be noticed and soon forgotten as the most valuable player in that year's World Series.

The effect Red Smith conveyed was of some privileged but infinitely pleasant uncle who had dropped by the toy department. There was no use trying to pick his pocket; the treasures of styles like his are locked away in secret hiding places. Our model for imitation was Red Smith's devoted friend Jimmy Cannon, who was not too much less a great man, although his greatness traveled those rougher paths when passion overrides certain niceties of execution.

Jimmy Cannon prowled the dressing rooms, ranting, preaching, weeping, and singing, and was altogether our image of *l'homme engagé* we all wanted to be. He also expressed our own reservations better than we could have dared when he observed, with the intensity of the sort of respect that needs a bit of envy to kindle to its fullest flame, that "Red Smith is wonderful, but he doesn't care about anything that happens outside the foul lines."

And then too the man we honor—I tremble about recalling this single dreadful trespass in Indiana of all devoted congregations—simply dismissed basketball as unworthy of the attention of persons of taste; and that was a prejudice that seemed inexcusable then and seems inexplicable even now to someone like myself who thinks of NCAA basketball as the only historical event upon which he can focus his fixed attention without having been paid to witness it.

And so I did not know Red Smith, which is to say that I had a proper veneration for the stuff he produced, but I did not know the stuff of which he was made. It took misfortune to reveal that essence; perhaps it always does in the special sort of man who is decently embarrassed about flourishing his virtues and brings them forth only when a crisis forces their display.

We are all owned by someone, and Red Smith was an artistic possession especially cherished by John Hay Whitney, publisher of the *New York Herald Tribune*. Whitney had graces rather beyond the average for newspaper proprietors; he had an immense hereditary fortune, which he had employed on works of the highest public and aesthetic spirit, and beyond, if not above, all that, he was a passionate sportsman. The Whitneys had owned and raced horses since Darby's Arabian was a foal, and, on the female line, they even owned a baseball team.

In 1967, a year of special infamy in the history of our trade, three New York newspapers went out of business, and Whitney's *Herald Tribune* was one of them. He was ever the sporting proprietor; and it was in character for him to announce that he was closing the paper with a telegram dispatched from the Saratoga racetrack.

The mourning period ran the brief course appointed for such misfortunes, and there were louder lamentations for John Hay Whitney in his mere disappointment than for his mill hands in their disaster. But it is always thus; set us to contemplate a man of wealth whose conduct minimally approaches the level of kindness and decency that we expect as mere form in our own class, and our hand goes up automatically to tug the forelock.

And, bondsmen as we were to the rich, we almost forgot to care about all the others who had been on the stricken vessel from which John Hay Whitney sailed away wiping a tear. Red Smith went into the water from that stove boat, and if his loss was smaller than the death of someone loved, I should have trouble imagining many others that could be worse.

He was living and writing in a city where what he wrote would not be read. I cannot expect you to understand what that means except by asking you to conceive Mike Royko's condition if he were in Chicago and still writing every day to be printed anywhere except Chicago. Of course, he would be a ghost, and that, for a while, is what Red Smith became. I don't suppose his income suffered; the rich may discard you, but, at least when they are the best sort of rich, they do not all that often let you starve, and Red Smith was still distributed by his syndicate. But that was not the point of his loss; he was not being read in New York, and although, next to myself, he would have been the first to agree that New York is hardly the apex of civilization, still it was where he lived and where his intimates walked, and if he was not speaking to them, he was not speaking to anyone he knew, and he was therefore a ghost.

And so, for four years, he had passed out of existence for me until one afternoon I happened to come upon the *Washington Post*, and Red Smith had written about Alex Johnson. Alex Johnson was always a somewhat recondite subject, and his errors and travails were forgotten long ago, but they made lively copy in 1970. The older among you may remember his brother Ron, who was his better along those lines that define the well-integrated personality and afforded many of the few pleasures available to those of us conscripted by the unkind gods to the New York football Giants.

Alex Johnson was one of those outfielders who show up on one roster this year and another the next. He was a performer with capacities that might well have flowered if he had ever had the experience of kindness. But he had that unfortunate variety of talent which is damaged by the knowledge that its owner has somewhere been cheated; he quarreled with his teammates, he affronted his managers, and he appalled the front office.

As it was, he was a troubled soul. In 1970, he went to the California Angels, who were all else but, and several of them were caught entering the dressing room equipped with pistols. They excused themselves by claiming that the abusive language of Alex Johnson had forced them to take the ordinary business precaution of equipping themselves for self-defense. Some of these bearers of arms were master workmen or as reasonably accurate facsimile thereof as the Angels franchise possessed, and Alex Johnson was only a journeyman. The club's executives adhered to the custom of proprietors when they have the choice between pieces of property when one has a higher retail value than the other, acquitted the gun-toters, and blamed Alex Johnson for having given them reason to tote guns.

I had myself no very strong opinions on the matter, but when I saw that Red Smith was about to express his, I assumed that his sense of propriety was of just the order most susceptible to affront by Alex Johnson's demeanor and that I was about to be elevated by a sermon whose charm could not quite obscure its essential snobbishness.

What confronted me instead was that rarest of all offerings available in the stockrooms of our journalism—an effort by an aging and comfortable white man to see life through the eyes of a young and troubled black one. Red Smith looked at Alex Johnson's case and did the hardest thing there is, which is to tell the difference between the victim and the bullies, and, when he had finished, he had hung Dick Walsh, general manager of the California Angels, so high that he does not exist in my memory now except turning and twisting up there on Smith's gibbet. The charm was still there—it would always be—but it was henceforth informed by a species of the sacred rage.

In due course the *New York Times* got around to bringing Red Smith back to the community of his neighbors, but not even the return from exile could ever again restore him to being again merely the popular entertainer. For he had learned the one great truth, which happens to be so elementary that prodigious and successful labors at obscuring it sometimes seem to constitute the major portion of the contemporary political philosopher's employment. Red Smith had found out that the world falls into two classes, those who own property and those who work for a living, and that even though each class, especially the second, ought to meet the other with a mannerly bearing, they have nothing in common. Those of you who are familiar with that minor Henry James, who is so much more the major than almost anyone else, will already have been taught that, even with the utmost of conscious goodwill, the Princess Casamassimas eventually lose interest in their little bookbinders and dismiss them, as John Hay Whitney did Red Smith and Dick Walsh did Alex Johnson, not with malice but with sovereign indifference.

Red Smith remained at home in the toy department, but he would never cease to remember thereafter that even it is divided between the few who own and the many they own and dispose of at their will. He had found what some of us had until then thought his only lack; the fanatic heart now beat in his work and would until he died.

He had been transmuted into one of those that Henry L. Mencken identified when he wrote to Theodore Dreiser, "It seems plain to me that the most valuable baggage that you carry is your capacity to see the world from a sort of proletarian standpoint. It is responsible for all your talent for evoking feeling."

The proletarian standpoint may seem a curious object of admiration for the Mencken so many of us think of as the Tory bourgeois incarnate. And yet he knew he was a proletarian in 1921 when he was writing to Dreiser and had taken up the sword and thrown away the scabbard for his great quarrel with the American consensus of the 1920s.

He was drawn to that war by an experience strikingly like the one that brought Red Smith to his. He too had been a cherished possession thrown into the discard for the convenience of its owners.

By 1917, Mencken had so abraded the readers of the *Baltimore Sunpapers* with his curious enthusiasm for the German cause in the First World War that his bosses felt compelled to put him on forced leave. He spent three years as a kind of internal exile, and when he returned, he was someone else; the iron of alienation had entered into his spine just as it seems to have into Red Smith's. Mencken had no cause to be grateful to the owners of the *Sunpapers* or Smith to John Hay Whitney, but the rest of us can thank them all; they were in their way splendid instructors because they instilled into their two victims that degree of alienation in whose absence no man can locate the best that lies within him. We cannot know wisdom until we have learned in the final sense that most of us are proletarians and that most of us are losers and that this knowledge can be very serviceable.

If it be not too drastic, victimage has substantial uses. But only the experience itself can provide them; they do not come packaged in the abstract. I do not suppose that Red Smith's ghost could be for me so vivid a presence if I had not gone through so many weeks trailing after the Democratic presidential candidates this year and did not arrive here oppressed by the contrast between his enrichment by even the adversities of reality and our politics' impoverishment by a search for the comforts of denying reality.

It is not so much that the mind comes to feel like a tired piano hammered by the repetitive assaults of Gary Hart's "nations" and "processes" or Walter Mondale's "these goshawful weapons." Each of them can be excused for the particular rag or tag he flourishes over and over as though it were a flag. I cannot fairly complain that I have heard that phrase since Iowa when most of us cannot by now remember Iowa or even Georgia or for that matter New York.

The surviving candidates have become like sad dromedaries plodding the desert in a caravan they can no longer be sure will ever reach Samarkand.

We can hardly in justice blame them if the events that cry out around them no longer reach their ears and if, as an instance, Walter Mondale could not protest the malign futility of the Marine beleaguerment in Lebanon until the polls assured him that he could speak without danger of public offense. They are so flayed, so vulnerable, so timidly conscious of the disaster that might attend any hint of the real self—by no means a bad one but subject to misunderstanding—that they seem to have forgotten every connection between the opinions they voice and the actuality of their lives. Otherwise how could Walter Mondale pay his respects to the movement for women's rights with a ritual embrace of the goal of "equal pay for equal effort" even while he himself incarnates the violation of that ideal as a lawyer paid $150,000 a year by a firm for which he hasn't had time to make any effort at all for eighteen months?

Twenty-two years have gone by since Mark Harris watched Richard Nixon writhe through a doomed California gubernatorial campaign and remembered Franz Kafka conjuring up the American political rally that reached its apogee when "the candidate went on uttering words, but it was no longer clear whether he was outlining his program or shouting for help."

So then it was Mr. Nixon who, in this case as in so many others, adumbrated the future tone of our politics; and those who mistakenly worried that the America of 1984 would be appointed by George Orwell might as well face up to the surprise of finding themselves in the Amerika of Franz Kafka instead.

I do not think that Gary Hart is mistaken in the conviction that he is the Democratic Party's future and that Walter Mondale is its past. If there is a definable degree of difference between them, it has to be that Mondale gives off a not unvaryingly confidence-inspiring odor of what used to be and that Hart carries a not untroubling scent of what is to come. That distinction would make him the more relevant of the two and therefore worth more reflection, which, with your patience, I should like to essay now in a spirit to a degree alienated but not, I pray, otherwise captious.

Hartism seems to me to be for politics what the master of business administration is to business. The business of business is to produce goods and services; the business of the MBA is to transform that process from the concrete to the abstract.

As a result, the swelling of the MBA degree's authority has so directly coincided with the decline of American productive efficiency that Felix Rohatyn observed a few months ago that he had at last begun to hope that we might catch up with the Japanese when he read that they had established their first graduate school in business administration.

Mark Hanna, who was a hands-on industrialist, once dismissed a defunct chairman of the board of United States Steel by saying that the first time he ever saw a blast furnace was a second or so after he died. The authority of that complaint no longer obtains; the received wisdom of today belongs more and more to experts who hold their licenses without ever having asked themselves or having been asked whether intimate experience with the subject at hand might in any particular way be relevant to their qualifications.

And such as they constitute the pool from which Gary Hart draws his advisers. The *Washington Post* recently favored us with the fruits of an examination of what it called his "deep intellectual roots."

Hart has, David Maraniss of the *Post* informs us, "an unusual mind, at once integrated and dialectic," or, as Hart himself puts it even more limpidly, he is involved in an unremitting struggle to achieve "both synthesis and consistency."

Unlike Freud, Einstein, and others of his predecessors on the voyage to the frontiers of thought, Hart has such small confidence in the uses of lonely meditation that one enduringly admiring former assistant told Maraniss that Hart's book *A New Democracy*, small offering though it is, "had more authors than the screenplay for *Tootsie*."

The workers in this ant colony labored between chores for the Corporation for Enterprise and Development, the American International Group, the Foothill Group, and like temples of academic abstraction.

We may assay their intimacy with the real when Maraniss introduces us to William S. Lind, the staff assistant primarily responsible for Hart's emergence as a military philosopher. We are told that Hart interviewed scores of applicants before settling upon Lind as his guide and counselor. It might have occurred to him that someone who had seen a war might have learned a little on the way; instead he preferred Lind, who, having eschewed the uniform from being too busy reading von Clausewitz, could tender a mind unclouded by direct experience.

Larry L. Smith, another former assistant, remembers continual strivings to find a slogan for the achieved synthesis: "I hoped that, out of five or six phrases, there would come something . . . connoting many things . . . that would somehow be the summary articulation of what we were doing."

Smith left in despair for Harvard, and the team finally came up with its slogan for the synthesis. It was "New Ideas."

That is just as well. "New Ideas" is at least a phrase with some root in the English language, and the sense that Gary Hart's style may be the permanent future of our political rhetoric had opened up the uneasy prospect that, once Ronald Reagan departs, we may never have another president who uses a familiar tongue not to make sense either.

But then Hartism is not so much about ideas as about the idea of ideas.

Now it so happens that the most distinguished scholar here present, Professor Max Lerner, once wrote a book he called *Ideas Are Weapons*, and wonderfully stimulating it remains. Still! and all, the idea of ideas has its pernicious side, which was most acutely isolated by T. S. Eliot in the critical essay which is almost forgotten except for the sentence that describes Henry James as having "a mind so fine that no idea could violate it."

The effect of those few words is quite different from what Eliot intended. Here is the entire passage:

> James's critical genius comes out most tellingly in his mas-
> tery over, his baffling escape from, Ideas; a mastery and an
> escape which are perhaps the last test of a superior intel-
> ligence. He had a mind so fine that no idea could violate it.
> Englishmen, with their uncritical admiration (in the pres-
> ent age) for France, like to refer to France as the Home
> of Ideas; a phrase which, if we could twist it into truth, or
> at least a compliment, ought to mean that in France ideas
> are very severely looked after; not allowed to stray, but

preserved for the inspection of civic pride in a Jardin des Plantes, and frugally dispatched on occasions of public necessity. England, on the other hand, if it is not the Home of Ideas, has at least become infested with them in about the space of time within which Australia has been over-run by rabbits. In England ideas run wild and pasture on the emotions; instead of thinking with our feelings (a very different thing) we corrupt our feelings with ideas; we pro-duce the political, the emotional idea, evading sensation and thought. George Meredith (the disciple of Carlyle) was fertile in ideas; his epigrams are a facile substitute for observation and inference. Mr. Chesterton's brain swarms with ideas; I see no evidence that it thinks. James in his novels is like the best French critics in maintaining a point of view, a viewpoint untouched by the parasite idea. He is the most intelligent man of his generation.

There is much that Eliot has said here—especially about Gilbert Chesterton—with which I disagree, but the spirit of the whole provides a most valuable caution. An idea *can* stand between us and true feeling, and it *can* bar us from those revelations that are available to us when we have absorbed all the lessons and made our peace with all the wounds of actual experience.

But then one does what one can, and Gary Hart may indeed have been onto something when he took note of Mr. Reagan's habit of describing the present in terms of reminiscence about the past and decided to counter it by describing the present by reminiscing about the future.

Too much has been made of the dimness of Gary Hart's recollection of the only past with which he is truly intimate: the alteration of his name and birthdate, the inflation of his family's social standing, the concealment of what he seems to have been sensitive to as his college's sectarian taint.

These fudgings do have some significance, but it is not as an indication of flaws of character but of defects in the powers of reasoning. For how can we hope to reason if we are so unable to absorb our own past and its experience that we cannot resist the devils prompting us to deny the past and distort its experiences?

And once we yield to those tempters, the imagined experience is just as worthy for us as the authentic one could be: We read von Clausewitz and we are soldiers; we have commissioned a poll and we are statesmen; we have cut the ribbon to open a bridge and we are engineers.

There is a social climber in all of us who would like to think that our country's history is so majestic that Henry Adams's *Democracy* is the novel about American politics that comes closest to their reality.

That, unfortunately, is far from the case: Our most perceptive political novelist is that obtuse and tone-deaf master, Theodore Dreiser. For Dreiser taught us pity. The Clyde Griffiths who is at once agent and victim of all the sufferings that haunt our recollections of *An American Tragedy* is a creature essentially innocent of any sins more profound than those of the coward and the fantast who cannot engage misfortune except by the ungainly flight to escape its immediate consequences that can only take him to worse ones. The point about him is not that he is unlucky—in general his luck is better than the average—but that it takes only one piece of bad luck to destroy him. He had, after all, a fair-spoken and even seductive bearing, and if the boat hadn't turned over, he might very well have made some figure in the world; the competition in upstate New York presents no towering obstacle to the aspirations of people like Clyde Griffiths. But, in due course, there would have been the odd mischance, and he would have made his own disaster out of it, simply because he was wanting in the strength of character that enables the real villain or the true hero to run intact through the blows of chance. Lack of fiber like his is hardly unfamiliar in our public men; there was always something about Mr. Nixon that vaguely suggested how things might have gone for Clyde Griffiths if the boat hadn't turned over, but then the boat was only waiting its time, and when he had lifted himself as high as he could go, he tipped it in his terror, and he and it did the job to which the gods had assigned it.

Those intimations of faint kinship with Clyde Griffiths are even louder in Gary Hart—a Dreiser childhood with a failed father and a mother illuminated dimly but fiercely with Protestant fundamentalism, and then the breaking free to a brighter, softer world at once menacing and beckoning, and stirring in the young man arrived from the provinces such a mixture of fear and desire that he does what he can to forget the past, lives uneasy with the present, and is happy only when he can dream about the future.

It is the hints both give of some linear descent from Clyde Griffiths that, for me at least, set the mind to resounding with echoes of Richard Nixon whenever I pause overlong with Gary Hart.

Both see signs—unseen by any other witness—borne by little girls at the sides of the roads they traverse on pilgrimage.

Nixon's little girl flourishes the banner "Bring Us Together." Hart's offers the assurance "We Love Our Future."

I do not mean to mark the resemblance in any spirit inimical to either party; the new political style must always remind us of Mr. Nixon because it is so largely his handiwork. His major contribution to our history was not the opening to China—which is no more than a high exercise of the special genius of American statecraft for making peace with countries with which we do not happen to be at war. His true achievement was that he was the architect of the politics we will live out our lives watching.

Thirty-two years ago, he divined the change that television would bring, and he understood in a flash that it was so almost cruelly domestic a form of communication that ways must be found to mask the self to escape the exposure that is the terrible risk of intimacy. His Checkers speech was the first great triumph of the new style, and *Variety* paid him proper respect by isolating his two television addresses in the 1952 campaign as the only ones important enough as technical breakthroughs to deserve extensive attention in the reviews it carries under the rubric "New Acts." No other candidate got that sort of notice, and no other had earned it.

Mr. Nixon was, of course, a far better director than actor; and eight years later, when he was preparing to debate John F. Kennedy, he was still so afflicted by stage fright that he remembers reminding himself over and over again that the really important thing was to seem sincere.

It has been said that Americans have taken now to voting not for policies but for attitudes. Perhaps they have always done that, and it is by no means a bad excuse for a choice. But the problem with any electorate that has been protected from experience as long as ours has is how it can choose when the attitudes become contrivances.

But that isn't all that hard a problem. The difference between the authentic and the false is in the tone. The true hero has digested the experience, looked the worst full in the face, accepted its lesson, and soldiered on without calling attention to a heroism he takes for granted. We recognize him when he is least grandiloquent. The Winston Churchill who thrills us most is not the one who made those great set speeches but the one who came back from France to tell his cabinet that England's strongest ally had thrown in the sponge.

"Gentlemen," he said, "we are all alone." There was a heavy silence while he paused and then he spoke again. "Personally," he said, "I find it rather exhilarating."

The same spirit breathes through the letter Vaclav Havel, the Czech playwright, wrote to a Swedish theater audience after he had been released from four years in prison for activities deemed subversive and learned that Stockholm was staging his latest play.

"There may," Havel wrote, "be people who think it is a mistake to have been born Czech. As far as I am concerned, I see it as a special task, which I, of course, did not set myself; but I accept it and wish to make the best of it."

That is the tone, as steadfast as it is modest, that we need only hear or read to know that here is the one true note beside which all others are false. The words look straight at reality and at once accept, define, and defy it, and the voice is not rhetoric but conversation.

I should suppose that this is just the tone that we most miss and almost despair of hearing again in our politics. It is only fair to forgive its practitioners the falseness of their tone because it is by now vocational. In most of the world those who govern and those who hope to govern depend for success upon the denial of reality. Because they cannot afford to confront the truth of life, they cannot learn from it; and they travel upward on a kind of escalator of abstraction.

Private man though Red Smith was, I do not think my protracted and digressive excursion into the public sector has taken us as far from him as it might seem to have. For his was most especially the particular note of intimacy with the human condition that our politics has all but discarded. And in his troubles and not his triumphs, he found the voice that was the glory of his autumn. For persons of character, there can be few better places to find it.

A Response and Some Reflections

MAX LERNER

I was sorry, as I listened to Murray Kempton on Red Smith, that Red wasn't present to hear it. The remark that Murray made, about our all being proletarians in a deep sense and our all needing alienation in order to bring out what is genuine in us, is (from everything I've heard about Red Smith) the kind of thing that he would really have appreciated.

But one man was lucky not to be here this evening. I need not say I refer to Gary Hart. Yet in one sense I'm sorry he wasn't. It's better to be lauded than roasted, of course, but when the roasting is as elegant as Murray has just committed on Gary Hart, it's something not to be missed, even if you're the victim.

And having heard Bob Schmuhl tell you that Murray and I worked together for years, you can imagine the kind of experience I'm having after so long a separation. We worked together on the *New York Post* when its opinion page, although not beyond reproof, merited some considerable attention and got it. We were companions on that page side by side for maybe fifteen years.

How shall I describe the experience? It was a sweet and sour time for me. The sweetness was in the comradeship of working newspapermen. We attended Democratic and Republican conventions together—even the Henry Wallace Progressive Party convention in 1948, with H. L. Mencken there and Rebecca West and Dorothy Thompson. This was in the days before television made our entire columnist profession defunct. And I remember Murray sitting at his typewriter at one of those conventions, with some further sweetening at his side, pecking out a wrap-up story about the convention, and laughing and laughing as he typed. And when I used to read those pieces the next morning I was caught up in some of that sense of joy that comes in the writing itself, actually. You know there's a kind of objective narcissism that all of us columnists have, and I have to say also that unless you have that sense of joy in the writing itself, or that sense of bitterness, or that sense of alienation, whatever it may be, you don't communicate it. That was the sweetness of it.

The sour part for me was the toughness of the competition. Appearing on the *Post* feature page regularly Monday, Wednesday, and Friday side by side with Murray was a continuing experience in the Stations of the Cross. I would pick up the paper each day with fear and trembling, and I would read

Murray's piece first, and then I would turn to my own and read it, and each day it was a continuing deterioration story for me. It was like falling off a cliff, step by step, and it got so I couldn't bear to read that paper, to read either Murray or myself. I ended it only by reading it only on those alternate days—Tuesday, Thursday, and Saturday—when we were not appearing on the page together. I was afraid then that if I read my piece the name above it would read as if it were signed not by Max but by Anticlimax.

I say this with some sweet and sour remembrance. Thus, as in all dialectic (and Murray has just mentioned the dialectic of Gary Hart), the sweet had a sour element built into it as its negation, but the sour also had the negation of the negation, which was sweet again. The sweetness was a kind of *agon* quality—the Greek idea that basically all sports and all creativeness were a wrestling with others and therefore with oneself. Writing alongside Murray was for me a loving wrestling. There was a long period when the wayward editor had us appear on different days, and then I have to admit that my product fell off in quality. I didn't have the *agon*. I missed him, because to read him was to be stretched, if not to your best, then to something that you wouldn't have to be ashamed of. Now that Murray and I are no longer on the same paper, I have to carry on this *agon* at a distance.

So here we are again together, for one enchanted evening anyway, talking as we also have been writing, playing the role all columnists have to assume—that of civilization watchers. Murray's campaign pieces are good short stories because they seize on the single symbolic episode, the single nuance, to light up the whole mood and enactment.

As you may suspect, there is a gap between us of some years, yet both of us have passed puberty by now, and we look back at a seemingly unending succession of candidates and presidents, and we have commented on all of them. At times we were too generous to some, at other times too niggardly. There is a squalor for newspapermen about the presidency and its campaigns. But there is also, to balance it, a patch of glory like the patch of sunlight on a threatening gray day. I find this patch of glory in our vocation of president watching and in the revisionisms that we are able to explore afterwards.

Murray, as many of you know, is a first-rate revisionist of presidents. His *Esquire* piece some years back on Dwight Eisenhower broke the finishing tape ahead of the rest of us runners. But this kind of revisionism we do comes so late in our perceptions of a president whom most of us have reviled that we can't help feeling we should have done it earlier. It comes when the president is no longer around to revel in our belated enlightenment. From that standpoint the best presidents are always dead presidents.

We find it hard to extend the same kind of rear-mirror insight to the campaign itself. What Murray said about Gary Hart, however rough, was important because it wasn't just about one man and one campaign. I heard him saying it also about an electorate which wants to be in on the discovery of a new star, whether in Hollywood or on the campaign trail.

One phase of what we do as voters in our democracy is to pick a star finally and turn him into a king, a democratic king. But then comes the other phase, when we bedevil and savage him. We're usually not content until we have broken his spirit and heart. That has happened to a whole succession of our presidents before 1984, all the way back.

There is something to be said actually for the *persona*. We look at what we call the *persona* and often curse ourselves for being content with so superficial a view. So we ascend to what we call "the issues." When we move away from the human to the issues, we forget that the total man, of which the *persona* is part, is more important than the sum of all of the ideas and controversies (most of them contrived) on which he pours his rhetoric. For the issues change, especially when you are no longer on the campaign trail but in the presidential office. But it is the total man who has to make the presidential decisions.

I have the feeling that journalism of this sort, from this angle of vision of the total person, may be able to reestablish a linkage between the authentically human and the realm of ideas and to reestablish the linkage also between the contemplative aspect of our lives and the human aspect, which includes personality and character but which also includes decision and action.

What we have heard this evening is a splendid demonstration of how the art of journalism can illumine the political dilemma of our time.

The Discussion Period

MURRAY KEMPTON AND MAX LERNER

MURRAY KEMPTON: I can't applaud that, Max; it's too nice, but thank you. I think it's always a good idea to keep in mind the fact that four fifths of what I have said is probably nonsense. If I am right about Eisenhower now, I was terribly wrong about him both times he ran, and if I'm wrong about him now, I was right about him both times he ran. Journalism is not what they call a rifleman's procedure. Journalism works more like a mortar. I was always very bad with a mortar, but I will try to remember what we tried to do. When you fire a mortar, you bracket it; you fire one to the left and one to the right, and then presumably your target is in the middle of these two, and you land on it that way. I don't know why the theory is that, but that's the theory. What journalism is, I think, is a mortar operation. It's a kind of continual bracketing, and I think that one of the great things about working this way is that the man you're writing about will eventually give himself away. You might as well have an open mind. He may give himself away and surprise you with his virtues. He may give himself away and surprise you with his vices. But he will give himself away, and so you don't have to worry. That's something it took me a long time to learn. You don't have to worry about making up your mind too quickly. But thank you, Max.

I just wanted to add the cautionary note about what I've said about Gary Hart. What I said about Red Smith I'm sure I have a firm grip on. What I've said about Gary Hart, who seems to be a rather incomplete fellow at the moment, is pretty incomplete, but perhaps it's wrong. I hope there was no malice in it.

MAX LERNER: About your reassurance, Murray, that eventually they give themselves away, I agree with you, but the trouble is that they give themselves away after they've been elected. Think of Jimmy Carter. He ultimately gave himself away, but we had to suffer four years of him before we found out. One thing that troubles me about our craft is the narrowness with which these fellows are usually looked at. Some of our colleagues look at them without any effort really to dig into the depths of the human psyche and the human heart. At some point the readers and viewers who trust us have a right, I think, to say that if we are trying to help them assess these fellows, we had better call on resources deeper and richer than those we have been calling on.

MURRAY KEMPTON: You know, one of the real problems of political writing is that we elect a president. He deals with great numbers of affairs about which the average political reporter knows very little. Even if you're in Washington, you know only what Washington is talking about at a given time. The result is that we are not terribly well educated. Since my vice happens to be writing bad novels about living people, I find myself reading mostly novels, or if I read histories they're not by any stretch of the imagination contemporary. We are in a sense very badly educated in terms of the issues that really matter. It's a big problem in this country.

Robert Heilbroner, when he was elected president of the American Economic Association, went back and looked at the meetings twenty-five years before of the American Economic Association, and he noticed quite quickly that none of the problems that bedevil the economists now, which in this case happened to be the oil shortage and multinational corporation, had even been anticipated twenty-five years ago, and in a sense, even the best of the academicians are unable to anticipate. Now it's worse with us because we live in a hurry; we discuss those issues which are the issues on the agenda of candidates at this moment. We never think of any others.

It is a little foolish for us to be sitting there debating in New York City whether or not the American embassy should be in Tel Aviv or Jerusalem, or whether or not political action committees should give money to Mondale, or whether or not Gary Hart voted against the Chrysler bailout. There have got to be other things. Then there are the matters of foreign policy in which these people can only attack one another by distorting one another's position, because their positions are otherwise almost the same. And in the end you have this problem that the agenda of this debate, which is quite silly, is set for us by the candidates, and it's full of irrelevancies, and we follow those irrelevancies.

What'll we do about entitlements? What'll we do about the distortion of the budget? What'll we do about Social Security? What'll we do about tax bills? It's very hard to read a daily newspaper and understand tax legislation. It's very hard to understand it anyway. But the problem is that those issues are not on the agenda of the political reporters. Taxes are in the financial page, or they're covered by congressional reporters, and those of us who follow the horse race are really not terribly well informed. Even the people begin to talk like us. I ran into a group of people standing around in Atlanta, and I said to this kid, about thirteen years old, "If you were voting, who would you vote for?" She said, "I'd vote for Hart. He's got momentum!" We get back what we hand. The wonderful thing about Red Smith's work is he almost never used sports clichés, and the awful thing about our work is we use them continuously.

QUESTION: *This is for Mr. Kempton. One evening I was watching the evening news and I saw Walter Mondale use the expression "Where's the beef?" five different times in five different cities, and I was wondering if something corny like that affects your judgment of the candidate?*

MURRAY KEMPTON: No. I think the "Where's the beef?" thing was a pretty good line when you consider the soggy stuff that we've gotten. These guys make the same speech over and over again. They never advance an issue, and "Where's the beef?" has a little life, and also you can put it in twenty seconds. I mean, it's that kind of speech. Nowadays, the way campaigns are run, television is *all*. What happens is that if you're campaigning, you go out with a candidate, you go to six different places, and you go for photo opportunities. Abraham Lincoln would not have given his Cooper Union Speech. He would have gone to a senior citizens' center, to a Hispanic market, and probably to a group of college students because they make very good pictures. He would have done four or five of those things, and there would have been no Cooper Union Speech. And he would have said the same thing at each one of them, and they would have selected some reasonably picturesque backdrops.

I spent one day with John Glenn, and we went to nothing but air bases. We went to a Marine repair depot and we saw six people and 4,285 tanks, and Glenn posed in front of these tanks and made a few speeches about the value of this and that and the other thing, and that was it. It was a photo opportunity. So the only paper which has really covered this campaign with genuine intelligence is the *Washington Post*, which simply sat Marty Schram down, and he did nothing but look at television because that's what people see. If you go to Syracuse, you could be on the local television station with an interview for half an hour because they're so desperate for time. You could be on there for half an hour, and that's more than the equivalent of one speech to five thousand people.

The only thing is that there's no reflection in that. In the dazed condition that these guys are in, when he comes upon a line that gets a response, he'll use it over and over and over again, because none of the other lines will get a response. It's an applause line. It used to be said that when television first came on it would be the end of comedy and vaudeville because you would use up your whole act in one day. And to some extent that's happened to these characters.

QUESTION: *My point is that to me he looked very corny. Did you think that?*

MURRAY KEMPTON: Well, I think there's something of the aging juvenile about Walter Mondale anyway. I mean, there is that look which he had all the time. I mean when he was riding high. There's always the look of faint alarm that comes into his eyes. And I don't mean to criticize him at all. I think that when he turned tiger, or closest approximation thereof, then he had a certain bluff, sort of empty, hectoring tone because it didn't fit his personality very well. But it worked much better for him than the other one, which was constantly this "oh my God, what are they going to ask me now?" look that he gave you. So that, I think, is corny. I think that a politician's act is so thin in many cases that if he does the same thing twice he's in real trouble.

Now, another point: Gary Hart loves show business; Ronald Reagan is show business. He has wandering around in the back of his mind 150,000 movie scripts. It's some sort of great videotape bank, and all he has to do is push some kind of computer button in his mind and up on the screen pops something. Whereas these other guys haven't got the videotape; they've got a tiny Rolodex, that thing you put telephone numbers on, and there's room for about six entries in it, and they close their eyes and read that. Reagan can give you variety. You spend a day with Reagan, and he will give a different brand of nonsense in each place.

MAX LERNER: I have to rise in defense of television here, along with some of its ephemeral qualities that attract us. I made the mistake of attributing the sudden rise in Hart's fortunes to television, and then I had my confidence restored by what happened to Hart afterward, still as a result of TV. Ultimately they reveal themselves, whatever the medium, or perhaps ultimately we see through them. Now Lincoln made the Cooper Union Speech, and it was a marvelous speech. But how much could those who heard that speech have told from it about the kind of man Lincoln was, and how he would rise to meet the testings of the Civil War? And we couldn't have told if we had heard it in our day, and if we had also heard the whole sequence of the Lincoln–Douglas debates for the Senate seat. The people who voted for Lincoln didn't really know him.

What I am saying is that to listen to a man's speech or listen to him in a debate, even if you hear him for hours, won't tell you about how he's going to respond, let's say, to the Cuban missile crisis, nor how he will act on Grenada or Lebanon. We are not going to learn it that way. To be sure, we don't learn it by watching them on television, but at least we get a chance over a period of months to see them in action, responding not only to ideas but also to human situations and relationships. In that sense I think that we've got a medium in television which cuts both ways.

We have to know what they will do on issues, but we also have to know something about the kinds of lives they have lived and how they have responded to crisis in those lives. This is something I think our profession of journalism doesn't much help the readers and viewers to get. That's what I meant when I spoke of the "whole man." We don't get the whole man. We get the television man, we get the *persona* man, we get the cognitive man to some extent. We do not get at the question of strength, of command, of the capacity to maneuver, of growth. Incidentally, I don't think we got it in the earlier republic either.

MURRAY KEMPTON: No, we didn't.

MAX LERNER: What we have not developed yet, I think, is the capacity of journalists to learn enough about these persons to judge them, to assess mind and character and the strength of the whole person in terms of the whole life.

MURRAY KEMPTON: Max, you know it's been a given in our politics for years that men grow in the presidency, but I'm wondering if Franklin D. Roosevelt was much different the first two years he was president from what he had been when he was governor of New York. I suspect not very.

MAX LERNER: He had more command as the president.

MURRAY KEMPTON: As governor of New York he was looked upon by Walter Lippmann, who was certainly a keen eye, keener than mine, as a very nice man who very much wanted to be president of the United States. Now it may be that to be governor of New York simply did not, as you said, give him the same command, the same national command that he had. And therefore his qualities did not show, as Kennedy's qualities did not show when he was a senator because it was not his kind of job.

But if anyone had predicted to me that Richard Nixon would be elected president of the United States and be—if I may use the expression in these precincts in the purely temporal sense—resurrected, I would have not believed him. But the Nixon who came to the White House was the Nixon who had been vice president. Probably not as good a man as the Nixon who had been vice president. He had an awful lot of scars by the time he got to the White House. Even though he was a very dim senator, I could imagine John Kennedy being something of a president. I could see that in Reagan as a candidate. I will go to my grave never voting for Ronald Reagan, but I can see something in him that the voters see, but I don't think the office has changed him at all. I don't believe the office ever changed Truman much. I think Truman was the same man. He learned a lot, and he did develop the sense of command.

MAX LERNER: Just a footnote about Walter Lippmann. He was as wrong as he could be about Franklin Roosevelt at that point. Sometimes a great journalist can commit an idiocy. I think Walter Lippmann did.

MURRAY KEMPTON: Particularly late at night he was wrong, but I think a case could be made for what he was saying. But, of course, Lippmann was looking at Roosevelt through the eyes of an Al Smith Democrat. I will tell you, if I had been writing in 1932, I would have had such round heels for Al Smith that I would have thought of Roosevelt as incomparably a smaller figure.

MAX LERNER: You wouldn't have thought then about his polio, just as Walter Lippmann didn't think about the polio. That had nothing to do with issues or anything else, but it had to do with the development of steel in his will.

QUESTION: *This is for both of you. Mr. Kempton mentioned the aspect of television. Do you feel that a candidate, and in turn a president, can be successful in America's eyes today without being a master of the medium, as so many say Reagan has become?*

MURRAY KEMPTON: I think you have to know how to use the medium. For example, Carter simply could not use it in an inspiring way. Nixon, if he had been a director, would have used it beautifully but actually used it quite badly. Reagan is such an incredibly natural performer. The odd thing about Reagan is he isn't as good as he was five years ago. Five years ago he really cooked.

But I think you have to know how to use the medium. I kept watching Gary Hart. He was on television; he looked like the winning quarterback. You know, he would come into the ring surrounded by about eight people, but they'd put the camera on him, and it'd look like a thousand. And he would come in with his shirtsleeves hanging out, and he'd look exactly as though he'd come back to the dressing room and was about to be interviewed by Howard Cosell. The only thing was, there never was a game. All you saw was the triumphant return to the dressing room. You never saw the game. And then when he got on television and anyone threw him any kind of curve, he just couldn't handle it.

The man has also got to be a master of a lot of the old techniques. He has to be able to give quick answers to questions. A guy that can answer questions very quickly is apt to be a little smarter than a guy that can't answer very quickly. And I think he has to have that, but I think you have to be able to use the medium.

If Roosevelt were president of the United States today, he could drive Reagan right smack out of our minds because he had a magisterial presence, and that's the only thing that Reagan really lacks. I keep thinking of politics in terms of domesticity. You know, I always think of Nixon as the perennial brother-in-law type and John F. Kennedy as the kind of boyfriend type, and Ford as the kind of husband type, but Reagan is not a member of the family. He is just that wonderful guy down the street. He's Uncle Ron, but he's not really your uncle. For what he does no one equals him.

Ted Kennedy said something to me once that was perfectly wonderful about Reagan. Kennedy was running for president in 1980, and he had this horrible hot style, as Nixon so nicely said, where he just blew wax all over the television studio. We were sitting in a cab somewhere, and he said something to the effect of, "They keep telling me that I've got to be more like Reagan and less like myself. You know I can't do that stuff. I watched him for hours, and I suddenly figured out if he were on a panel and somebody handed him an AP bulletin and it said 'Indian Point nuclear plant just blew up; 50,000 dead, 500 million fleeing for the ocean,' Reagan would look at it and he'd say, 'Gee, I wish things like that didn't happen.'" And that's true. Kennedy had caught what was wonderful about Reagan's technique, which makes it possible for him *not* to be responsible for anything particular that happens. It is an honest feeling. He doesn't feel responsible. He believes implicitly that nature is the best cure of all ailments. This is the best style in the world, but the average politician simply can't do it because he hasn't got Reagan's saving grace of knowing in his heart of hearts that it's not his fault. I don't know where he gets it from, but he knows it, and he makes us think it's true.

MAX LERNER: I think we have to go a little beyond the question of the media here. I think of two men. One was president, and the other wants to be: Harry Truman and John Glenn. Neither of them with any charisma really. Now if you try to think of them in terms of the media, it wouldn't be a natural for Truman, and yet somehow Truman would be able to get some of that authentic quality of his across, just as he used to do in the whistle stop campaigns. I recall the 1948 Democratic convention. It was hot, sweltering. We were practically doomed. And suddenly this fellow in a cool white suit gets up there on the platform to deliver his acceptance speech, and with his first few sentences we sit up and we find ourselves then climbing on the table and cheering.

I try to think of Truman on television. He wouldn't be like Reagan. He hasn't got that skill. Yet somehow the authentic quality of his would come through there, too. Now that isn't true of John Glenn. I think he's an authentic man, and I think he would have made a good enough president. But Glenn can't get across on any medium, whether it be television or a direct speech to an audience. This, of course, is troubling, because one of the tasks of a president is to relate to people publicly. A man like Glenn can relate very well privately, but publicly he doesn't relate. We have a deep need within us for the dramatic, however it be expressed. But the dramatic is not necessarily what's going to be able to run the country. It doesn't follow that if you have this dramatic flair you are therefore going to govern America.

MURRAY KEMPTON: Well, there's no way President Truman could ever have been president of the United States and gone the primary route. I think he and Glenn probably have one quality. I just can only imagine it in Glenn, but I think you can see it. There are certain kinds of people who cannot take command until they have command. In other words, I think Roosevelt was capable of taking command without having it, but there's a man who says, "I will accept this and do my best." I don't think Glenn would dare quarrel with his commander-in-chief. I don't think Truman would dare. To quarrel with your commander-in-chief is somehow a breach of courtesy and really a breach of your patriotic duty. But make either of those guys commander-in-chief, and then he *is* commander-in-chief. When Truman got that office, he said, "Okay, that is the name of the game, and that is the game I want to play."

QUESTION: *It seems to me that journalists in print and on television come across as being bored with the electoral process. Is this true, and why is it?*

MURRAY KEMPTON: Most people are not bored who cover political campaigns. It's a very glamorous and exciting beat to them. I think if I can blame political reporting for one thing, it's the feeling that the United States of America needs to have a primary system which begins at Christmas and runs until the following August. I don't think the political process needs that at all, but I think we who cover it need it. We become very serious men. We run into our publishers, and they say, "Well, how's it going out there?" and we talk to them and we become very consequential. Take away this primary process, and it would be a blessing to everybody.

Gary Hart had 16 percent in Iowa. I turned with my usual stupidity when I filed from Iowa, and somebody asked if I were going to listen to Gary Hart. I said, "You mean to tell me that you think 16 percent of the vote is a breakthrough? You call that a breakthrough?" And I walked out and paid no attention to Hart's press conference. I went to New Hampshire, and this guy was rolling like a big wheel because everybody kept saying he got 16 percent of the vote in an Iowa caucus. You know what 16 percent of the vote of the Iowa caucus is? About the number of people who are in this room.

Anyway, political reporters built him up. They're trying to give the illusion that there's a fight on. Mondale is the nominee, and there is no stopping him. Hart is drowning and we keep pounding that Gary Hart stuff and pounding that Gary Hart stuff and assessing it because these guys want to stay in Howard Johnson's motels until August, and I don't. So don't accuse our boredom as what's doing it. As far as I'm concerned, I don't want to see another one of these things, unless they call me. But I don't count. I'm not typical. By the time most of these guys are my age, they will be fed up with it and be publishers themselves and be saying to some other kid, "What does it look like?" and I'll probably still be out there covering it.

Harry Truman Returns

RED SMITH

NEW YORK HERALD TRIBUNE

AUGUST 16, 1956

CHICAGO—The old champ came striding down the aisle with outriders in front of him and cops behind, and memory recaptured the classic lines which once described Jack Dempsey's entrance in a ring:

> Hail! The conquering
> hero comes,
> Surrounded by a
> bunch of bums.

This was Harry ("Give 'Em Hell") Truman, last Democrat to hold the heavyweight title, coming out of retirement now to slug it out with the clever young contender, Ad Stevenson. The arena was a hotel ballroom, the ring a curving battery of microphones, the crowd made up of working stiffs assigned to a press conference. Stevenson wasn't there in the flesh, but you could sense his presence, a stick-and-move guy, tough for even a young adversary to hit solidly.

The old champ looked fit, square of shoulder and springy of tread, his skin clear, his eyes bright behind the glittering glasses. No roll of middle-aged flesh showed under the gray double-breasted; his blue polka-dotted bow tie spread wings for bold flight.

But how about the old legs?

At the bell, the left flicked out in a practiced jab. "I am deeply touched by the anxiety of the press and so many of our illustrious columnists about my political judgment." It was a light jab, but he felt it get home.

He glanced about the room with a cocky, crooked grin. McGurk used to give that same grin to the fighter he drew to illustrate H. C. Witwer's *Leather Pusher* stories. Jim Braddock's ruddy kisser wears it today.

Inwardly, a ringsider applauded. "Attaboy, Harry! Tell 'em what you did to Pawling Tom Dewey."

A moment more of light sparring, then Harry moved to the attack. His voice was cold and level. Stevenson's counsel of moderation "was, in fact, a surrender of the basic principles of the Democratic Party." "I am shocked that any liberal Democrat would advocate or encourage the abandonment of the New Deal and the Fair Deal as out of date." Stevenson is not "a dynamic and fighting candidate." "He cannot win the election by himself."

"There is nothing personal about my attitude toward Governor Stevenson." In the room there was undeceived laughter, but the old champ kept his face straight, going through with the feint. "In fact, I like him personally.

"That's all." He stepped back, as though to let his adversary fall forward.

Stevenson didn't go down. The attack had been meant to shatter him, explode his title pretensions, and leave the field to Ave Harriman, but Ad was still on his feet and coming in. Questions hit Harry from all directions.

"Mr. President, you just said that recent events showed that Adlai Stevenson lacks a fighting spirit. What recent events are you referring to?"

"I didn't say that; I said his recent actions show that he lacks the fighting spirit to win an election."

"Which recent events would you refer to, sir?"

"His moderation, his tie-up with the conservatives of the Democratic Party."

"Any specific actions?"

"Your judgment is as good as mine."

He was backing and circling, grabbing and parrying, doing a Missouri waltz, and the legs were going. He came up on his toes. "I think he [Stevenson] would need the help of an old man from Missouri," and he laughed with the crowd.

Ken Overlin was like this in his last days as middleweight champion, still sure he could lick any bum they threw in with him. The young ones came along, though, and licked Ken. They always do.

Once Harry slipped but recovered swiftly. He said he had told Stuart Symington by telephone, "Get yourself out here if you expect to—uh"—win the nomination?—"do anything about the Missouri delegation," he finished, laughing over the slip with the others.

Toward the end he seemed impatient for the final bell. "Gentlemen," he said, "I think that is enough," and he lifted his hands. Somehow, one was reminded of Abe Attell as an old man fighting a kid in St. Louis. A few fast rounds, and then Abe turned to the crowd.

"Gentlemen," he said. "I am Abe Attell, featherweight champion of the world. I have always given you a good show. This is as far as I can go."

The old champ had come in briskly. Now he went out slowly. They never come back.

JAMES J. KILPATRICK In 1964, James J. Kilpatrick became a syndicated columnist, after several years as a reporter and editor at the *Richmond News Leader*. Once the most widely syndicated political columnist in America, he continued to write columns that focused on the U.S. Supreme Court and "the writer's art" for Universal Press Syndicate (now Universal Uclick) until early in 2009. Kilpatrick is the author or editor of many books, notably *The Foxes' Union* (1977), *The Writer's Art* (1985), and *Fine Print: Reflections on the Writing Art* (1993). He delivered this lecture on April 17, 1985.

JAMES J. KILPATRICK

The Art
of the Craft

From time to time, such is my good fortune, I am able to escape
from the Washington Zoo and travel abroad in the land. Some of
these travels involve the observation of political candidates, a most
interesting species; some travels take me to the lairs of big business, where
drinking and eating habits of predators may be recorded; but the most
pleasant travels wind up at schools where journalism is taught or at the
meetings of state press associations.

Here my custom is to begin with a moderately respectful bow to
broadcast journalists—you will not overlook the qualifying adverb and
adjective—and then to speak directly to those of us in print journalism
who write for a living. I speak to the operative verb: Whatever else we
may be, whether we are editors, columnists, reviewers, critics, reporters,
or analysts of trends on the market, we are first of all *writers*.

Our task is deceptively simple. It is as deceptively simple as the task
of carpenters, who begin by nailing one board to another board. Then
other boards are nailed to other boards, and, lo, we have a house. Just
so, as writers we put one word after another word, and we connect those
words to other words, and, lo, we have a news story or an editorial or, if it
goes badly, a plate of spaghetti. This was the lamentable fate of a certain
Southern college president who recently wrote an op-ed piece for the
Birmingham News. His topic was "Silent Scream," an anti-abortion movie
that has caused much controversy. He said that, first, the film demonstrates
a power to move us. He continued, "Second, it documents the perversity
of realizing rational resolutions to unusually emotion-laden means of mass
communication—means which, if widely utilized, would make virtually
impossible the operation of democratic processes."

This is the kind of thing that I had in mind when I remarked that the
crafts of writing and carpentry are deceptively simple. The carpenter has
to begin with a plan; the writer must begin with a thought. There must be

at least the germ of an idea. Before the first board is nailed to the second board, or the first word connected to the second word, there has to be some clear notion of where we expect to be when we have finished nailing or writing. The college president who penned that wretched sentence had no clear idea of where he had been or where he was going. If he had been building a house, the roof would have fallen in on his head.

All this is elementary, but it is astonishing how often we lose sight of the elements of our craft. We must have something to say. And that brings me to the art of Red Smith, whom we honor tonight. He brought all kinds of gifts to his work. He had a nice hand for simile and metaphor. He had a wonderfully funny, pool ball sense of humor; he could play caroms and cushions before hitting his target. He had a great sense of perspective; he never lost sight of the fact that he was writing about the games men play, and he never took himself or the games too damned seriously.

Most of all, he had something to say. He started with facts—good, seasoned 2×6 facts, aged in the record books. He built his columns on solid foundations. If he said the score between Saginaw and Lansing was 5–5 at the top of the ninth with an 0-for-4 infielder leading off for Saginaw, that was the way it was. You could look it up. I won't say that Smith never wrote a thumbsucker; I'm sure he did, for all of us do, but he wrote very few. He started with joists and worked his way to the rafters; his columns had beginnings, middles, and ends. He was a good lumberman.

Smith was much more. He wrote not only with a bell-like ring of authority but also with grace and wit. Like all first-rate writers, he had his little devices. He had a trick of the apparent afterthought, a red caboose that trailed his train of thought. Once he watched Rocky Marciano beat Ezzard Charles to a pulp and thought it strange that other boxers should covet so brutal a whipping. "Still, it's a living," said Smith, "provided a guy does live." Again, he wrote about ballplayer Billy Loes, who was suspended for throwing a temper tantrum. Loes announced that he would appeal to commissioner Ford Frick. "If he does, he'll get a hearing," said Smith, "though it probably ought to be in juvenile court."

A part of Smith's art was to keep his similes short and homely. Grantland Rice's affection for the old Sunshine racetrack near Tampa was "like a parent's feeling for a small, soiled child." At Squaw Valley for the winter Olympics of 1960, he watched cars swerving on icy roads. They were "swinging their sterns like starlets on parade." In Havana in 1958 he covered the kidnapping of race driver Juan Manuel Fangio: "Rumors were thicker than gulls on a sea wall." He could draw a vivid image from a single perfect verb; a rich woman on a cold day was "turtled down into her minks."

Smith had a big head, as oval as the track at Churchill Downs, and he had eyes as sharp as a good pair of binoculars. He could see sham a mile away. Back in 1953 he covered a football game between Notre Dame and Iowa. In the closing minutes a Notre Dame lineman "stopped the clock by falling into a melodramatic swoon." The time thus gained was employed by Notre Dame to tie the score, 14 to 14.

Because Notre Dame was involved and Notre Dame is always in the spotlight, this created a national crisis, and the government teetered perilously. There was agitation for a rule forbidding fakery, though it was not clear how an official could enforce the same without a lie detector. Ultimately the lawgivers put the points of their heads together and promulgated the doctrine that to tell or act a lie was untruthful.

Smith turned his glasses on golfers to the same effect:

> The fact is, there are golfers who are vile mathematicians and can't count for sour apples. There are shuffling, unwary walkers who wouldn't dream of kicking a ball out of the rough, except by accident. There are myopic players who can't see all the way down to a clubhead grounded in the sand. The divine right of any golfer to concede himself all putts under 12 feet is honorably established, and if a man happens to sneeze while announcing his handicap, so it sounds like 13 instead of 3, he can hardly be blamed for his head cold.

In 1958 Smith took a judicious look at a new rule in baseball prescribing that any pitcher who throws at a batter on purpose becomes subject to a fine of $50. "If he persists in his unneighborly attitude, a severer penalty will be imposed." The difficulty, Smith foresaw, would lie in the brushback. The ball whips toward the plate, way inside, high and tight, and the hitter flings himself backward in exaggerated terror. The umpire, said Smith, is not to be deceived. "Get up, you bum," says the ump. "You wanta live forever?"

Suppose, however, that the pitch is half an inch farther inside. Is this due to faulty control or misanthropy? "Ball one," says the believer. "Fifty bucks," says the skeptic. These are questions that try men's souls.

Smith was mostly an even-tempered fellow, easy to get along with, but he had an unsuspected capacity for anger. He despised the hypocrisy evidenced by the Olympic committee members, and he developed a real loathing for "Happy" Chandler, whom he regularly identified as baseball's greatest living ex-commissioner. "Mr. A. Benny Chandler," Smith once wrote, "a swashbuckling amphibian revered by Kentucky game wardens as the Duckslayer of Versailles, recently delivered himself of a wonderfully detached, unbiased disquisition on the present state of baseball." Lesser targets Smith covered with a solemn irreverence: "At 12:01 P.M., Governor Rockefeller, Mayor Robert Wagner, and five assistant pants cutters assumed a Matt Dillon stance at the finish line [of the new Aqueduct track], drew seven pairs of gold-plated scissors, and snipped."

Smith loved the English language. In 1960 he urged all sports reporters, especially broadcast reporters, to undertake an evolutionary experiment. Its purpose: to deliver their reports in English. Like all of us, he had his crotchets. "Reforms could start," he suggested, "by eliminating the barbaric and indefensible use of defense as a verb." He understood the special languages by which we communicate—one language for medicine, another for sports, another for Madison Avenue. "These private tongues," he said, "serve as a sort of stockade, giving insiders the cozy sense of belonging, mystifying outsiders and keeping them outside."

Red Smith worked for papers in Milwaukee, St. Louis, and Philadelphia before he joined the *Herald Tribune* in 1945. Once there he stayed at the top of his league until his death in 1982. Before flying to South Bend this afternoon, I read maybe a hundred of his columns. In the same way that rookies study Ted Williams's swing, young writers would do well to study Red's style. Let me mention half a dozen characteristics that made Smith so consistent a heavy hitter.

He taught himself to look intently at whatever he was writing about. At a racetrack he was not content to write generally about a colorful crowd or a fine spring day. Through his eyes we saw the jockey's silks, kelly green and buttercup yellow; we enjoyed a 5-knot breeze and a temperature in the 60s. At Yankee Stadium, if the details were necessary to his point, he could report the progression of balls and strikes on a given hitter, the sliders and slow curves and fastballs. He looked; he looked *intently*, with unremitting concentration, and he carefully stored images for the hour he could put them to use—images of gulls and sea walls, of starlets on parade, of small soiled children.

Second, he put clarity first. He obeyed St. Paul's famous maxim to columnists, reporters, and editorial writers: Without clarity we are nothing. Pore over Smith's pieces as you will, you will find few long and involved sentences, few unfamiliar words, almost no lapses into a foreign language. He wisely avoided dialectal writing, though in the milieu of the games he covered, the temptation to phonic transcription must have been almost irresistible. As a consequence of this restraint, Smith's stuff reads delightfully well aloud.

Third, he knew how to sustain a tone. When he wanted to be serious, as he was serious in hating racial segregation in Birmingham in 1954, he was serious all the way. In his obituary pieces on various athletes and writers, he set a tempo in his lead—largo, or adagio, or whatever—and he held it. He could write with deep emotion, but he kept that emotion under tight rein, close to the rail, and did not let it drift. Most of his stuff was light stuff. He was writing about "men who devote their lives to children's games," and he recognized that children's games are played on the lowest slopes of Olympus. Smith tuned his typewriter to the key of mock serious, and he made it play beautiful music.

Permit me a word about that elusive virtue known as *taste*. Smith worked among a breed of men, professional athletes, not usually identified with a pristine purity of speech or conduct. Because he loved the track and he loved the prize ring, he was necessarily close to gamblers and to their shadow world. It would have been understandable if Red had salted his columns with profanity or with the kind of ribald anecdote beloved in locker rooms. He never did. He was one of the all-time great yarn spinners, but in his work he kept his yarns clean. I am reminded of Jody Powell, who once said that the first duty of a president's press secretary "is never unintentionally to mislead you." Well, Red never unintentionally gave offense to anyone. When he wanted to jump on the high muckety-mucks of the PGA, he could give them a capital drubbing, but he never struck a low blow. You could read him aloud to your grandma.

Of the next observation I cannot be sure, because I never sat in a press box with Smith and only once watched him actually at work, but I will make a small bet that he wrote slowly and read his copy right to the moment he had to put it on the wire. This I infer from internal evidence: In all of Smith's columns I read, I did not mark a single clumsy sentence, not a dangling participle, not an orphaned clause wandering about in search of a subject to call its home. To the best of my knowledge, Smith never went into print with a compound verb on which mayhem had been committed. All this suggests rigorous copy editing; it suggests the kind of sandpapering and polishing that raises the craft of the carpenter to the art of the cabinet maker.

Let me urge all of you who would be writers to follow Smith's high example. One shortcoming of so many writers today is that they do not take pains, they do not recast their flawed sentences, they do not edit their copy for the sense of it, and they wind up with what I have come to call mangles and tangles.

There was a feature writer for the *Miami Herald* who let us know that "after injuring his leg on the farm, Daniel Neuharth sold it and opened a creamery in Eureka."

In a science newsletter, this captivating image: "Long thought to be relatively flat and shaped like huge Frisbees, the scientists have found that some galaxies are actually oblong in shape."

From a novel called *Full Circle*: "And on Sunday night, after a quiet dinner he cooked her himself on his barbecue, she flew back to San Francisco alone."

The *New York Daily News* described a stroll by Tyrone Power, Jr., on Park Avenue: "Besides his eye-catching good looks, he wore white sneakers."

Irv Kupcinet, in the *Chicago Sun-Times*, quoted the president of the former Chicago Boys Club on why the club had changed its name to the Boys and Girls Club: "Of the 31,000 inner-city youths we serve, almost 30 percent already are girls."

From the *Baltimore Sunpapers*: "Two years before he was born, Mr. Falwell's father killed his own younger brother in a violent shoot-out."

And there was something profoundly informative in a flyer from the Frye Mansion in Seattle, telling patrons about an exhibition of Bob Timberlake's paintings: "Timberlake was born in his native North Carolina." We are reminded of the nun who traced her Irish ancestry to her parents.

Once we start examining mangles, it is hard to stop. British Airways put out a pamphlet promoting a visit to London: "Sitting in Kew Gardens' outdoor cafe the other day, suddenly a fleeting shadow passed overhead." From a paper in Johnson County, Kansas: "Bundled up in a borrowed coat, tears rolled down Mrs. Hayes' face as her teeth chattered in the freezing temperature." The Associated Press reported from Poland that a police officer "beat the priest with his fists and a club wrapped in a rag at least four times." In Vero Beach, the *Press-Journal* had an item about a thirty-three-year-old woman who had been suggestively approached by a man with a golden retriever: "After saying hello to the woman, the dog ran off and the man continued the conversation."

When we get hurried or preoccupied, we come up with words that are patently the wrong words. There was the worried reader who wrote to the medical columnist that he was in moral terror of prostate trouble. This might have been the faculty member at the University of Washington; according to the student newspaper, he underwent prostrate surgery. The other day I read of an actress who reaped celebrity with her appearance on Broadway. In Alabama, we had an editorial praising a departed statesman whose goal was to be the penultimate public servant. A biographer said of Bette Davis that if the vultures of the women's clubs had known of her affair with her director, "they would have swept down on her like so much carrion." A writer in the Greenville, South Carolina *News* noted that the alligator, "which was once nearly instinct in the state," has recovered. And a feature writer in North Carolina let us know that "after lying decadent for several years," the restored railway yards at Salisbury are alive again.

It always has been important for writers to search for the right word. I don't know that this quest is any more important today than it has been in the past, but the dizzying speed and volume of communication persuade me that we of the press have an increasingly sensitive task to perform. I fell in love with the writing art at the tender age of five and was weaned on a Corona portable typewriter. Later I labored on a series of beloved Underwood manuals. As a boy I learned to hand-set type and to handfeed a press. For twenty-five years on a daily newspaper I dealt with hot metal. As a reporter I used the telephone to dictate copy or notes.

These days I find myself bewildered by new forms of communication. Typewriters have disappeared from our city rooms. Hot metal long ago yielded to cold type. My brethren in broadcasting bounce signals off satellites as if they were banking a six-ball into the corner pocket. At the Democratic convention in San Francisco last summer, I watched in awe as correspondents talked to their editors through computers. And I am aware, as we must always be aware in areas of technological change, that today's marvelous devices of communication soon will be yesterday's telegraph key.

So much speed! So many words! The demands upon writers and broadcasters compel us to produce—to meet deadlines—but they leave perilously little time for us to think. Precision always is a difficult task, whether we are dealing with machine tools or a budget analysis. Somehow we must find the time for reflection, for the long view, for the slow examination of ideas, and for the painstaking search for words to express ourselves precisely.

These are serious undertakings, but on an evening of remembering Red Smith I have no idea of leaving you with portentous thoughts. Let me express a prayer that those of you studying journalism who will pursue professional careers will take up your quest with the same joy that Smith brought to his own career. "Retire?" he once was asked. "No, never," he said. "If I don't write I'll die." There was a true writer speaking. Yet Red understood, as all of us in newspapering understand, that we are not writing for posterity; we are not aiming at a box seat in a pantheon of immortals. Once Red went to a birthday party for Granny Rice. He remarked that the party "will be settling into stride about the time these pages become a shroud for some obsolete haddock."

In that vein of philosophical acceptance, I leave you. For the most part, we write upon sand. History flies by as swiftly, as evasively, as ducks past a hunter's blind. We get an occasional wingshot, not much more, and perhaps the wonder is that the editorial judgments of newspapermen stand up as accurately as they often do. Ours is a great business; in our best moments maybe we can term it our profession. Ours is a craft that sometimes rises to an art. However it may be defined, as Red Smith knew, newspapering is more fun than anything—not more rewarding, in any material sense, but more fun. Nothing else even comes close. I am proud to be a part of it.

Alexander Woollcott long ago summed up a feeling that Red Smith most certainly shared. I have quoted the old Town Crier a hundred times and will quote him to my grave: "I count it a high honor," Woollcott said, "to belong to a profession in which the good men write every paragraph, every sentence, every line, as lovingly as any Addison or Steele, and do so in full regard that by tomorrow it will have been burned, or used, if at all, to line a shelf."

Questions and Answers

QUESTION: *How long are you going to continue to write your column?*

JAMES J. KILPATRICK: My tentative plan is to continue writing it through August 1989, because that will mark a nice round twenty-five years since I began, and twenty-five years is enough. I will then have been almost forty-nine years in newspapering, milking a cow every day, and that's a lot of milking. But I have to add that the closer I get to August 1989, the more tentative my decision is likely to be.

QUESTION: *What was the most difficult article you can recall writing?*

JAMES J. KILPATRICK: It would be awfully hard to say. Some columns are difficult in the sense of analysis. You take a state or municipal budget and try to make it coherent in a thousand words, and you have problems. Or you wade your way through a long, complex opinion of the Supreme Court, and you are writing against a deadline, and it's not easy to extract the real significance in the time you have to work on it. But these difficulties are part of everyday life.

Some pieces are difficult just because of the physical conditions under which they're produced. In a presidential campaign year, for example, you may be up at four o'clock in the morning, being certain that your bag is in the hall by 3 A.M., and you take off with the candidate. You fly somewhere, and you get in a bus, and you fly some more, and you get in another bus. You go watch the candidate shaking hands at a factory gate, or maybe visiting some old folks, and you get back in a bus and then back in the airplane. You fly to some other airport, and maybe you've had a square meal during the day, and maybe you haven't. You're always running late. The candidate is a bore; he's had nothing new to say all day; you have to wring eight hundred to a thousand words out of his inane remarks. You finally get to bed at midnight in some distant hotel, and then you're up again at 4 A.M. I myself haven't done too much of this. I go out on the trail for only a couple of days at a time, but I have enormous respect for the people who follow campaigns the whole way through. When they get through they're more dead than alive.

QUESTION: *Who are your favorite journalists, to read or to watch?*

JAMES J. KILPATRICK: I could name quite a few, sir, on both the liberal and conservative sides. Ellen Goodman, who writes for the *Boston Globe,* is a beautiful writer. Mary McGrory of the *Washington Post* writes lovely stuff. I couldn't agree less with her political views, but she has a wonderful way of putting things. For humor, Art Buchwald, Russell Baker, and Calvin Trillin are first-rate humorists. Their columns can stand up with anything that Addison and Steele used to write. The other day I found an old copy of Hilaire Belloc's essays. The pages hadn't even been cut. I read it with fascination. How that guy could write!

So many others: Bill Safire of the *New York Times,* George Will of *Newsweek* and the *Washington Post,* Bill Buckley of *National Review.* Don't let me forget Murray Kempton. He's in a class by himself. There are lots of first-rate writers out there. The *Post* has a sportswriter, Thomas Boswell, who's a jewel in that newspaper's crown. The fellow who covers horse racing for the *Post,* Andrew Beyer, is a joy to read. I'm afraid to mention many more for fear I will leave out some and at midnight tonight I will say, "Why did I leave out so-and-so?"

QUESTION: *Is there a liberal bias in the press, as so many politicians claim?*

JAMES J. KILPATRICK: The only way I can answer this is to ask, what do you mean by "the press"? There are in this country about six thousand weeklies, seventeen hundred dailies, scores of magazines of general circulation, and a great proliferation of locally owned television and radio stations. All these together constitute "the media," hated word, or "the press." It's almost impossible to generalize about the press so defined. If you could analyze all the weeklies and all the small-city dailies—and nobody could analyze them all—you'd probably find extremely little political bias in the news columns. It just isn't there.

But ordinarily your question is understood to mean bias at the very highest levels of journalism—the three major TV networks and such great organs of print journalism as the *New York Times,* the *Washington Post,* the *Los Angeles Times,* the *Miami Herald,* and so on. If you confine your question to that high, thin, but very influential level of the media, yes, there is in my judgment some evidence to back up the charge of a liberal bias.

Now I don't believe this bias is as great as my beloved friend Jesse Helms thinks it is, but now and then I get a pretty good whiff of it. I think there is some there. And I think it is inevitable that it should be so. Those of us in either print or broadcast journalism are not disembodied spirits. In a way we can be compared to judges on the state and federal benches—judges who come to their high judicial stations with a presumed objectivity. They are to call the law as best they can. But a justice who goes on to the United States Supreme Court, or a columnist who sits down to write a presumably objective column, brings to that task the sum total of all the experiences of his lifetime. It is inevitable, absolutely inevitable, that in the end these biases—these prejudices, these predilections, these accumulated observations—are going to be reflected in his judicial opinions or in his writing. It couldn't be otherwise.

I don't think it will happen, but suppose ol' Jesse does win control of CBS. He fires Dan Rather, puts me on as anchorman, and gets me a new sweater. I am now going to select the twenty-two items that will be on tonight's *Evening News*. This is the disconcerting fact: I would pick twenty of the same twenty-two my friend Dan Rather would pick, because on any given day, the twenty top stories are probably obvious: a major storm, a sensational trial, a significant court opinion, a speech by some prominent political figure, what happened today to the Dow Jones average. That sort of thing. It would be only on the marginal two or three items that our choice would vary. Dan's judgment would be, "This is news; we must cover it." My judgment would be, "This other story is more important; we should use it tonight instead." These would both be honest judgments on our part, but his editorial judgments would reflect his "bias," and my judgments would reflect mine.

There is no greater truism in our business than a truism known to us who have been in the news business all our lives. Every editor is asked constantly, *"What is news?"* His reply is, "News is what I say it is." That sounds arrogant, and it may be arrogant, but that's the way it is. It is our responsibility—ours alone—to declare and to define what is news tonight, or what is news in tomorrow morning's paper, and to make hard choices when the news hole is small and something has to be spiked. I don't think a free country would want it any other way. We don't want some federal commission ruling that this is news and this is not news. So, yes, to return to the gentleman's question, I think there is some bias—a liberal bias—at the highest levels of the media, but I don't think this tilt is anywhere near as pronounced as some of my good friends think it is.

QUESTION: *Since you mentioned Hilaire Belloc, could you give any reflections on his contemporary, G. K. Chesterton?*

JAMES J. KILPATRICK: I love Chesterton. Now you're talking about stylists, and you have named two of the great ones. Belloc had a wonderful stylistic device. It was the simple declaratory sentence—four or five words, subject, predicate, object. I came across a line in one of Belloc's essays: "Lucidity is the soul of style." I'm not at all certain that is true, for I think of Joyce and Faulkner, who were not the most lucid guys who ever came along, but they were great stylists. Chesterton's trick was antithesis. Read some of Chesterton's essays, his criticisms, his literary pieces. He had a lovely way of balancing sentences.

We have some good stylists turning out stuff today, not perhaps at that level, but their work is distinctive. Cut off the bylines, and give me one hundred words of Bill Buckley, one hundred words of Art Buchwald, and, say, one hundred words of Kurt Vonnegut or Norman Mailer, and it wouldn't be much of a puzzle to name the authors. Our own contemporaries may not be up to Macaulay and Gibbon, not up to Burke or Chesterton, but not bad, not bad.

QUESTION: *Do you ever have days when you don't know what to write, or don't feel like writing, or can't write?*

JAMES J. KILPATRICK: Sure, you bet. Every one of us who writes for a living has days like that. I keep on my desk a 4 × 6 scratch pad that's headed "Column Ideas." Some days I will have four, five, six possibilities on there. At the moment, my list includes "National Labor Relations Board," because I've gotten interested in how many certification elections the unions have been losing lately. It's a column idea. I'm interested in the Navy (I have a son who's a chief petty officer, career Navy), and I have a note to do a piece on the role of women in the Navy. I may do a column on spring coming to the Blue Ridge Mountains. I have four or five possibilities, and two or three of them will materialize into columns.

There are other days when the 4 × 6 scratch pad is absolutely blank. I have nothing I really want to write about; I have a deadline of eleven o'clock in the morning, and it's now eight o'clock in the morning. I feel the first sweaty sense of panic. I still work on an old Underwood manual typewriter. I roll in a piece of paper, and just to get something on that piece of paper, I rattle out my byline and release date. Then that typewriter looks up at me like an unfed dog. What now?

I sympathize with what I believe is the thrust of your question. All of us know these desperate moments of intellectual paralysis. You don't have an idea; you don't have anything, and it's now 8:30 or a quarter to nine, and the morning papers fail to inspire a single thought. But you will find, if you've been in the business long enough, that you have stored a little extra firewood somewhere. You have a little kindling tucked away. You had an idea on the scratch pad two weeks ago and discarded it because it wasn't good enough, and you didn't think it would make a whole piece. But it's now 9:30, and you know what? That discarded idea is looking a whole lot better. So you retrieve your abandoned notes, and you type in a dateline: Washington. Then you must hit a typewriter key. You compel yourself to write that critical first word. Then a second word, a whole clause, a complete sentence; you just force it out. It may not be a good first sentence, and you may wind up in a little while by throwing it away and starting over, but you have to get that first sentence out. The next sentence is not that much work. Now you've done a whole paragraph, and you're into it. It's an inelegant simile, but you know what they mean in those TV commercials when they talk of occasional irregularity? It happens to us all, but all of us get over it.

QUESTION: *Do you have a staff or research people who feed you things?*

JAMES J. KILPATRICK: No, I am me. What you see is what you get. My "staff" is one beloved young lady named Jinnie who handles everything in the office. I tried a couple of times to employ someone to do research for me, but it didn't work. They never asked the questions I would have asked, so I wound up having to do all the reporting myself. But, believe me, I have lots of people who feed me things. I must be on the mailing list of every lobbyist in town.

QUESTION: *Which article of yours generated the most public response?*

JAMES J. KILPATRICK: Let me answer in this way: Half a dozen times a year I will write what we call my "country columns." These are literary exercises in which I flutter my butterfly wings. I write about spring in the Blue Ridge, or about the bird and animal life. I write a column every July in the form of a letter to my oldest grandchild. Heather will be fifteen this summer. Well, my birthday columns to Heather generate a tremendous mail. It is absolutely astonishing how many little girls named Heather dwell in the United States of America and how many of them are thirteen, fourteen, fifteen years old. Nineteen-seventy must have been a bumper year for Heathers. Anyhow, these offbeat columns produce an amazing amount of mail.

When I write about an issue that is both timely and hotly controversial, the mail pours in. Recently I wrote a column in opposition to the MX missile. It startled my conservative readers and delighted my liberal readers, and we were weeks digging out from under the avalanche. If I dare to write a piece in favor of even a little bit of gun control, I will trigger heavy fire from the National Rifle Association. But if I devote great thought and care to an analytical piece on the budget or on tax reform, I get nothing. Zilch. I write a great deal about the Supreme Court. My most learned pieces on the exclusionary rule will draw about four letters. Social Security is a hot topic. I will tell you the American Association of Retired Persons is a very nimble outfit. So it goes. I try to spread out. I write about education, I write about health, I write about problems at the Pentagon, but the columns that I work hardest on ordinarily generate the least mail. It's the columns that touch people, or find some common bond, that bring in the letters.

QUESTION: *Do you respond to letters?*

JAMES J. KILPATRICK: Yes, sir. The rule in my office is that I will respond to every reasonably civilized letter that comes in. The anonymous ones, of course, we dump out. We have a file called the "nut file," and it stays full. Letters come in, written in red and black typewriter ribbons all the way across the page, leaving no more than an eighth of an inch on either side, and I look and see that they're quoting the Bible. Out they go.

But after you've tossed the libelous letter, the form letters, the copies of letters to President Reagan, and all of the morning's nut letters, I still will average fifty letters a day that have to have responses. Drafting responses to these letters, even when a third of them can be disposed of with identical form letters, takes an inordinate amount of time. I probably spend more time on reader mail than I can justify, but I think it's useful public relations. The trouble is that if you write really good and thoughtful responses to the good letters, then readers write back. First thing you know, you have a pen pal, and that really can eat into your time.

QUESTION: *Over the years have you become more or less impressed with sportswriting?*

JAMES J. KILPATRICK: Yes, I've become more impressed with the quality of sportswriting since I was a boy following the St. Louis Cardinals through the *Oklahoma City Times*. It's better now. Go back to Red Smith. Red was singular. There were other great ones: Scotty Reston, Westbrook Pegler. Both of them began as sportswriters and went on to other fields of journalism. They were first-rate, but the general quality of sportswriting today, as I read it, is much better than it used to be. I think we are developing in sports, as in so many other fields of newspapering, the informed specialist. We find restaurant critics these days who have been through the Cordon Bleu school in Paris. We have people writing about health news who could qualify as paramedics. They're knowledgeable about health and medicine and surgery. We have science writers who really know their science. At the U.S. Supreme Court, where I spend so much of my time, we have a cadre of reporters who are graduates of law schools.

This same encouraging development carries over into sports. We have better writers—and better-informed writers—than I recall from the past. On the larger papers, the sportswriters get travel budgets that let them go to Las Vegas to cover a fight or to Louisville to cover the Derby. This is true not only of the greater newspapers but also true of papers with circulations up to 150,000. They're sending competent craftsmen and skillful writers to report news of sports, and every now and then their craft also rises to an art.

And a Grasp of Millionaires

RED SMITH

NEW YORK HERALD TRIBUNE

DECEMBER 12, 1952

Every now and then one of the brothers in this lodge, generally a rod-and-gun editor because they are the most erudite, manages to fill a column with a glossary of sporting terms and thus gets a day off so he can go shoot a fox or dynamite a trout. This is a harmless dodge that deceives nobody and often entertains the reader, especially if the discussion concerns those agreeable collective nouns applicable to the animal kingdom.

No matter how familiar they may be with the words, most people are obscurely pleased to be reminded that when Moby Dick was among friends he helped make up a gam of whales, that several incipient fur coats at play constitute a pod of seals, that a flock of geese at rest are a gaggle of geese, and in flight they are a skein. We have also a pride of lions, a covey of quail, a yard of deer, an exaltation of larks, a shoal of fish, a drove of oxen, a pack of wolves, a swarm of bees, a farrow of pigs, a flight of swallows, a clutch of eggs, a hatch of flies, a span of mules, a herd of antelope, and a bevy of broads.

All these are terms in common use, to be heard bandied over a slug of carrot juice in practically any health bar at practically any hour of the day or night. In addition, there are sporting terms of narrower circulation which have almost disappeared from the language. At considerable expense, an effort to restore them is now made here.

For example, there is a current tendency to refer to any pack of basketball players as a team or squad. This is loose usage. Strictly speaking, a number of basketball players who are just standing bonily around with their knees sticking out are a gangle of basketball players. When they are in action, cognizant of the point spread and the significance thereof, they are a sniggle, or fix, of basketball players.

Some collective nouns may be used in the plural or singular, interchangeably. One of these is the accepted term for one or more sports broadcasters—a yammer of radio announcers.

Baseball players, of course, employ their time in various pursuits. Sometimes they collect around an umpire and squall about his decision. Sometimes they buttonhole the official scorer and tell him that the play he scored as an error yesterday should have been called a hit. Sometimes they sit in the hotel lobby and bellyache about their salaries or night games or their manager's failure to understand them.

At all times, they are known collectively as a grouse of ball players. Their managers are not gregarious by nature. As a rule, they herd up only at World Series time and during the winter meetings. On such occasions they can be lumped together as a conceit of managers.

The generic term for umpires varies according to the user. In the view of players and managers, they constitute a braille of umpires. Fans group them as a guilt of umpires.

There is a sizable body of men, specializing in football and basketball, whose waking and sleeping hours are passed with a whistle clamped between their fangs. They are a skirl of referees.

When owners of baseball clubs assemble in executive session to revise the waiver rule or deal with the bonus problem, they make up a dawdle of magnates. A sitting magnate cornered at contract time by one of his players is simply a niggard.

In boxing there are three major groups—a quiescence of fighters, a venality of managers, and a dissonance of commissioners.

Other proper group names include a doze of race stewards, a scheme of jockeys, a prevarication of golfers, and a vagrance of amateur tennis players. At any track meet the spectator may find a decolletage of athletes and a setting of officials, sometimes called a calcification.

College football coaches, athletic directors, and presidents are all covered by the single phrase a flatulence of educators.

When editors herd together, this is called a congealing.

As everybody knows, sports reporters in bulk constitute an indigence of writers. A friend insists that at certain seasons this species should be described as a bibulation of sportswriters. As to that, this deponent cannot testify.

CHARLES KURALT First as a reporter and columnist for the *Charlotte News* and then as a correspondent and anchor for CBS News, Charles Kuralt tried to explain—in his phrase—"the jigsaw puzzle of America." His "On the Road" video postcards introduced viewers to subjects in ways that broadened the definition of news while telling the country more about itself. Recipient of ten Emmy Awards and three Peabody Awards for his work in television, Kuralt also wrote several books, including *On the Road with Charles Kuralt* (1985), *A Life on the Road* (1990), *Charles Kuralt's America* (1995), and *Charles Kuralt's American Moments* (1998). He died on July 4, 1997. He delivered this lecture on April 23, 1986.

CHARLES KURALT

The View from the Road

W e are gathered in memory of a stylish writer, one of the best: Red Smith, whose life and work honored Notre Dame and honored human beings as a species. So the subject, at least the first subject, is writing. I'll begin with a few random thoughts about writing. I met Elmore Leonard, who writes good crime novels. He said he had three rules for writing: Number One: In dialogue, never use the word "besides." "Besides" is a transition word, he said, used by a speaker to change the subject. It's a lazy device for a writer. Never use "besides" in dialogue. Rule Number Two: Use no more than one exclamation mark per fifty thousand words of manuscript. Rule Number Three: As an author on a book promotion tour, never agree to be met at the airport by a limousine, because in this way a writer is captured by the trappings of success. This last rule, Elmore Leonard told me, he had broken, however, once people actually started *offering* to meet him at the airport in a limousine.

I have fallen into all the traps that await the unwary writer. As a young writer at CBS News in the '50s, I had Douglas Edwards wish everybody a "fulsome" Christmas. And that is how I learned the hard way that "fulsome" is a synonym for "nauseating." I have learned that "livid" does not mean flushed and crimson; it means "black and blue." I discovered, much to my surprise, that a "hale fellow, well met" is actually a "h-a-i-l" fellow, not "h-a-l-e." He is well-greeted, not hale and hearty. When I read about a car careening down the street, I know the writer meant "careering" down the street, although the car may "careen" or tilt sharply if it goes around a corner.

I treasure all these small distinctions, and I think they are worth preserving—now that *I* have gone to the trouble of learning them. I understand that the language changes by majority vote, by usage, but I agree with Theodore Bernstein, the old *New York Times* man who has written about the language a good deal, that there are some fields of human activity in which a count of noses does not provide the best basis for law and order.

I have served on the usage panel of *The American Heritage Dictionary*. They send us ballots and ask us to vote whether to accept new usages. I always vote "no." The pilot says on the public address system, "We are presently at 32,000 feet over Kansas City." Do you accept this popular usage as a synonym for "at present"? "No," I always say. Presently, I may change my mind, but I doubt it.

I don't think the young writer is wasting his time who browses through Fowler or Eric Partridge or Bergen Evans from time to time, or who keeps Otto Jespersen's seven-volume *Modern English Grammar* on a shelf in the bathroom.

Proper usage, of course, is only the foundation of the house the writer is trying to build, however. The risers, beams, and rafters are subject matter, and the wallpaper and furniture of the house are all style. I think good writing comes from good reading. I am sure of that, in fact. I think writing is imitative. When I sit down to write, I know that I hear in my head the rhythms of writers I have read and admired. Sometimes, I can even remember *which* writer's rhythm I am hearing. I think all the good writers hear the music of good writing they've read. The *great* writers like Red Smith compose new music for the rest of us to hear when we sit down at the typewriter.

I was surprised to discover that he learned to write the same way I did. He wrote better, but here's what he said about it. I was just reading *The Red Smith Reader* on the airplane coming here. I came here from Moscow, and I took this book with me—so I had plenty of time to read it on the way back. In an interview one time Red Smith said, "In my later years I have sought to become simpler, straighter, and purer in my handling of the language. I've had many writing heroes, writers who have influenced me. Of the ones still alive, I can think of E. B. White. I certainly admire the pure, crystal stream of his prose. When I was very young as a sportswriter I knowingly and unashamedly imitated others. I had a series of heroes who would delight me for a while and I'd imitate them. . . . But slowly, by what process I have no idea, your own writing tends to crystallize, to take shape. Yet you've learned some moves from all these guys and they are somehow incorporated into your own style. Pretty soon you're not imitating any longer."

I think it was E. B. White—no longer alive—who taught us all that one could write movingly about small things—the birth of a spider, the death of a pig. Red Smith also wrote about small matters with an insight that gave them importance. And now we have all learned from him. It was E. B. White, his model and mine, who said that good writing elevates people, and bad writing depresses people. I believe the aspiring writer (I assume there are some in this room) has a responsibility to himself to read much, and to learn to recognize the difference between good writing and bad writing.

I believe good writing takes patience. Red Smith said it was the one part of the job he didn't enjoy, sitting at the typewriter. But he knew it was important to sit there until he remembered the right word. Mark Twain said in an inspired moment, "The difference between the right word and the nearly right word is the difference between the lightning and the lightning bug."

Eric Sevareid once said it differently. He was one of the better writers who ever worked around CBS, one I always admired and whose work I used to read. From time to time, he collected his pieces into books, and I found those books in my high school library, and I admired Sevareid's essays greatly. But when I got to know him, I found that he was never entirely comfortable with television, the lights, cameras, and all the things you have to put up with to do a story in television. He said it was like "being nibbled to death by ducks." Once, when he was feeling particularly grumpy about television, I heard him murmur, "One good word is worth a thousand pictures."

Words matter, even in a picture medium. Not many good words are used in television these days, I think. The characteristic young television journalist is more interested in images, especially his own image, I'm sorry to say. There are so many young men and women who are good at performing, or producing, or shooting pictures, and so few who are good at writing, that whenever a writer shows up at CBS, people treat him with respect and whisper behind him in the halls, "He's a writer, you know." Charles Osgood and Bruce Morton and Andy Rooney are among those who are whispered about as they walk down the hall, and a few others.

But if it's writing in which a young journalist excels, probably, to tell you the truth, he would be well advised to shun television and enter some other field—newspaper or magazine writing, or writing for the wire services. As things stand today, all of those options offer a better opportunity for the writer to practice his craft. The writer will be frustrated by the abbreviation of his work in television—television news stories are short and getting shorter, as you may have noticed, and the writer will be distracted by the flashing graphics and shifting gears and ringing bells that are characteristic of most television news programs these days.

It might have turned out differently. When I came to work for CBS News twenty-nine years ago next month, there were writers on the premises. Stylists. Eric Sevareid, Winston Burdett, Dick Hottelet, Charles Collingwood, and many others. Hottelet was the last to retire, last fall in the same week that Collingwood died. And there was Edward R. Murrow, who reminded us that a television set is only a box with wires until innovative and thoughtful and resourceful men and women give it substance. Murrow, surrounded by powerful egos, deplored the egotism of broadcast journalism. Sometimes at the end of the day he would say, "Well, we've done as much damage as we can do for one day. Let's go have a drink." And that was an invitation all of us who were kids accepted eagerly because we knew we were going to have more than a drink. We were going to have a little seminar, a little discussion about this thing we were doing.

News on the air was being invented in those days, and Murrow was its Edison. One thing I heard him say more than once was, "Look. Just because you have a loud voice, just because 16 million people hear you every time you open your mouth, don't think that makes you any smarter than you were when your voice only reached the other end of this bar!" Probably that ought to be engraved and put on the walls of television newsrooms. Murrow recognized that amplification did not confer wisdom.

If he could come back today and walk into our newsroom, I think he would be impressed by many things. I think he would be impressed by the size, by the fact that CBS News has grown so much, from the small collection of talented individualists he assembled to a mighty and far-flung and bureaucratic organization upon which the country has come to rely, together with its competitors. I think he—who spoke of lights and wires— would be impressed by how much more advanced our lights and wires are. I don't know how it works, but I was over in Moscow yesterday, and the day before that we put on a program which people saw right away. We didn't have to process the film and put it in a can and give it to some Pan Am passenger to give it to a customs guy in Frankfurt and hope that it would somehow get back to America. It all arrived in America instantaneously. Murrow spoke into an old ribbon microphone and was heard, scratchily, in people's living rooms. We flash pictures in color into those same living rooms across oceans from Moscow or across space from the moon. He would love all that.

I think he would notice other improvements. Because he was fair-minded and humane, I think he would be pleased that not everybody who is on television these days, or working behind the scenes, is white and male. I remember thinking when Diane Sawyer was reporting from the State Department in the days of the Iran hostage affair a few years back, that her work, which was so calm and full of information and full of insight, would have just knocked Murrow out. Nobody appreciated great reporting more than he did.

He would love the technical advances. He would love the human advances. He would be encouraged to notice that we still talk ethical principles at lunch, which is more than can be said for the employees of most other enterprises in America, I think. Those seminars in the bars still go on, though without Murrow to lead them. He would be glad to see that most of the professional standards he raised have not been much lowered. We haven't become the supermarket newspaper, though the temptation must have always been there. As Andy Rooney remarked the other day, we even could have been as bad as British journalism! But instead we manage to appeal to a daily news audience with *New York Times* standards. Murrow would appreciate that. I think he would appreciate the fact that we have competition now. Really, back in those earliest days, we didn't have any competition that we were worried about or respected very much. That's all changed. There are good people on all the networks now, and good people like MacNeil and Lehrer. That's good and he would think so.

I think he would deplore the show business aspects that are creeping into our line of work. He would be dismayed that all these years after *See It Now* there is no place in the schedules of any of the networks for documentary treatment of important subjects. He would be surprised by the extent to which good writing has been devalued. By the way, he would notice the same old egos in the newsroom, though in many respects we have less to be egotistical about than did Murrow and his colleagues.

Events sometimes conspire to bring you back to Earth. I have told the story about how one day in Fort Myers, Florida, we parked the "On the Road" bus on a residential street. People are forever coming up offering story ideas or praising us for all the sweet little stories we do. A woman came out of her house smiling, and I smiled, and she smiled, and I opened the door to accept the usual pleasant remarks and she said, "I think I would like a couple of loaves of rye today, please." She thought we were the bread truck. We've also been mistaken for the X-ray van and the Bookmobile. That's good for you, you know. The reporters who genuinely begin to think of themselves as important—and you see them, you can almost tell them on the air, the ones who have a greater interest in themselves than in the story—those are reporters who are not doing themselves or their craft any good. And people like the lady in Fort Myers will always help you remember that you're not such a big shot as you may be tempted to think.

It's been nearly twenty years for the three of us "On the Road"—Izzy, Larry, and me—and we have learned, if we have learned anything, not to come on like a big-time television news crew. I hope not to be lofty and philosophical in these remarks. I'm really trying to give practical advice to some of you who I suspect are going to enter this field. Most of the people we do stories about have never been on television before, and they are likely to feel a little apprehensive about the experience. So we try to put them at their ease just by being ourselves. It helps, to tell you the truth, if you're in my line of work, if you're fat and bald. That's the truth. Because people look at me and they say, "If that guy can look like that and talk like that, then I can just be myself." Which is what you're hoping for, of course.

We have adopted what we call the "tricycle principle." We watch a lot of local television; everywhere we go we see the local news. Izzy and I were in his motel room someplace watching the local news when a story came on about a children's tricycle race, little kids trying to ride their tricycles fast. Pretty cute story. And Izzy said, "You know what? Before this story is over that reporter is going to ride a tricycle." And I said, "No, he wouldn't, because that would ruin it." Sure enough, he signed off—"Joe Doakes, Eyewitness News," and the camera pulled back to watch him pedaling down the sidewalk on the tricycle. Then and there we adopted the tricycle principle, which is very simple: "Don't ride the tricycle." Try to keep yourself out of the story if you can. Don't appear on camera at all if you can avoid it. People are not interested in the reporter, or shouldn't be, and if the reporter does his work well, people will be interested in the story he is telling. If they end up thinking about him instead of the story, he has succeeded as a celebrity but failed as a storyteller.

Which brings us back to substance, which brings us back to writing. I don't think a journalist can be a very good writer unless he is first a pretty good thinker. I have encountered television journalists who know a lot about television, and even a little bit about journalism, but not much about anything else. I am happy with your arrangement here at Notre Dame; I am glad this talk is sponsored by the Department of American Studies. I think the reporter's mind should be cluttered, and my own is cluttered with American studies—not the systematic sort which might gain me a passing grade in a course at this great university but a chaotic jumble of facts which nevertheless comes in handy. I know that daffodils bloom in Savannah the last week of February, but they don't bloom 'til the second week of April in Hartford. I know that there was a member of Custer's Seventh Cavalry in Major Reno's outfit who was there at the Little Big Horn and who didn't die until 1950. I am intrigued by all the things Americans use to hold their mailboxes up—welded chain and wagon wheels and old plows and cream separators. I know that the whistling swans migrate every year from Siberia to the Chesapeake Bay. I know that the weakest coffee in America is served in Brookings, South Dakota; that a barrel is 31 gallons if it's beer, but 31 and a half gallons if it's water, and 40 gallons if it's a barrel of whisky; that starting in 1917 if you wanted to immigrate to America, you had to be able to read; and that if you need to stop a cut from bleeding what you do is say the sixth verse of the sixteenth chapter of Ezekiel while walking toward the sunrise, or so they say in the mountains of North Carolina, where I come from.

Now, most people can get through life perfectly well without knowing all these things, but if you are a reporter you need to know them. And if you are a feature reporter, you can find a way to do a story about every one of them, and as a feature reporter, I have. And I have done stories about musical saw players and swimming pigs. The swimming pig was one of our big ones. The Remarkable Swimming Pig of San Marcos, Texas. We even rented an underwater housing for the camera to get underwater pictures of that little porker paddling along. We made a big thing out of it. Afterwards, a lot of farmers wrote me letters and said, "You idiot! Any pig can swim!" It would have been helpful to have known that before we did the story, but all knowledge is imperfect and incomplete.

Red Smith had a lovely cluttered mind of the perfect sort. It was just an accident, you know, that he got into sportswriting. He could have done anything. He told how it happened. Let me read you another passage from this interview in *The Red Smith Reader*. He was working on the copy desk of a newspaper called the *St. Louis Star*. He said in this interview:

> That fall the managing editor, a man named Frank Taylor, fired two guys in the sports department, and he came over to me on the copy desk and he said, "Did you ever work in sports?"
> And I said, "No"
> "Do you know anything about sports?"

And I said, "Just what the average fan knows."
"They tell me you're very good on football"
"Well, if you say so."
And he said, "Are you honest? If a fight promoter of-
fered you ten dollars would you take it?"
I said, "Ten dollars is a lot of money."
And he said, "Report to the sports editor Monday."

After that he never was at a loss for something to write about. You have to have something to write about. It's all right with me if Red Smith's mind was cluttered with facts about the Kentucky Derby, which it was; or if the reporter's mind is cluttered with facts about corruption in Chicago, as Mike Royko's mind is; or the political philosophy of William Howard Taft, as George Will's mind seems to be. But I am sure that felicitous writing comes only from felicitous musing on the contents of a kind of jumbled file cabinet or wastebasket of the mind. Good writing comes from consummate curiosity and keen observation. Curiosity, that's the thing, and from an inborn sympathy for human beings and the human condition, and always from broad, even if disorganized, knowledge. If I were hiring a reporter, I would sooner hire one from American studies here than from a full-fledged school of journalism someplace else, because the American journalist-to-be who has studied America has his priorities straight. Journalism is not so complicated that you can't learn it on the job, but America is complicated and deserving of much contemplation.

It is a country full of surprises, you know. After all these years of meandering through it, we have been to every part of every state many times by now. I believe the country to be more neighborly, and more just, and more humane than you would think from reading the papers or watching the evening news.

The country I have found is one that presses upon the visitor cups of coffee and slices of pie and great gobs of local history, and always wants you to stay longer than you have time to stay—and doesn't bear much resemblance to the country that makes it to the front pages, which have room only for wars and politics and calamities—or perhaps I should say politics and other calamities—and not enough room for telling the story of people living and working and trying to be good neighbors. But that country is there, as we all know. Journalism, by its nature, rushes about shouting. The country, by its nature, moves slowly and talks softly.

I don't mean, of course, that we in journalism shouldn't be telling the story of everything that goes wrong. That is why we are doing our work. This kind of country cannot work unless we persist in rushing and shouting and pointing out everything that goes wrong. But I have wondered whether the historians, whose job it's going to be to sift through the refuse we reporters deposit on the pile of history, might not find some articles of value we didn't much notice at the time—impulses of humaneness and decency and the will for justice.

There's such a thing in this country as a national conscience, or so I have come to believe. Things are a lot fairer than they used to be for a lot of people in our country. And besides that we have reached the conclusion that we really shouldn't pave every meadow, or terrace every hillside, or pollute every trout river, that we have to leave a bit of wild America for our children to love as we have loved it. We have faced a lot of problems of our people and our land. The technical problems don't worry me so much. Technical problems, which admit of purely technical solutions—we're just wonderful at solving those in America. I bet we live to see the day of abundant energy from unexpected sources just because that's become identified as a big problem. It's these very much more difficult human problems that we have gone to work on as a people in the last twenty years and actually found a few solutions to. We're not much for congratulating ourselves. We would much rather go galloping off in search of new problems to solve, but I think there are grounds for modest self-congratulation in the history of our country in the last twenty years or so. We cover government, but these impulses I'm talking about sprang up outside of government, sometimes even in spite of government. Well, very often in spite of government. They didn't originate in Washington. One woman wrote a book, Betty Friedan—the book which Alvin Toffler said "pulled the trigger of history." One woman decided that, no, she was tired, she thought she would not move to the back of the bus. And in these ways—these human ways—the country is changed forever.

My first grandchild was born last month. I hope he undertakes American studies when he gets to college, because he won't understand from the papers and the television news alone how profoundly his country has changed. If American journalism has one great weakness, it is that we lack a sense of history. I advocate a journalism of context. It would take a conscious effort. It would require writers with exquisitely cluttered minds, and editors able to relate today's wire service bulletin to events of the past.

It would immeasurably improve our newscasts and newspapers, however, and it would serve the country.

Well, I have been talking as if I know something about journalism, and I am not sure I do. Red Smith said pounding a typewriter is a pretty easy way to make a living—a lot better than lifting things, he said. I have worked myself at the edges of the craft; it's been a long time since I covered anything important. I have tried to keep importance and relevance and significance entirely out of my work, in fact, on the grounds that with everybody else covering the Senate hearings, somebody has to cover the greased pig contests and the guy who has a car that runs on corncobs. And that's been me.

I seem to have pleaded here for better writing, smaller egos, broader knowledge, deeper understanding. I suppose those are unexceptionable ideals and that nobody in the room will wish to argue about these modest goals for journalism, but if you do wish to I am about to give you your chance. I may not be able to answer profound questions, for reasons I have already explained. Mine has not been a profound career. And I would welcome trivial questions, of course. But I'm ready to try anything.

Questions and Answers

QUESTION: *My friend and I were talking about how stories in the news, big stories, seem to go to the back of the newspaper once they've lost their fizzle, so to speak. I'm curious about Northern Ireland and Ethiopia. I wonder what has happened in Ethiopia after the money that has been sent to them. Has the help even scratched the surface? I want to hear your comments about how these stories get pushed aside.*

CHARLES KURALT: I have very little to add to what you said. I think that is a valid criticism of journalism. We all cover a story and then forget about it and move on to the next thing. That's a little bit of what I was trying to say. We don't even remember what happened last month in our intense desire to cover well the thing that's happening this minute. It happens that I have seen some follow-up stories about hunger in Ethiopia. The problem has been to a very large extent temporarily solved, apparently. All of that outpouring of sympathy and money and food was not in vain.

I was the Latin American correspondent for CBS, and I was doing stories years ago, I mean back in the very early '60s, about the problem that Nicaragua was going to someday become. Every reporter in Latin America was doing stories like that, but it was very hard to get them printed or get them on the air. Because in those days, who cared? You had to put Fidel Castro into every lead to even get your story on the air. Every now and then I would send a story in, and it would sit around on the shelf in New York for three or four weeks and it would be a lovely story, one that I had dug up myself. So then I would tell a friend from UP or some wire service, and he'd look into it and run a wire story. They'd see it in New York and they'd say, "Hey, we have this very story on the shelf," and then they'd run it the next day because it had been confirmed by the UP.

QUESTION: *I wanted to thank you so much for showing us that outpouring or groundswell of affection that the Soviets had for Vladimir Horowitz. It was beautiful. Did you feel as awed as perhaps we did?*

CHARLES KURALT: The question is about a program we did the day before yesterday from Russia about the concert of Vladimir Horowitz, the great old piano virtuoso who went back to the place he was born and played his first concert in sixty-one years in Moscow on Sunday. It was indeed a moving experience. It was for me, too. I'm dying to see the program. You know what happens when you're working is that you're thinking, "Okay, I've got to be ready." I have to think of what I'm going to say next, and so I didn't hear the Schubert with the same lack of distraction that people who were sitting at home did. I want to sit down quietly someday to look at that program and see what happened.

I'd never been to the Soviet Union before. Since the subject is journalism tonight, let me tell you this: I've listened to Radio Moscow a good deal. I go fishing out in Montana, and some nights you can't get any AM or FM. So I tune to shortwave, and sometimes the only shortwave I can get is Radio Moscow. The contrast between Radio Moscow and Western radio last week was interesting to me. I was very proud as an American the week of the bombing of Libya. I don't mean that I was necessarily proud of what the U.S. did in Libya. Radio Moscow had a wonderful time reporting the death of children at the hands of the U.S. Air Force. It made you wonder whether those who made the decision to bomb Libya had taken into account more than the possible military gain. It made you wonder if they'd taken into account the possible propaganda loss. Not only in the Soviet Union but in Western Europe and other places. But anyway, what made me proud was then finally, later on in the evening, to hear the Voice of America. For some reason I had assumed that Charles Wick and that crowd had kind of ruined the Voice of America and compromised it. But the lead was roughly as follows: "This is the Voice of America broadcasting from Washington. Here is the news: Demonstrations against the American bombing of Libya continued in the Third World, in Western Europe, and even in the United States today."

That sent chills of pride down my back—to know that you could, even in Moscow, tune in one station to hear what was really happening and that station was an agency of our own government. I think it's the best propaganda of all, to have a place where people around the world know they can turn to hear the truth. Do you understand what I mean? It made me proud to hear what actually was happening after listening to Soviet radio talk about genocide. Radio Moscow reported while I was there that in the raid not only was the French embassy destroyed, but that the French ambassador was killed. And they never corrected it.

QUESTION: *It's kind of a given that the media have become a powerful force in our society. Do you think the media are powerful enough to affect*

policy decisions in the executive branch, and as a sidelight to that, do
you think perhaps the media are too big for their britches and trying to
be too influential?

CHARLES KURALT: Sure, the press has always been too big for its britches,
and there is a natural tension, I think, between government and press. But
it's always been that way. Go back and read what Washington thought of
the press of his day. He had something to complain about. There was no
such thing as a *New York Times*, a place where you could reasonably expect to read the truth. Everybody was grinding his own axe and very often
at President Washington's expense. Jefferson, who said if given the choice
between a free press and a government he would instantly take the press,
said that before he became president. Afterwards he was quite bitter about
his treatment in the press. And so on down to our present times.

It is in the nature of the press to want to find out things and tell people
about them. And it's in the nature of the government to try to keep things
quiet. So it just seems to me that there's always going to be that struggle.
But it is not an even struggle. Remember the press cannot arrest and im-
prison people. The press can't bomb Libya. The press can't do any of the
things that a powerful government can do. All the press can do at its best
is try to tell people what's going on. Politicians and even presidents often
don't like that. But I think, on the whole, it's a healthy thing.

It helps if you can develop a reputation for fairness. Some of you will
remember those days when the Nixon administration launched a concerted
effort to undermine the credibility of the press. Spiro Agnew made that
famous speech in Des Moines in which he suggested that Walter Cronkite
slanted the news by the way he raised his eyebrows or something like that.
Cronkite was a handy man to have around all those years, because people
had seen him and they had seen Spiro Agnew, and they tended to trust
Cronkite. They were right, as it turned out, to do so. So when politicians
and others complain about the almighty power of the press, I've never been
able to weep for them.

Besides, they've learned to use us, you know. The Reagan administration has probably perfected the art better than anybody else. The last political campaign I covered was Kennedy versus Nixon in 1960, and I always
thought the reason Kennedy won—it was a very close election, people
forget—was that Kennedy really enjoyed the give-and-take with the press,
and he really knew how to use us. We resisted being used, of course, but

he'd invite you in for a fifteen-minute private conversation and give you a little nugget of information you could have exclusively. He enjoyed all that, and Nixon was diffident about it, suspicious of the press, and made no friends in the press corps.

Now, all these years later, the technique of exactly when to make an important announcement, that is, twenty minutes before the evening news goes on the air, all of those little tricks have been refined by the people of this administration. And I think that in the struggle between the national government and the press, the national government has all the best of it.

QUESTION: *You mentioned that Edward R. Murrow might be a little disappointed with the way the media have overdramatized things. With the recent wave of terrorism we've seen a lot of critics of the media say that the overdramatization of certain stories gives voice to the people who cause these terrorist acts and in effect adds fuel to their desire to continue on with these attacks. Does coverage on television of terrorist acts encourage more terrorism?*

CHARLES KURALT: I don't know, maybe so. The Barbary pirates did what they did in the Jefferson administration long before there was any television. They didn't do it for news coverage. There'd been that kind of action in the world a long time before we came along to cover it, and there arises the question: What would you have us do? *Not* tell you that a cruise ship has been hijacked, or that a hole has been blown in the wall of a TWA plane in flight? In the end you have to come down on the side of "Please tell us; we would like to know these things." Would terrorism stop if there were no television to cover it? I have grave doubts.

QUESTION: *I have two questions. One, I wonder if you would elaborate on the coffee in Brookings, South Dakota? And then if you could, in relation to all those facts you speak of cluttering your mind, where would a young journalist begin to get the clutter—reading from the past or reading from the present, or just going out after work and hitting the local bars?*

CHARLES KURALT: First, about the coffee. I've thought and thought and thought about it. The coffee gets weaker as you move west. You first start noticing it around here. Izzy and Larry and I decided that the pioneers going west ran out of coffee, and they had to keep reusing the same grounds.

By the time they got around Salt Lake City they liked it that way. They still drink the coffee that way. It certainly is true that until you reach the Donner Pass the coffee gets weaker and weaker and weaker. Then as you come down the hill into San Francisco it's okay again.

Concerning the cluttering of your mind, I think it's a question of reading, of setting out to read a lot, and then savoring the experience you gain in the course of a journalism career. If you have curiosity you build up that cluttered mind. I suppose the trend today is toward specializing; having an uncluttered systematic body of knowledge might be even better. But for the general assignment reporter it is really helpful just to be curious about all kinds of things. And the point I was hoping to make was that the techniques of journalism—how to make up a page, how to read a newscast—those are things you can learn fairly readily. But if you haven't that passionate curiosity to begin with, you probably ought to go into some other line of work—wholesale grocery business or something like that.

Don't you have any trivial questions at all?

QUESTION: *What would you like to have done if you were able to do it over again?*

CHARLES KURALT: From the time I was a little boy I cannot remember a time when I did not want to be a reporter. I don't know where the idea came from. It just seemed romantic to me. And it has been a little bit romantic. I think it is a lovely way to spend one's life, being curious and asking questions. I was never very good at being a real reporter, which I had to do. I was in Latin America as the bureau manager, and I was the Los Angeles bureau manager and covered stories out there. The whole time I was in Latin America I was afraid Dick Valeriani of NBC was sneaking around behind my back, finding out something I didn't know which would make me look bad the next day. And he was! The competitiveness of it and the intensity of it never did appeal to me. Nowadays, if we ever came upon another camera crew, we would leave. We'd figure it's a media event, too big a deal for us. So we never have to worry about that competitiveness. But the way I'm spending my life now is entirely satisfactory. CBS doesn't even know where I am. They don't care where I am.

And it's almost as if people are expecting us to show up. We went to Sopchoppy, Florida, to do a story about worm grunting. You may not know about worm grunting at Notre Dame. What you do is you pound a stake into the ground, preferably using a truck spring to pound it in, and you rub very hard with the truck spring across the top of the stake. It sets up a vibration in the ground, which earthworms find very disagreeable. To escape it they pop to the surface, and you pick them up and go fishing. I didn't believe that, but sure enough there are people around Sopchoppy, Florida, who make a living at it. (It will not surprise you to learn that if you do it in the national forest you have to have a federal worm-gathering permit. That's the truth. You put it in the window of your pickup truck.) There's not much in metropolitan Sopchoppy. The big thing is Mr. M. B. Hodge's bait store, and we went there to ask where we could see some of this going on. We parked the bus and I got out, and there was a guy leaning against the door whittling. Not carving anything, just making a pile of shavings, the way we do in the South, and as I walked by he just glanced at me and said, "Ah, I knew you guys were going to show up here sooner or later." So, to make a career of just showing up, I don't know what else I could have done.

QUESTION: *Don't you believe that oftentimes the news media are pressed to create news that they might not want to or they don't present news that should be presented? For instance, the Bay of Pigs was never made public to the American people. It was never really played out to the fullest extent. Don't you think a lot of that goes on?*

CHARLES KURALT: There's a lot of sloppiness and all that, but I always come down on the side of going ahead and telling people things. In the case of the Bay of Pigs, the *New York Times* found out about it two or three days before it happened, and they were going to print it. President Kennedy begged them not to reveal it because it would abort the mission. Of course, it was a terrible calamity for Kennedy and for U.S. policy, and for those poor guys who landed and were wiped out on the beach. Later on Kennedy admitted that he wished the *Times* had gone ahead and printed it because it would have stopped this thing. I recognize there are times when there are genuine national security considerations, but I'm one of those who believes that in this kind of country, go ahead and tell everybody everything. Ninety-five percent of the stuff stamped "Secret" in Washington is not secret from the Russians in the first place. It's just secret from us. The reason it is called secret is to protect some bureaucrat rather than to protect the national security. There's an awful lot of hanky-panky going on under the broad blanket of national security. As to the other part of your question, about being rushed sometimes into putting some stuff on the air that we wished we hadn't. It does happen sometimes, sure it does, especially under the competitive pressure. But whenever it happens that's just bad journalism. It shouldn't happen. People don't stay misinformed long because that same competitiveness brings us the truth as quickly as it can. We're just so fast now; we can make mistakes in a big hurry. When I was coming along as a young newspaper reporter usually you had time to correct them. You could stop the press, but there's no stopping the press in television.

QUESTION: *Does one "On the Road" story stand out above all the rest?*

CHARLES KURALT: I like the ones about people doing outrageous things. Gordon Bushnell up there in Minnesota who always thought there should be a straight highway from Duluth to Fargo, North Dakota, and the state wouldn't build it so he decided he'd just have to build it himself. He started in to do so, and worked for twenty-five years on it. When we met him he'd finished about eleven miles, had about 180 miles to go, and he was seventy-eight years old at the time. But he just struggled on, sure that someday the state would see the wisdom of it. Mr. Bushnell was not crazy by any means. He was just in love with that road and thought it was a good idea.

I guess my favorite story concerns George Black. It takes an hour and a half to tell, but I'll try to tell you in five minutes. For a journalism discussion this is particularly good because it shows you how journalism works, and it also tells you a little something about how the government works.

We did a story in my home state of North Carolina about Mr. Black, an elderly black brickmaker. He'd been making bricks since 1889, and when we met him he was making bricks yet. He had a mud mill, a mule who walked in circles to stir up the mud, and Mr. Black would take the mud and form it expertly into these big outsized bricks, exactly the way bricks were made in the colonial period. And his bricks were much in demand in places like Williamsburg in Virginia, and Old Salem in North Carolina, and other places where old buildings were being rebuilt. Many of our stories really have been silly or trivial, but this time, as we walked about town with him—he showed us this brick church, and this brick schoolhouse, and this brick walk and this wall—we suddenly realized that he had made the building materials that had made that city, almost alone. He said Mr. R. J. Reynolds came riding out on a white horse one time and said to him, "Mr. Black, do you think you could make a thousand thousand bricks, for I have in mind to build a tobacco factory?" And Mr. Black said yes, he thought he could and did, and there they still are in this enormous building.

The story was just one of those stories that worked. It was more than that. It was a tribute to one of these people I really admire. Well, the morning after it was on the air, I was sitting on the edge of the motel room bed scratching and trying to wake up and figure out where we would go next, and the phone rang. It was Marvin Kalb, our State Department correspondent at the time. Of course, that was a red letter day for me right there, getting a phone call from Marvin Kalb, and he said something to the effect that "There's a fellow here in the State Department who wants to talk to you. I don't know what he wants to talk to you about, but I wish you'd call him and get him off my back. His name is Harvey J. Witherell, and he's on the Guyana desk at USAID. I think he is the Guyana desk over there probably, but call him." I said, "Sure." And I did, and Harvey J. Witherell's voice was just trembling with excitement. He said, "I hear you did a story about a brickmaker last night," and I said, "Yup." And he said, "Gosh, I've been looking all over the country for a brickmaker. Forbes Burnham, the prime minister down in Guyana, told us if we want to give them some foreign aid that would do them some good, send them a brickmaker. He said they have a five-year plan to rebuild the country in brick, and there's no shortage of raw materials, of course—there's plenty of mud in South America—but they don't want to build a big brick factory. They want somebody to teach the people village by village to do it for themselves," and I said, "Well, I've got just the man for you, Harvey, but he is ninety-two years old." And Harvey Witherell said, "I don't care how old he is. I think he's the last one." So I told him how to call Mr. Black. I believe the very next day, on official government business, Harvey packed his suitcase and flew down to Winston-Salem. They met and they struck perhaps what is the best foreign aid deal the country's ever had. For $1,000 ($100 a day) Mr. Black would go to South America for ten days, would go village to village, would take his daughter and a couple of kids from the neighborhood, and they would show those people how—his daughter is also an accomplished brickmaker—and they would do the job for the U.S.A. And Harvey J. Witherell was excited. Mr. Black was excited—he had rarely if ever been out of the county, and here he was going off abroad on a government mission. I was excited. I had been the Latin American reporter, as I said, and I still had credit in the bars down there in Georgetown, and I thought it would be nice to get back and see old friends, and it became a pretty big deal, as these government things do.

They called this one Operation Black Jack, and cables flew back and forth between Washington and Georgetown. I have a stack, somebody sneaked them out of the State Department for me. It's not another Pentagon Papers Case; they were not classified documents, but they stand a foot or two high.

As this thing was planned it became a bigger and bigger deal. The FBI came down and fingerprinted Mr. Black to make sure he was not some kind of dangerous subversive going abroad to represent the country. You can't imagine how big it became. But somebody high up in the State Department looking this thing over said, "Wait a minute. This man is ninety-two years old. That's just ridiculous." He stamped the whole thing "canceled," and down it tumbled through the bureaucracy, and it all landed on Harvey's desk. And he called me this time practically in tears. He said, "After all this, it's all over. They say he's too old." I said, "Way it goes, Harvey." I tried to cheer him. He's one of those bureaucrats we're always reading about. He'd been there twenty years, and here he was trembling on the brink of actually doing something. He'd been so excited, and he'd been shot down.

But here comes the journalism. This is the way it works. Mr. Black had been telling people in the neighborhood how he was going to go to South America, and the *Winston-Salem Journal*, a pretty good paper, sent a reporter and photographer around. They did a page-one story, "Mr. Black's Going to South America," as a result of this television program. And the UPI reads the *Winston-Salem Journal*, and they said that's not a bad story. They picked it up and ran it nationwide, "A" wire with a wire photo, "Mr. Black's Going to South America." And the *Washington Post* subscribes to the UPI, and they said that's a pretty good story, and they picked it up and ran the picture. And the White House reads the *Washington Post*, as we all remember, and somebody at the White House said, "Wouldn't it be wonderful if President Nixon would see this man off?"

The timing was just exquisite. The very week that the State Department had canceled the whole thing, the White House was inviting Mr. Black to come meet the president on his way to South America. And Harvey J. Witherell, sitting there in the wreckage of his dream, let his eye fall on the president's appointment schedule for the week and it said, "10 A.M. Wednesday, George Black, who is going to South America for the State Department." So, of course, that made Harvey feel better, a lot better. And he, whistling a little tune, cut that item out and attached it to his canceled project and sent it up through the bureaucracy again, and, sure enough, as he knew it would, all the wheels that had been running backwards started running fast forward. The canceled project became a high-priority project, and Mr. Black came to Washington. Of course, nobody at the White House thought to ask how he was going to get to Washington, so he came on a Greyhound bus the way people do, and they said, "Bring your family." He did. He brought thirty-two of them.

At the White House the guards said, "Oh, no, this is too many people," and they argued about it, and finally they said, "We'll let half of you in." And President Nixon said, "It's a very nice family you have here, Mr. Black." Mr. Black said, "You know, it's only half of them. They made the other half stand out there on the street." So President Nixon, to his credit, said, "I'll see the other half this afternoon at three o'clock." So Mr. Black got to see the president, not once but twice, and did go to South America and ran all the people ragged who thought he was too old. They all came back exhausted. He came back feeling great.

But the great moment was the day Mr. Black went to the White House. They opened the Oval Office doors for three minutes, and all these animals rushed in, the press, taking pictures and taking notes. I was one of the animals that day, straining to see what was happening. And some big burly photographer pushed Harvey J. Witherell right out of the way. "Excuse me, buddy." To take a picture. In his moment of glory, you know, he's shunted aside. But I have a picture on my office wall. It's terrific. It shows President Nixon in the middle, and it shows a sea of handsome black faces—half of Mr. Black's family—and one white face sticking in from the corner. Harvey J. Witherell got in there.

I'm sorry. That's what happens when you ask a simple question of a long-winded reporter. Well, you have had better speakers in the three previous episodes of the Red Smith Lecture than you have had tonight. I have the greatest admiration for Murray Kempton and James Reston and Jack Kilpatrick, and I hope that you have more profound speakers in the future than I have been able to be. But you won't have any who will have as much fun as I have had with you tonight, and I thank you very much.

Person to Person

RED SMITH

THE SIGN

JULY 1960

The advertisement for a new book by H. Allen Smith says he "tells hilarious, scandalous tales about his Westchester neighbors, he reveals the sacred secret of what goes on behind a *Person to Person* interview."

Well, I haven't read *Let the Crabgrass Grow*, though I mean to, because Allen Smith is my favorite namesake, and I try not to miss anything he writes. However, as to that sacred secret behind *Person to Person*, that bugs me. That sacred secret has been a glowing coal in my bosom ever since the scandals broke about television's rigged quiz shows and Ed Murrow quit *Person to Person* because it was disclosed that this show was rigged, too. (Ed had always believed that when his cameras picked up Fred and Clara Nusspickel impaled against their living room sofa with Pepsodent simpers pasted on their faces, they were no less astonished by the chance encounter than he was.)

May a survivor tell what It is really like? In our house, that fateful night is always referred to as It. We look back on It with much the same sentiments that Washington's soldiers cherished for Valley Forge. And although more than a year has gone by since the performance, we are still encountering "audience reaction," as we call it in show biz.

One of us gets introduced to somebody in Logan, Utah, or Lexington, Kentucky, and with the handshake comes a faintly puzzled frown. Then the expression clears.

"Oh, yes," our Public says, "I saw you on *Person to Person*."

There is a silence, receptive on our part, strained on his. Our new friend bites his lip.

"Staying here long?" he says. "Or just passing through?"

The way it all started, this friend of mine who is a friend of Ed Murrow's called up and asked, "How about going on *Person to Person*?" and I said, "Well, I don't know," and the kids said, "Aw, come on, Pop, it'll be fun," so I said, "Well, okay then."

We didn't exactly finalize the deal right then, as we say in TV biz.

In fact, by the time a date was set the kids were (a) married and living in Milwaukee and (b) away at college.

We live in Connecticut at the end of a little lane, four houses in from the road. A month before the appointed day, men arrived to photograph our humble Cape Cod and measure rooms, which seemed just a little snoopy of CBS. Two weeks later, telephone linemen popped out of the woods, pulling down old poles and putting up new ones festooned with transformers, cyclotrons, and Buck Rogers death-ray disintegrators, stringing wires, laying waste to our neighbor's crepe myrtle. After them came the structural steel men.

I forget which tobacco company sponsored *Person to Person*, but this I know: If I had foreseen, when I started smoking, what trouble it would put people to just to sell a carton of cigarettes, I'd never have switched from corn silk.

One day I was awakened before noon by a cry, "Get an ambulance!" and a pounding on the door. A glance out the window told what had happened. Obviously, Danny Arnstein, having completed the Burma Road, had moved his entire force and all trucks, cars, armor, and heavy equipment onto our half-acre. A Jack's beanstalk of spidery steel had sprouted overnight and now towered above the trees. Our

neighbor across the lane burst out of her house with blankets for two men stretched on the frozen earth.

A big truck had slipped its brakes, rolled down an incline, and pinned the men against another truck. It was feared that one had a broken back and internal injuries, but later when the ambulance had carried them away and three carloads of police had arrived to take reports in triplicate, word came from the hospital that the only serious injury was one compound leg fracture.

The tower, we were informed, was needed to pick up "the signal" and toss it to the next Connecticut ridge, where an identical structure was being built to pick it up and fling it into New York. Without these monsters, and a garageful of electronic gadgets that crowded our car out into the winter, America could not have heard that deathless cue:

"Well, Red, as a sportswriter you must meet some mighty interesting people."

The entertainment world would never have been thrilled by the response:

"Well, Ed, now's you mention it, I guess I prolly do, at that."

On an evening early in The Week, two directors of It arrived with notebooks. Real nice guys named Charley Hill and David Moore. We had a couple of slugs and talked, and they made notes. They went away, and peace reigned until Friday, peace broken only by the tourists.

Evidently there is a race that reads up on approaching TV attractions and then goes snooping. Sightseers kept pulling in to park in the driveway, stroll about the premises, peer into windows, back their cars across the lawn, and drive away, looking disdainful. A midwinter thaw gave their tires excellent deep traction in the turf.

Shortly after noon on Friday, Charley and Dave came back with crew, mobile unit truck, and scripts. Based on the notes they had made earlier, the scripts read like this:

Mr. Murrow: Good evening, Kay.
Kay: Ad lib.
Mr. Murrow: Good evening, Red.
Red: Ad lib.

That's the part they said was rigged.

It is said that on occasions like this your entire life flashes before your eyes, and lots of people never appreciate what a fascinating life they've had until they see this review. I know only that the details of that day are all fuzzed up in my memory.

It seems to me we went through the script once or twice with Dave or Charley impersonating Ed Murrow and the other holding a stopwatch while we tried to make up answers.

Meanwhile the crew took our house apart. They shifted furniture, rearranged pictures, covered mirrors in pale blue chiffon, strung fine wires along all the wall moldings, ran cables in through open windows, set up cameras and spotlights, concealed sundry tools of Satan in the fireplace.

Mom and I went out for hamburgers—no, it was Friday—tuna fish salad. We returned to a freezing house, where the winter wind whistled through all the windows that couldn't be closed on account of the cables. There were twenty-eight guys in our house, and it is a small house.

A man hid a microphone about the size of a walnut in the lining of my necktie. He strapped on a shoulder holster under my jacket, holding batteries and stuff. He ran a wire down my leg and clipped it to the pants cuff. I think I was disappointed when he didn't slit my trousers and shave my head for the electrodes.

They gave Mom a mike to hide in her bosom and a girdle with pockets for the batteries and stuff. We were now wired for sound, and it was about 7 P.M. The show wouldn't go on until 10.

We had what they call a "walk-through" with Mr. Murrow. No speaking parts, really, just a rehearsal of the business so everybody would know when it was time to go downstairs and show Ed a picture of Yogi Berra. We never did get to see our interlocutor, but his voice came through squawk boxes in each room.

I was showing him the swimming pool. When we bought this house the pool came with it, and I was self-conscious about it because we're not the Hollywood type. However, it's no bigger than a billiard table and costs no more for upkeep than a steam yacht, so I quit trying to pretend it didn't exist. I was standing back there under a mess of floodlights, and all of a sudden I heard Ed's voice, very snappish:

"You people over there, near that white thing. Will you get out of there, please?"

His camera had picked up another batch of tourists who had come around behind the house and were standing alongside a little white bathhouse, or dressing-room, that we like to call our cabana. That's what burned me up, "that white thing."

Well, they chased the tourists and we got back into the house, where the temperature was now around zero. Reluctantly, the directors let Mom put on a light sweater. It was air time.

"Good evening, Kay," came the mellifluous greeting, "Good evening, Red."

"G-g-g-g-good-d-devng, Mizzurmur," we said through chattering teeth. It was a smash hit, though I never did get to complain to Ed Murrow about calling our cabana that white thing. I meant to, but the fact is I've never met Ed.

DAVE KINDRED Besides being named State Sportswriter of the Year on fifteen occasions in three states and National Sportswriter of the Year in 1998, Dave Kindred received the Red Smith Award from the Associated Press Sports Editors in 1991 for his major contributions to sports journalism. A columnist for the Louisville *Courier-Journal*, the *Washington Post*, the *Atlanta Journal-Constitution*, and *The Sporting News*, he also served as associate editor and columnist at *The National*, the daily sports newspaper that was published from January 31, 1990, until June 14, 1991. Kindred is the author of several books, including *Heroes, Fools and Other Dreamers* (1988), *Glove Stories: The Collected Baseball*

Writing of Dave Kindred (2002), and *Sound and Fury* (2006), about the relationship between boxing champion Muhammad Ali and sportscaster Howard Cosell. He delivered this lecture on April 17, 1991. **BOB HAMMEL**, who earned many awards for sportswriting during a newspaper career spanning more than a half-century, responded to the lecture. He's the author of eight books, including *The Bill Cook Story: Ready, Fire, Aim!* (2008). **JANE LEAVY** visited Notre Dame within days of the Red Smith Lecture and offered her views on Smith and sportswriting to a campus audience. She's the author of the baseball novel *Squeeze Play* (1990) and *Sandy Koufax: A Lefty's Legacy* (2002).

DAVE KINDRED

90 Feet
Is Perfection

I can't tell you how many times I've come to a difficult spot in a column and said, "What would Red do here?" So now I come before you at a ceremony honoring Red's memory and his contributions to journalism. I don't know what to do. What would Red do? Red would tell you the truth.

The truth is, I've never been so honored. Red Smith was my hero, and journalism is my life. To be invited to speak to this distinguished group on subjects so dear to me—it reminds me of a line the former Kentucky governor Happy Chandler always used. Happy began his speeches saying, "I'm like the mosquito that flew over the fence into the nudist colony. I don't know where to begin."

Sportswriters are not accustomed to being honored, unless you count it an honor to receive mail from offended readers.

I once got a letter from a farmer in Berea, Kentucky. I had done a column suggesting that the University of Kentucky's basketball team would lose an important game to Indiana. When Kentucky happened to win that important game, the farmer in Berea went to work collecting his letter, and it arrived a couple days later. There was a note. And there was a plain plastic bag with some brown stuff in it. The note said, "Dear Dave: Here's some pure Bluegrass horse manure, the same stuff that column was made up of."

Coaches in particular have little forbearance with sportswriters. My friend and yours, the basketball coach at Indiana University, once said he thought he'd like to be a political cartoonist because a political cartoonist needs only one idea a day. "But then," Bob Knight said, "I decided I'd be a sports columnist because a sports columnist doesn't need any ideas."

Norm Van Brocklin was a great pro football player and mediocre pro football coach. Sadly, he developed a brain tumor. But he didn't lose his sense of humor or his sense of what a sportswriter is. "If I get a brain transplant," Norm said, "I want a sportswriter's brain. That way I'll get one that's never been used."

A sportswriter buddy of mine, Dick Fenlon, once called Adolph Rupp late at night. Rupp was the great Kentucky coach and curmudgeon who believed in a bourbon or three before bedtime. Fenlon introduced himself and asked if they might talk. Rupp said, "Fenlon, Fenlon. I know two writers in Louisville. One's Fenlon and one's Kindred. One's a good guy and the other's a son of a bitch. Which one are you?"

Fenlon quickly claimed to be the good guy. Which leaves you with me. Again, it's an honor to be here, and it's a certain honor to be the first sportswriter asked to do this lecture.

In April of 1967, I walked into the old press barn at Augusta National Golf Club and stood in the back of the room looking over rows and rows of typewriters with men working while they faced a giant scoreboard at the front. I had asked at the check-in desk where Red Smith was sitting. Most sportswriters arrive at Augusta National the week of the Masters golf tournament to see some golf. Not me.

I'd been reading Red Smith for ten years by then, and all I wanted at Augusta was to see the great man at work.

Once upon a time, I wanted to be a major league baseball player. I believed myself, in the fashion of all teenage phenoms, to be quite the prospect. I could hit, I could field, and I could run. How I could run. I believed I was very fast—until the day my father challenged me to a race to first base.

He was a carpenter. That day he wore his carpenter's shoes, big ol' things that he called clodhoppers. He had a carpenter's pencil shoved up under his cap. He said, "Let's race to first base."

So I figured I'd show the old man what the new generation was made of. We took off from home plate together. We stayed together for a few strides. Then I began to notice something. I noticed I was no longer stride-for-stride. I was a distinct second in a two-man race.

My father beat me to first base by a step that day. As we slowed down on the outfield grass, he looked at me. I looked at him. And I did what any teenage phenom would have done. Without hesitation and with no remorse whatsoever, I lied. I told him I hadn't been really trying. I told him we'd have to do it again sometime.

That was the day, I think, that it dawned on me that maybe, perhaps, could be, I would never make it as a big league baseball player. It was a little lesson in mortality.

And soon enough my dream changed. I couldn't be a big-league ballplayer. Well, I'd be a big-league sportswriter.

That's when I began reading Red Smith. Happily for me, his columns were carried in my local newspaper, the *Daily Pantagraph* of Bloomington, Illinois.

I loved the laughter in those columns. Red went places and did things and talked to famous people. All of that was good. But what I liked most was the simple pleasure of reading words written by a man so clearly happy to be writing them.

By that April day in 1967 when I stood at the back of the Augusta National press barn, I'd been reading Red Smith for ten years. I was then twenty-six years old and writing golf stories for the Louisville *Courier-Journal*. I remember standing at the back of the barn just watching Red Smith type. He had a little portable typewriter. I remember he used two hands to guide the paper into the roll. He typed with two fingers, and he typed slowly. As I stood at the back of the room, I imagined he was writing poetry on that clackety-clack machine, poetry from a press barn, poetry about Arnold Palmer most likely—but poetry nonetheless.

I have been disappointed many times by journalists of great talent and fame. I have found them to be mean-spirited frauds. In the fifteen years I knew Red Smith, he never once disappointed me. He was everything his work suggested him to be. He was kind and gentle and caring.

I count it as one of my life's blessings that Red Smith took an interest in a kid golf writer from Atlanta, Illinois.

So I'm happy to be here today because nothing means more to me than to have a chance to tell people that Red Smith is what journalism ought to be.

Red worked with a talent given to very few people. Yet the reason that talent shone so brightly is that Red worked very hard to give it a foundation. That foundation was reporting. He always thought of himself first as a reporter digging up stories. With the stories in hand, Red then turned them into little jewels shining with touches of his writing brilliance.

Red attended the first night baseball game in St. Louis, the first one under the newfangled arc lights, and wrote an account of that game from the point of view of a glowworm made melancholy because the night no longer belonged to him.

Red always told me, when I asked the secret, "Be there." Be there. Reporters go to where the stories are. No story ever came to my front door and demanded to be written.

But if I went to Moscow, there was a story. If I went to Yankee Stadium, if I went to the Kentucky Derby, if I came to South Bend to see O. J. Simpson on a day when Terry Hanratty would throw seven interceptions and wind up sitting on the bench, an ice pack on his battered brow—if I did those things, then I had a chance to do the reporting that journalists are paid to do. Red always said, "I'm a reporter, just a working stiff trying to write better than I can."

I can't think of a better recipe for great journalism.

Unfortunately, today's journalism is not that at all. Today too many newspapers believe in devaluing reporting. Worse, newspapers have become the enemy of writing.

It began, I think, with the emergence of *USA Today*. Over the last seven or eight years, every newspaper in the country has made changes based on what they've seen in *USA Today*. Those changes, I believe, have hurt journalism as a whole. It's all packaging now. It's color graphics and pie charts and news nuggets. I call it Wizard of Oz journalism. No heart, no brain, no courage—and when you look behind the colorful front, there's nothing there. It's empty, a trick, a fraud.

Not that I'm criticizing *USA Today*. My criticism is directed at publishers and editors who have been seduced by the *USA Today* formula. I don't criticize *USA Today* because it is exactly what it set out to be: a quick read off the top of the news. Some people have said *USA Today* is the newspaper for people too busy to watch TV—and I'm sure the *USA Today* folks consider that a compliment. They have defined a market niche, and they have created a product that sells.

Fine. More power to them. I just don't think the *USA Today* formula ought to be applied to every newspaper in this country. And that's what is happening.

Newspapers have convinced themselves that people don't have time to read. They have convinced themselves of this by doing surveys which report less and less time spent reading newspapers. So they react to this information by creating newspapers which can be read in a hurry. The stories are short. There are summaries of stories everywhere, sort of a *Cliffs Notes* version of the news. Newspapers are assuming the worst for a business that depends on the printed word. They're assuming that no one wants to read and so must be lured into the odious act.

Then why, tell me, are booksellers doing greater business than ever in history? Why are there more magazines sold today than ever in history? People are reading. They'll always read. There is a tactile pleasure in reading that cannot be replicated by television. Red Smith said people go to games to have fun, and they pick up the paper the next morning to have fun again. They pick up the paper because there's a heft to it. There's a real touch. They may see a story on the eleven o'clock news, but they'll read the paper the next day to see what happened.

Television is the appetizer. Newspapers are the steak and potatoes.

Yet newspapers are bent on transforming themselves from the substantial to the trivial. Let *USA Today* do that, just as Charles Kuralt goes on the road and does his act and I go to ball games and do mine. There's a market for the superficial, for human interest, for entertainment.

But newspapers as a whole should resist with all their might the seductive lure of superficial journalism. People will read if we give them reason to read. That's because people do what they like to do. If people tell survey takers they just don't have time to read newspapers, I say it's because newspapers have failed in their mission. People will make time to do what they must do. People will make time to do what they like to do. That should be the goal of newspapers: to be essential even as they are entertaining.

Coverage of the Persian Gulf War is persuasive evidence that good newspapers are important to readers. It was a television war. We saw it before our eyes. And yet we bought more newspapers than ever because for all we saw on the television, there still was a need to understand it. As brilliant as Gen. Norman Schwarzkopf was in explaining the coalition's ground war strategy, I read three newspapers and two news magazines before I understood just why, how, when, and where we ran that "Hail Mary" play with two hundred thousand soldiers.

During the Gulf War, I wrote several columns with war themes. I didn't like the overheated patriotism I saw at the Super Bowl. Nor did I like the Seton Hall story in which the Italian basketball player Marco Lokar was basically run out of the country because he wouldn't wear an American flag on his jersey.

On those issues, I was in a minority so small as to be invisible. Even my wife, my best friend, asked why I wrote columns that ran so directly against public sentiment. I had to do them, I told her, because sports is more than just games. It's a real part of our lives, and we need to understand what sports tells us about ourselves.

I always come back to Red. He said the best sportswriting is done by writers who pay attention to what's happening outside the white lines. I have tried to do that. People even have thought to praise me by saying, "Gee, sports is a metaphor for life, the way you write about it." I thank them and move on, because if sports is more than a game, it's also more than a metaphor. To say it's a metaphor is to say that sports stands for nothing on its own. To say it's a metaphor means it only makes sense when understood in terms of real life. We see sports demanding "pride" and "dedication" and "commitment" and "sacrifice" and "courage." Those are values important to real life, and so we assign a metaphorical value to sports because it inspires those values in us.

I think sports does much more than that. It's much more than a metaphor. It's the real thing. Howard Cosell tells us that sports is a fantasy world where greed and duplicity are ignored rather than confronted. As always, Howard is telling it like it is. Corruption and hypocrisy are part of our games as surely as they are part of politics, religion, and journalism. Yet there is an undeniable value in sports. That value speaks to the heart of American principles and beliefs. It's why Red Smith worked fifty-five years in sports journalism. The *60 Minutes* people came to Red after he won the Pulitzer Prize in 1976 and basically asked him why he'd wasted his life writing sports. Red's kind and gentle answer to Morley Safer was, "The only thing still standing in Rome is the ballpark." By that Red meant there's important work to do in understanding why people gather in coliseums and arenas and ballparks.

Today's sportswriters are better than ever. George Solomon, my friend and the assistant managing editor for sports at the *Washington Post*, says it's no longer possible for a sportswriter to be simply a fan going to the ball games. Now they must be able to do the broad range of work demanded of any journalist in the building: issues, ideas, features, profiles, deadline reporting. I'm proud to be one of those folks, though, I admit, I've been writing sports for thirty-two years, and there have been hundreds of times when I wondered why I kept at it. Why didn't I grow up? I always came back to Red. If a man of his class and talent did sports forever, there must be something there. I spent years wondering why our games have such a hold on us.

I keep my old baseball glove on my desk. It's a Wilson A2000 and it's beautiful and it's the best baseball glove ever made. After all this time the leather is a golden color under a patina of dirt carried away from infields all over Illinois. If I slide my hand into the glove, I feel the leather a little dry, but it's soft. It's soft enough that when you feel it against your palm you remember a kid's dreams. To feel the A2000 is to imagine it carrying you toward a sharply hit ground ball behind second base. To touch the glove now is to remember a time when you were young enough to do anything, even outrun your dad to first base.

That's why I keep that glove there. And I'm not alone. George Bush keeps his old first baseman's mitt in a drawer in the Oval Office. Richard Nixon suggested plays to the Washington Redskins. Ronald Reagan said games are good because they're clean hate. The Spanish philosopher George Santayana said in the 1920s that his three favorite things about America were our kindness, our jazz bands, and our football. Historian Jacques Barzun said anyone who would understand the heart and mind of America first must learn baseball.

Rev. Timothy S. Healy used to be president at Georgetown University. He said, "Games are beautiful in their complexity, their rhythm, as well as in the beauty of their players. The ancient Greeks knew that it was a good thing for all of us to watch beauty, above all when that beauty involved movement, suddenness, and improvisation. Watching anyone do anything well enlarges the soul."

I saw Larry Bird score 3 points once at an important time in a big ball game. He did it with an improbable move to the basket and with a free throw. It was only one play, only 3 points—yet it was all of a man's life.

Larry Bird's mother raised six children as a $2-an-hour short-order cook in French Lick, Indiana. His father had been something of a hotshot kid basketball player until he quit school after the eighth grade. Between drinks, Bird's father was said to be the best piano tuner in French Lick. He killed himself a year after the divorce. The boy Larry Bird was seventeen.

He went from his little nowhere town to the big state school, Indiana University. But he left after a month. He'd looked into his roommate's closet and seen all the new clothes he could never have. After making his millions with the Celtics, he took to calling himself "the hick from French Lick."

There'd been a time at seventeen when he'd never thought much about life after high school. He guessed he would work construction, pour concrete, something. All he cared about was basketball. Still, he would say, "I went to class and did my homework," because he believed it would catch up to you if you didn't do your work.

He once said, "The guy who won't do his schoolwork misses the free throw at the end. In high school," he said, "we used to shoot fouls at 6:30 in the morning before class, but one of my best friends never showed up. In the regional finals our senior year, he missed three one-and-ones in a row, and we lost in overtime. I never said nothing to him. I just looked at him—and he knew."

For Larry Bird, the game is no metaphor. It is real. It is joy. It is Pete Rose explaining his rough-cut face by saying, "You'd look this way, too, if you'd slid head-first for twenty years." It is Al Campanis, a Dodger scout at the time, saying he'd seen a great young pitcher named Sandy Koufax—and Campanis said, "When I stood at the plate against Koufax and saw that fastball coming, the hairs stood up on my arms. The only other time that happened was when I saw the Sistine ceiling."

The novelist W. P. Kinsella wrote, "Within the baselines, anything can happen. Tides can reverse, oceans can open. That's why they say, 'The game is never over until the last man is out.' Colors can change, lives can alter, anything is possible in this gentle, flawless, loving game."

And we are connected to the games. We're connected in ways we seldom acknowledge and may never understand. We may get no further as a player than sandlot games. We may race our fathers one day and discover we're not all we hoped to be. But when we go to the ballpark, the place of our dreams, we feel a connection to the game. We vibrate in tune to the game's eternal rhythms. It all feels right, as few things in life feel all right.

I love the games because they show me how good we can be, and by that I mean good in every way: morally, spiritually, physically. To see Michael Jordan in motion, that great, angular body sprinting across a floor, now flying, now doing something even more impossible than the impossible thing of last night—to see Jordan is to know that God's in His heaven and well pleased.

I write about different sports in different tones of voice. For golf, I am soft and pastoral. Football makes me angry. Basketball quickens my heart. Boxing scares me. These moods then are reflected in what I write.

As natural and predictable as that may sound, the connection never occurred to me until one day I tried to figure out why I feel so good at the Masters and so lousy at the Super Bowl. Well. Golf is poetry, football is war. I like poetry better.

So the games changed me, even as a spectator, even as an objective reporter. They changed me by seducing me into their rhythms. It seems only natural and predictable, then, that the games would have touched me in more substantive ways. If I am changed by the casual rhythms of golfers and the simple geography of 200 acres, then how am I changed by the senses of order, fairness, and justice which are the underpinnings of our games?

For the better, I would hope. We see greatness in Joe Montana, and we draw from his example a feeling of strength and excellence. We put that feeling to our own uses, perhaps in work as difficult as a mother's rearing a child, perhaps even in the writing of a sentence. We would be as good in every way as our games have shown it is possible to be.

The world, an imperfect place, seeks harmony above all. Our games already have it. Red once wrote, "Ninety feet between bases is the nearest to perfection that man has yet achieved."

Truth is all we want from this world. Finding it at ball games gives us reason to think we can find it somewhere else.

I once went to a little coal town in eastern Kentucky to write about a high school basketball team that played its games on the second floor of the school building. They had chicken wire over the windows to protect the glass from wayward basketballs. People in the first row of bleachers—there were two rows—pulled back their feet whenever play came their way.

The coach took me to his house for dinner that night, and while we talked I heard an odd noise in the room. The noise came every two or three seconds, like someone breathing, except this sounded like dirt rattling through a sifter. I looked around the table and saw that the sound came from the coach's father.

He was a small man made to seem smaller by the way his back was bent. It was a coal miner's humped back produced by a lifetime bent double bringing up coal from mine shafts 3 feet high.

His terrible and terrifying work never got the coach's father enough money to move away from the place called Kingdom Come. What he got, by breathing coal dust, was black lung disease—and the noise I heard at the table was the rush of air being sucked into a dying man's lungs.

I wrote about it. I wrote a little bit about basketball and a lot about life in a hell called Kingdom Come. I told how the father had sacrificed his life to give his son an education that led him into teaching and coaching. Sports touches real people in real ways. The theologian and writer Michael Novak wrote, "Most of what Americans know about the humanistic traditions—about excellence in act, about discipline, about community, about unity of body and will and spirit—they learn first-hand from their experiences in sport."

One of today's best sportswriters is Tom Callahan. He knew Red better than I did, and he learned from the great man. Tom says of sports, "There's something there that buoys people. If you write about sports long enough, you're constantly coming back to the point that something buoys people, something makes you feel better for having been there. Something is hallowed here. I think that something is excellence."

It's Ted Williams at bat. It's Vince Lombardi and Bob Knight creating teams of simple purity. It's Larry Bird inventing a wonder when a wonder is the only answer. It's Walter Payton running, Muhammad Ali floating like a butterfly. It's ordinary people doing extraordinary things and extraordinary people doing unimagined things. We see these things done by men, the Sistine ceiling painted by a man, and we know at these moments that we are part of something greater than ourselves.

We come away from these moments as the British essayist Bernard Levin came away from a production of *Nicholas Nickleby*. He said he came away "not merely delighted but strengthened, not just entertained but uplifted, not only affected but changed."

A Response

BOB HAMMEL

My listed function is to respond, which I hope does not imply a contesting, opposing voice. I can only endorse not only what David has said but also his very presence: as the first sportswriter to give the Red Smith Lecture. What imaginative casting on Notre Dame's part.

But also, what splendidly proper casting. Dave Kindred is my choice as the very best practitioner of the art that the late and great Mr. Smith illuminated for all of us.

I imagine there was a point in Dave's career development when the experience of reading Red Smith brought the same inward reaction that I know I had, and another writer from another field and another era describes:

> If I come across by chance in the good authors, as I often do, those same subjects I have attempted to treat, seeing myself so weak and puny, so heavy and sluggish, in comparison with those men, I hold myself in pity and disdain. Still, I am pleased at this, that my opinions have the honor of often coinciding with theirs, and that at least I go the same way, though far behind them, saying, "How true!"

How very true.

The "good authors" do indeed include some sportswriters, though it doesn't take any of us long before a certain sense of worthlessness sets in, a feeling that surely there is something of considerably more benefit to mankind that could be pursued.

Dave's one boss at *The National*, Frank Deford, wrote, "I can't imagine that any of us worth a dime doesn't go through a phase in which we question whether it is a fulfilled life in the toy shop. . . . I could visualize grandchildren coming up to me in my dotage and saying, 'Big Daddy, what did you do during Vietnam?' And I would reply that I had been at the NBA playoffs. Or, 'Poppy, where were you during the Civil Rights movement?' And I would explain that I missed that because of the Stanley Cup. But, finally, I resolved the issue with myself: that I am a writer, and that incidentally I write mostly about sports, and what is important is to write well, the topic be damned."

I'm sure Dave has experienced that questioning of values. I know I have, many times. And each time, I have thought the whole thing over, considered the things that I could do, that I am trained to do, educated to do, capable of doing, and I ended up grateful that Red Smith did invent sportswriting and spared me the unemployment line.

But any sport is just a game, questionable in its worth for the time we give it. A writer/player said of his sport,

> I hate it and avoid it because it is not enough of a game and too serious an amusement. . . . See how our mind swells and magnifies this ridiculous amusement. . . . What passion does not excite us in this game: anger, vexation, hatred, impatience, and a vehement ambition to win in a thing in which ambition to be beaten would be more excusable. For rare and extraordinary excellence in frivolous things is unbecoming a man of honor.

Let me identify the "athlete," the same person whose self-doubt on writing I read earlier: the sixteenth-century French essayist Montaigne, who was referring to chess.

The people we cover are comparatively new to the concept of visual aids. Only in relatively recent times have young athletes been able to study films or tapes of the greatest players doing just what they are trying to learn to do. It's a wonderful shortcut, a great teaching tool.

But we in any field of writing have had such visual aids available to us forever, at the public library. Montaigne may have hated sports, and not even conceived them in the sense we do today, but what he said about writing would serve any young sportswriter well:

> I want the substance to stand out, and so to fill the imagination of the listener that he will have no memory of the words. The speech I love is a simple, natural speech, the same on paper as in the mouth; a speech succulent and sinewy, brief and compressed, not so much dainty and well-combed as vehement and brisk.

He said, "Eloquence that diverts us to itself is unfair to the content." What a succinct and beautifully phrased attack on overwriting.

We can study reporting techniques that go back much further than
Montaigne. In *The Innocents Abroad*, Mark Twain wrote,

> It is hard to make a choice of the most beautiful passage in
> a book which is so gemmed with beautiful passages as the
> Bible. Who taught those ancient writers their simplicity
> of language, their felicity of expression, their pathos, and,
> above all, their facility of sinking themselves entirely out
> of sight of the reader and making the narrative stand out
> alone and seem to tell itself?
>
> Shakespeare is always present when one reads his
> books. But the Old Testament writers are hidden from view.

Mark Twain speaks of a vanishing art in the field Dave and I share. Less
and less is there on the sports pages the work of writers who put the story
first, who cherish as much as Mark Twain the "facility of sinking themselves
entirely out of sight of the reader and making the narrative stand out alone
and seem to tell itself."

Today's style is to write to be noticed, to cut, to be regarded as brave.
Red Smith and Dave Kindred could slice to the bone when the subject merited it, but do it with an elegance that said the pleasure was in the precision
and perfection of the slicing, not the cut itself.

The thought regularly occurs to me: Can the writer whose style com-
pels him to cut and slash daily go home at night pleased? Happy?

Deford wrote,

> I always marveled at Red Smith that, as fine as his work
> was, he could go on turning out the same-length piece, day
> in and day out, for bloody decades. It must be a real art,
> for him or for all the best columnists—Dutch miniaturists.
> Most of the best sports columnists today do, at least oc-
> casionally, venture into other territory, writing books or,
> anyway, articles. But Smith was the purest columnist. I
> was always very envious of him, imagining that he must
> have been the happiest of writers, the happiest of men.

Still, Deford contends that sportswriting is better today than in olden
days, my days. He should be right, for one major reason: Women are in

the field, too, another senseless barrier down. The effect must be improvement, just as baseball has to be better now than in the "golden" '20s and '30s because it no longer is whites-only, to its vast benefit.

But sportswriting is simply an aspect of news writing in general, and there is evidence of a lack of conscience or responsibility there that a growing segment of the public finds distasteful. Freedom of the press is not an issue the public would vote in today, and maybe never would have.

In his book *Statecraft and Stagecraft*, Professor Robert Schmuhl, among other things director of this university's Program on Ethics and the Media, noted how consistently and prominently the newspaper industry flaunts the 1787 statement of Thomas Jefferson: "Were it left to me to decide whether we should have government without newspapers or newspapers without government, I should not hesitate for a moment to prefer the latter."

But twenty years later, six years into his presidency, Schmuhl notes in his book, Jefferson said in a private letter,

> It is a melancholy truth, that a suppression of the press could not more completely deprive the nation of its benefits, than is done by its abandoned prostitution to falsehood. Nothing can now be believed which is seen in a newspaper. Truth itself becomes suspicious by being put into that polluted vehicle. The real extent of this state of misinformation is known only to those who are in situations to confront facts within their knowledge with the lies of the day. I really look with commiseration over the great body of my fellow citizens, who, reading newspapers, live and die in the belief that they have known something of what has been passing in the world in their time.

Is that true today, on the news pages? On the sports pages?

I hear repeatedly from champions of today's free-firing young sportswriters that it's a good thing ol' beer-guzzling, womanizing Babe Ruth came along when writers were idolaters, because he would have been cut to pieces today. But did you read anywhere of Pete Rose's immersion into gambling before there were formal charges? Did you read of Wade Boggs's affairs before there were charges? Where were the revelations about Sugar Ray Leonard before a court transcript spelled them out?

The primary difference today is that rudeness and ridicule have replaced Smith- or Kindred-style eloquence as the quickest and surest ways up the sportswriting ladder. H. L. Mencken in news and Jim Murray in sports showed there can be art and style in those, but that part is lost in today's rush toward irreverence.

How nice that tonight we honor an exception—two, really: Dave Kindred and Red Smith.

Sportswriting: A Woman's View

JANE LEAVY

U ndoubtedly the greatest lapse of my sportswriting career is that I never covered a game at Notre Dame. Still, I always thought I got my start here. I became a sportswriter, as so many of us did, because of Red Smith, the legendary Irish quarter-miler, also known as the late sports columnist for the *New York Times*.

In fact, the first time I ever set foot in a professional locker room I was wearing credentials that said, "Red Smith, *New York Times*." This was back in 1976, when I was a student at the Columbia University Graduate School of Journalism writing my master's essay about Red. The powers that be didn't think too much of sportswriting—we were all supposed to want to be Woodward and Bernstein. But they made an exception because the subject was Red. I spent six months sitting at his elbow asking why he put commas where he did and following him to ballparks and saloons. And finally to the AFC Championship Game in Pittsburgh.

It was 16 degrees at kickoff. To give you an idea of Red's courtliness, suffice it to say, he gave up his seat in the heated press box with the hot food and the stat sheets hot off the presses to sit outside in the auxiliary press box with me. Along about halftime, Red allowed how he didn't really need to see the rest of the game live, and why didn't we just go inside and watch the rest on TV? I was too young and too dumb to realize what it meant for a working journalist to do this. My gratitude and admiration have grown over the years.

At the end of the game, Red followed his colleagues downstairs to interview the victorious Pittsburgh Steelers. And I followed Red. I found myself outside the Raiders' locker room staring up at a 7-foot-tall Pinkerton guard whose nose was almost as long as he was tall. "Ladies' Day today?" I said. He gazed down at my credentials. "You're Red Smith?" I nodded as modestly as I knew Red would.

"Go right in," he said.

So I did. On my left, I saw the Oakland Raiders sitting completely dressed and completely silent except for the occasional chattering of teeth. On my right, I saw coach John Madden, his huge head in his huge hands, trying to absorb the enormity of the defeat. He looked up and saw me standing in his doorway and said, "Who the bleep is she?"

The Pinkerton straightened as tall as he knew how and said, "Don't worry about her, Mr. Madden. She's Red Smith."

When I broke into the business, women were not allowed in locker rooms except with Red Smith's credentials. You had to get some guy to do your legwork for you, as Red used to say. Now, fifteen years later, the federal courts and the commissioners of every professional league have ruled that female reporters must have equal access to the locker room. As Lisa Olson of the *Boston Herald* learned last fall, equal access does not necessarily mean equal treatment. In the tumult of last fall's events, much was said about the impact of Zeke Mowatt "wiggling his waggle" in Olson's face. Very little was said about the impact of female sportswriters—there are now an estimated five hundred of us—on sports reporting. That's what my novel, *Squeeze Play*, is about: a woman's view of sports. And that's what I'd like to talk to you about tonight.

The truth is, in sportswriting gender is a double-edged sword. For every time I had a guy pin me against the outfield fence and say, "Women! That's for me!" there was a time when I was treated with uncommon chivalry. Emphasis on the uncommon. I have no doubt that I was hired by the *Washington Post* in 1979 in part because I was a woman. I also have no doubt that I got some stories I wouldn't otherwise have gotten because people were more comfortable talking to a woman.

I don't think it undermines a woman's right to be in the locker room to admit that it is different to be a woman in a man's world. The biggest difference is that from the moment you cross that threshold into the locker room, you know you are an outsider, which is what a reporter is supposed to be. I think you can make the argument that gender may give a female sportswriter more distance, and therefore more perspective on the world of sports. In other words, you are never tempted to think you are just one of the guys.

I learned this my first month at the *Post* when I was sent to Houston to interview the Oilers' running back, Earl Campbell. Earl Campbell did not want to be interviewed by me. In fact, he was so determined not to be interviewed by me that he preferred to spend five hours standing in a men's room rather than come out and face me. Being a new and conscientious reporter, I was just as determined to talk to him as he was to avoid me. So I stood outside the men's room for five hours waiting for Earl to change his mind. It was an insane stand-off. I couldn't leave, and he wouldn't leave.

At the end of five hours, he made a break for it. I introduced myself. Earl Campbell said, "No comment."

It was, to say the least, a formative experience—in the power and the powerlessness of the press. I had the power to make a grown man stand in a bathroom for five hours. He had the power to keep me out. From that moment on, I knew that my experience as a female sportswriter was going to be different from, say, Red Smith's.

But different does not always mean worse. My first time in the locker room (after my initial debut as Red Smith), I went to talk to the New York Knicks about jocks getting all pretty and sissified. I was terrified. After I had spent five minutes standing around hiding behind my notebook, Phil Jackson, now the coach of the Chicago Bulls, put his arm around me and said, quite gently, "Is it your first time?" Needless to say, I was quite taken aback and only in part because he was stark naked. After I admitted it was my first time and explained why I had come, Phil Jackson proceeded to go around the locker room and interview his teammates for me. He handed me my story. Athletes do that sometimes. In this case, I have no doubt that he did it because I was a woman and because he was trying to make me feel comfortable.

In my experience, male athletes tell female sportswriters things they don't tell other males. There are several reasons for this, one of which is very simple. As Ken Singleton of the Baltimore Orioles once told me, "You ask different questions." And that may be because female sportswriters are not interested in competing with men unless they happen to be other journalists.

Go into any baseball locker room in America and you'll find some radio guy sticking a microphone in some pitcher's face and saying, "That was your red dot slider, wasn't it, big guy?" A female sportswriter is much more likely to ask, "What was the pitch?" She is also unlikely ever to call someone "big guy." The difference is the radio guy is trying to prove something with his question. The woman is just trying to find something out.

There is another reason why athletes tell women different things. In *Squeeze Play*, my heroine, A. B. Berkowitz, a baseball writer for a slimy Washington rag, says, "I'm short. I'm small. And if there's one thing I've learned this season, it's that big guys tell small girls things they do not tell other guys. I look harmless. And it works. Sometimes they tell me I remind them of their little sisters."

Let me give you an example. I had a friend who covered hockey for years. One season, the star of the team was in a terrible slump. The tabloids were full of headlines about him. Did he need glasses? Were his legs gone? Was he concealing an injury?

One day, the player took my friend aside and told her, off the record, that the problem was he was infertile. He wouldn't let her write it. But he didn't want her writing inaccurate stories either.

I don't think it's a coincidence that the reporter he told was a woman. Nor did I think it was a coincidence when Al Bumbry of the Orioles took me aside one day in the dugout at Memorial Stadium and told me about growing up as an illegitimate child and being teased about it and developing a speech impediment and how he and his wife had just separated and he was worried about his daughter developing a speech impediment, too.

Both these stories became part of the plot in *Squeeze Play*. Though it's a comic novel, and I hope it makes people laugh, it's also about ethics in journalism and what you do when people hand you a part of themselves. Reporters, as you may know, are not philosophers. They are pragmatists. They'll do anything to get people to talk, even if it means being nice. In a way, reporting is a seduction. You use empathy to undress someone. As A. B. says at the beginning of the book, "There's maybe one guy per 24-man roster who understands that nakedness is a metaphor."

In ten years as a sportswriter, I came to wonder whether the resistance to women in the locker room really had to do with nudity or, as A. B. says, "with being seen for what you are." If nakedness per se is the issue, it's easy enough to put your pants on. If nakedness in the sense of being perceived is the issue, it's not so easy to cover up.

We live in the era of personality journalism. The ability to undress someone, metaphorically speaking, is a marketable skill. As television has usurped more and more the reporter's task, telling you the score, sports pages have concentrated more and more on what athletes feel, what their lives are like, what their personality traits may be. This is great, except, of course, when the personality in question doesn't have one or is smart enough to understand he's going to sound dumb trying to have one. Which brings me back to Earl Campbell standing in a bathroom for five hours rather than talking to me. My editor had decided Earl was going to be a personality whether he liked it or not. I didn't blame Earl for avoiding me. In his position, I might have done the same. After all, just because he had great legs didn't mean he could go one-on-one with me. I had all the advantages: education, language, and the ability, if I chose to use it, to make him look stupid.

Standing in that parking lot outside that men's room, I remember feeling something for the first time, something I felt over and over during my ten years at the *Post*, something you're not supposed to feel as a reporter. I felt responsible for how he was going to sound. For a reporter, the problem with feeling responsible is that it leads to paralysis.

Once some years ago, I wrote a piece on the legendary Russian pairs skaters, the Protopopovs, who had defected to the West after an illustrious Olympic career. The promoter of the show they were appearing in, wanting to hype the story, told me off the record, which is to say not for attribution, that the KGB was harassing their relatives back in the Soviet Union. The Protopopovs had not been able to reach their relatives for weeks. But, the promoter said, being troopers they were prepared to skate anyway. It was a great story.

When I told the Protopopovs what I had learned, they begged me not to write it for fear it would make the plight of their relatives worse. The managing editor of the *Post*, the late Howard Simons, told me to go with it. I'll never forget what he said: "Who are you to play God?"

I think ultimately that is why I left reporting. Jane the outsider had gotten too good at getting close to people. The process of distancing myself from them to fulfill my obligations as a reporter had become wrenching and morally unclear.

As A. B. says in *Squeeze Play*, "Sometimes when it's time to write I can barely make it upstairs to the press box. It's like every word, every sentence, every quote, is a weight I can't support. What if I'm wrong? What if it's all wrong? I can't bear the weight of my own power. I seduce them into doing this, into telling me what they don't want to say. Then I have to think of a way to do what I have to do without betraying them. It's a pact with the devil is what it is and the devil is me."

So I left the *Post* to write this novel. You can imagine what a relief it was to be able to make up the quotes and not worry about someone saying I had gotten it all wrong or taken it out of context. I worked for two years on the book without hearing any of the voices of the game except those in my head. I wrote all the stories I could never put in the paper and all of my doubts about them too. I didn't have to worry about being respectful. I could quote people the way they really talk (a value instilled by Red Smith). I could be as irreverent as I pleased.

Undue reverence is a problem for sportswriters, even the best of them. Red used to tell the story about being accused of going to spring training and frolicking in the sun and "godding up" all the ballplayers. Partly that is a function of proximity, just hanging around. Partly it is a function of writing nonfiction; facts and libel laws behoove you to be careful and respectful, especially in a family newspaper. And partly it is a function of male bonding. Most sportswriters grow up speaking the language of the locker room and use the jargon as a way of fitting in, a way of showing they know their stuff.

As a woman writing a sports novel, I had the advantage of being removed from all these conventions and inhibitions. I came to feel I could tell more of the truth in *Squeeze Play* than I ever could as a reporter.

But then a funny thing happened just as I was finishing the manuscript. I began to have anxiety attacks. In my distance from the game, I had found perspective but now also self-doubt. I began to ask myself, "What if I made it all up?"

I kept telling myself this was fiction, that I was supposed to make it all up. But being rational didn't help. Finally, I did the only thing I could think of. I decided to go back to baseball. I needed to hear the voices of the game to make sure the fiction was real.

It sounds pretty silly, I know. But I was scared to go to spring training. I was so scared, in fact, that I arranged to have my friend, Dave Kindred, this year's Red Smith Lecturer and winner of the Associated Press Sports Editors' award for best sports columnist, meet me at the stadium. I was not about to confront this sudden fear of double knits alone. Of course, he stiffed me. So there I was, fifteen years after my rookie season, an outsider again, trying to summon the courage to step back into that world and find out if my wacky, whimsical, and somewhat outrageous fictional version bore any similarity to the original.

I was standing by the third baseline. Batting practice was over. Rookies were trotting by spitting sunflower seeds and worse at my feet. Across the field, I saw Luke Appling sitting on a bat signing autographs and chatting up the fans. I walked over and put my foot up on the bench. Sportswriters always put their feet up when they talk to athletes. I don't know why. Anyway, I couldn't help but notice Luke staring at my pasty white northern shins—he was staring at them hard. Finally, I said the first thing that came into my head. "Like that white skin, huh, Luke?"

Luke Appling, all eighty years of him, winked and said, "I *always* liked white skin."

That's when I knew I was home. Luke may not have been one of the fictional guys, but he could have been. I flew home again the next morning feeling real again.

The Babe Was Always a Boy— One of a Kind

RED SMITH

THE NEW YORK TIMES MAGAZINE

SEPTEMBER 16, 1973

Grantland Rice, the prince of sportswriters, used to do a weekly radio interview with some sporting figure. Frequently, in the interest of spontaneity, he would type out questions and answers in advance. One night his guest was Babe Ruth.

"Well, you know, Granny," the Babe read in response to a question, "Duke Ellington said the Battle of Waterloo was won on the playing fields of Elkton."

"Babe," Granny said after the show, "Duke Ellington for the Duke of Wellington I can understand. But how did you ever read Eton as Elkton? That's in Maryland, isn't it?"

"I married my first wife there," Babe said, "and I always hated the gawdam place." He was cheerily unruffled. In the uncomplicated world of George Herman Ruth, errors were part of the game.

Babe Ruth died twenty-five years ago, but his ample ghost has been with us all summer, and he seems to grow more insistently alive every time Henry Aaron hits a baseball over a fence. What, people under fifty keep asking, what was this creature of myth and legend like in real life? If he were around today, how would he react when Aaron at last broke his hallowed record of 714 home runs? The first question may be impossible to answer fully; the second is easy.

"Well, what d'you know!" he would have said when the record got away. "Baby loses another! Come on, have another beer."

To paraphrase Abraham Lincoln's remark about another deity, Ruth must have admired records because he created so many of them. Yet he was sublimely aware that he transcended records, and his place in the American scene was no mere matter of statistics. It wasn't just that he hit more home runs than anybody else, he hit them better, higher, farther, with more theatrical timing and a more flamboyant flourish. Nobody could strike out like Babe Ruth. Nobody circled the bases with the same pigeon-toed, mincing majesty.

"He was one of a kind," says Waite Hoyt, a Yankee pitcher in the years of Ruthian splendor. "If he had never played ball, if you had never heard of him and passed him on Broadway, you'd turn around and look."

Looking, you would have seen a barrel swaddled in a wraparound camel hair topcoat with a flat camel hair cap on the round head. Thus arrayed, he was instantly recognizable not only on Broadway in New York but also on the Ginza in Tokyo. "Baby Roos! Baby Roos!" cried excited crowds, following through the streets when he visited Japan with an all-star team in the early 1930s.

The camel hair coat and cap are part of my last memory of the man. It must have been in the spring training season of 1948 when the Babe and everybody else knew he was dying of throat cancer. "This is the last time around," he had told Frank Stevens that winter when the head of the H. M. Stevens catering firm visited him in the French Hospital on West 30th Street, "but before I go I'm gonna get out of here and have some fun."

He did get out, but touring the Florida training camps surrounded by a gaggle of admen, hustlers, and promoters, he didn't look like a man having fun. It was a hot day when he arrived in St. Petersburg, but the camel hair collar was turned up about the wounded throat. By this time, Al Lang Stadium had replaced old Waterfront Park where he had drawn crowds when the Yankees trained in St. Pete.

"What do you remember best about this place?" asked Francis Stann of the *Washington Star*.

Babe gestured toward the West Coast Inn, an old frame building a city block beyond the right-field fence. "The day I hit the adjectival ball against that adjectival hotel." The voice was a hoarse stage whisper; the adjective was one often printed these days, but not here.

"Wow!" Francis Stann said. "Pretty good belt."

"But don't forget," Babe said, "the adjectival park was a block back this way then."

Ruth was not noted for a good memory. In fact, the inability to remember names is part of his legend. Yet he needed no record books to remind him of his own special feats. There was, for example, the time he visited Philadelphia as a "coach" with the Brooklyn Dodgers. (His coachly duties consisted of hitting home runs in batting practice.) This was in the late 1930s, when National League games in Philadelphia were played in Shibe Park, the American

League grounds where Babe had performed. I asked him what memories stirred on his return.

"The time I hit one into Opal Street," he said.

Now, a baseball hit over Shibe Park's right-field fence landed in 20th Street. Opal is the next street east, just a wide alley one block long. There may not be five hundred Philadelphians who know it by name, but Babe Ruth knew it.

Another time, during a chat in Hollywood, where he was an actor in the film *Pride of the Yankees*, one of us mentioned Rube Walberg, a good left-handed pitcher with the Philadelphia Athletics through the Ruth era. To some left-handed batters there is no dirtier word than the name of a good left-handed pitcher, but the Babe spoke fondly: "Rube Walberg! What a pigeon! I hit twenty-three home runs off him." Or whatever the figure was. It isn't in the record book, but it was in Ruth's memory.

Obviously it is not true that he couldn't even remember the names of his teammates. It was only that the names he remembered were not always those bestowed at the baptismal font. To him Urban Shocker, a Yankee pitcher, was Rubber Belly. Pat Collins, the catcher, was Horse Nose. All redcaps at railroad stations were Stinkweed, and everybody else was Kid. One day Jim Kahn, covering the Yankees for the *New York Sun*,

watched two players board a train with a porter toting the luggage.

"There go Rubber Belly, Horse Nose and Stinkweed," Jim said.

Don Heffner joined the Yankees in 1934, Ruth's last year with the team. Playing second base through spring training, Heffner was stationed directly in the line of vision of Ruth, the right fielder. Breaking camp, the Yankees stopped in Jacksonville on a night when the Baltimore Orioles of the International League were also in town. A young reporter on the *Baltimore Sun* seized the opportunity to interview Ruth.

"How is Heffner looking?" he asked, because the second baseman had been a star with the Orioles in 1933.

"Who the hell is Heffner?" the Babe demanded. The reporter should, of course, have asked about the kid at second.

Jacksonville was the first stop that year on the barnstorming trip that would last two or three weeks and take the team to Yankee Stadium by a meandering route through the American bush. There, as everywhere, Ruth moved among crowds. Whether the Yankees played in Memphis or New Orleans or Selma, Alabama, the park was almost always filled, the hotel overrun if the team used a hotel, the railroad depot thronged. In a town of five thousand, perhaps seventy-five hundred would see the game. Mostly the players lived in Pullmans, and somehow word always went ahead when the Yankees' train was coming through. At every stop at any hour of the night there would be a cluster of men on the platform, maybe the stationmaster and telegrapher, a section gang and the baggage agent, watching the dark sleeping cars for the glimpse of a Yankee, possibly even the Babe.

It was said in those days, probably truly, that receipts from the preseason exhibitions more than paid Ruth's salary for the year, even when he was getting $80,000, which was substantially more than any other player earned, or any manager or baseball executive. It was more than President Herbert Hoover received, but if this was ever pointed out to Ruth he almost surely did not reply, as the story goes, "I had a better year than he did." He would have been correct, but the Babe was not well informed on national affairs.

Crowds were to Ruth as water to a fish. Probably the only time on record when he sought to avert a mob scene was the day of his second marriage. The ceremony was scheduled for 6 A.M. on the theory that people wouldn't be abroad then, but when he arrived at St. Gregory's on West 90th Street, the church was filled and hundreds were waiting outside.

A reception followed in Babe's apartment on Riverside Drive, where the Eighteenth Amendment did not apply. It was opening day of the baseball season, but the weather intervened on behalf of the happy couple. The party went on and on, with entertainment by Peter DeRose, composer–pianist, and May Singhi Breen, who played the ukulele and sang.

Rain abated in time for a game next day. For the first time, Claire Ruth watched from a box near the Yankees' dugout, as she still does on ceremonial occasions. Naturally, the bridegroom hit a home run. Rounding the bases, he halted at second and swept off his cap in a courtly bow to his bride. This was typical of him. There are a hundred stories illustrating his sense of theater—how he opened Yankee Stadium ("The House That Ruth Built") with a home run against the Red Sox, how at the age of forty he closed out his career as a player by hitting three mighty shots out of spacious Forbes Field in Pittsburgh, stories about the times he promised to hit a home run for some kid in a hospital and made good, and, of course, the one about calling his shot in a World Series.

That either did or did not happen in Chicago's Wrigley Field on October 1, 1932. I was there, but I have never been dead sure of what I saw. The Yankees had won the first two games, and the score of the third was 4–4 when Ruth went to bat in the fifth inning with the bases empty and Charlie Root pitching for the Cubs. Ruth had staked the Yankees to a three-run lead in the first inning by hitting Root for a home run with two on base. Now Root threw a strike. Ruth stepped back and lifted a finger. "One." A second strike, a second upraised finger. "Two." Then Ruth made some sort of sign with his bat. Some said, and their version has become gospel, that he aimed it like a rifle at the bleachers in right center field. That's where he hit the next pitch. That made the score 5–4. Lou Gehrig followed with a home run, and the Yankees won, 7–5, ending the Series the next day.

All the Yankees, and Ruth in particular, had been riding the Cubs unmercifully through every game, deriding them as cheapskates because in cutting up their World Series money the Chicago players had voted only one-fourth of a share to Mark Koenig, the former New York shortstop who had joined them in August and batted .353 in the last month of the pennant race. With all the dialogue and pantomime that went on, there was no telling what Ruth was saying to Root. When the papers reported that he had called his shot, he did not deny it.

He almost never quibbled about anything that was written. During the 1934 World Series between the Cardinals and Detroit Tigers, the *St. Louis Post-Dispatch* assigned its Washington correspondent, Paul Y. Anderson, to write features. His seat in the auxiliary press box was next to Ruth, a member of the sweaty literati whose observations on the games would be converted into suitably wooden prose by a syndicate ghostwriter. Babe was companionable as usual.

"You see the series here in '28?" he asked.

"No," Anderson said, "was it a good one?"

"That was when I hit three outta here in the last game."

"Gee," Anderson said, "a good day for you, eh?"

"Yeah," Babe said, "I had a good day. But don't forget, the fans had a hell of a day, too."

Paul Anderson was at ease with men as dissimilar as Huey Long, John L. Lewis, and Franklin D. Roosevelt, but he had never encountered anyone quite like this child of nature. He devoted his story to the bumptious bundle of vanity seated beside him. To his discomfort, a press box neighbor asked Ruth the next day whether he had read the story. Ruth said, "Sure," though he probably hadn't. "What did you think of it?" the other persisted while Anderson squirmed.

"Hell," Babe said, "the newspaper guys always been great to me."

A person familiar with Ruth only through photographs and records could hardly be blamed for assuming that he was a blubbery freak whose ability to hit balls across county lines was all that kept him in the big leagues. The truth is that he was the complete ballplayer, certainly one of the greatest and maybe the one best of all time.

As a left-handed pitcher with the Boston Red Sox, he won eighteen games in his rookie season, twenty-three the next year, and twenty-four the next before Ed Barrow assigned him to the outfield to keep him in the batting order every day. His record of pitching twenty-nine and two thirds consecutive scoreless innings in World Series stood forty-three years before Whitey Ford broke it.

He was an accomplished outfielder with astonishing range for his bulk, a powerful arm, and keen baseball sense. It was said that he never made a mental error like throwing to the wrong base.

He recognized his role as public entertainer and understood it. In the 1946 World Series the Cardinals made a radical shift in their defense against Ted Williams, packing the right side of the field and leaving the left virtually unprotected. "They did that to me in the American League one year," Ruth told the columnist Frank Graham. "I coulda hit .600 that year slicing singles to left."

"Why didn't you?" Frank asked.

"That wasn't what the fans came out to see."

Thirteen years after Ruth's death, when another right fielder for the Yankees, Roger Maris, was threatening the season record of sixty home runs that Babe had set thirty-four years earlier, I made a small sentimental pilgrimage in Baltimore, where the Yankees happened to be playing. The first stop was the row house where the Babe was born. A gracious woman showed visitors through the small rooms. Next came a drink in the neighborhood saloon Ruth's father ran when Babe was a boy. Nobody ever came in who remembered the Ruth family, the bartender said. The tour ended at St. Mary's Industrial School, which the wrecker's big iron ball was knocking down.

St. Mary's was Babe's home through most of his boyhood because his parents weren't interested in rearing him. He left the home on February 27, 1914, three weeks after his nineteenth birthday, to pitch for the Baltimore Orioles of the International League. Jack Dunn, the owner, paid him $600 and sold him late that summer to the Red Sox for $2,900. He was 6-foot-2 and an athlete, thick-chested but not fat.

"A big, lummockin' sort of fella," said a waiter in Toots Shor's who had worked in a restaurant near the Red Sox park where young Ruth got sweet on one of the waitresses.

When his hard-pressed employers sold him to the Yankees, he was still a trim young ballplayer who had hit twenty-nine of the Boston club's thirty-two home runs that season of 1919. He hit an unthinkable fifty-four in his first New York summer, fifty-nine in his second, and became a god. His waistline grew with his fame, until the legs that nobody had considered spindly began to look like matchsticks and his feet seemed grotesquely small.

He changed the rules, the equipment, and the strategy of baseball. Reasoning that if one Babe Ruth could fill a park, sixteen would fill all the parks, the owners instructed the manufacturers to produce a livelier ball that would make every man a home-run king. As a further aid to batters, trick pitching deliveries like the spitball, the emery ball, the shine ball, and the mud ball were forbidden.

The home run, an occasional phenomenon when a team hit a total of twenty in a season, came to be regarded as the ultimate offensive weapon. Shortstops inclined to swoon at the sight of blood had their bats made with all the wood up in the big end, gripped the slender handle at the very hilt, and swung from the heels.

None of these devices produced another Ruth, of course, because Ruth was one of a kind. He recognized this as the simple truth and conducted himself accordingly. Even before they were married and Claire began to accompany him on the road, he always occupied the drawing room on the team's Pullman; he seldom shared his revels after dark with other players, although one year he did take a fancy to a worshipful rookie named Jimmy Reese and made him a companion until management intervened; if friends were not on hand with transportation, he usually took a taxi by himself to hotel or ballpark or railroad station. Unlike other players, Ruth was never seen in the hotel dining room or sitting in the lobby waiting for some passerby to discard a newspaper.

St. Louis was one town where he was always met. When the team left St. Louis, his friends would deliver him to the station along with a laundry basket full of barbecued ribs and tubs of home brew. Then anybody—player, coach, or press—was welcome in the drawing room to munch ribs, swill the yeasty beer, and laugh at the Babe's favorite record on the Babe's phonograph. He would play Moran & Mack's talking record, *Two Black Crows*, a hundred times and howl at the hundredth repetition: "How come the black horses ate more'n the white horses?" "Search me, 'cept we had more black horses than white horses."

Roistering was a way of life, yet Ruth was no boozer. Three drinks of hard liquor left him fuzzy. He could consume great quantities of beer, he was a prodigious eater, and his prowess with women was legendary. Sleep was something he got when other appetites were sated. He arose when he chose and almost invariably was the last to arrive in the clubhouse, where Doc Woods, the Yankees' trainer, always had bicarbonate of soda ready. Before changing clothes, the Babe would measure out a mound of bicarb smaller than the Pyramid of Cheops, mix and gulp it down.

"Then," Jim Kahn says, "he would belch. And all the loose water in the showers would fall down."

The man was a boy, simple, artless, genuine, and unabashed. This explains his rapport with children, whom he met as intellectual equals. Probably his natural liking for people communicated itself to the public to help make him an idol.

He was buried on a sweltering day in August 1948. In the pallbearers' pew, Waite Hoyt sat beside Joe Dugan, the third baseman. "I'd give a hundred dollars for a cold beer," Dugan whispered. "So would the Babe," Hoyt said.

In packed St. Patrick's Cathedral, Francis Cardinal Spellman celebrated requiem mass, and out in 5th Avenue thousands and thousands waited to say goodbye to the waif from Baltimore whose parents didn't want him.

"Some 20 years ago," says Tommy Holmes, the great baseball writer on the *Brooklyn Eagle* and *New York Herald Tribune*, "I stopped talking about the Babe for the simple reason that I realized that those who had never seen him didn't believe me."

EUGENE L. ROBERTS, JR. Gene Roberts shared the Pulitzer

Prize for history with Hank Klibanoff for their book *The Race Beat:*

The Press, the Civil Rights Struggle, and the Awakening of a Nation

(2006). His career in journalism includes stints as a reporter and

editor at the *Goldsboro News-Argus* in North Carolina, the *Norfolk*

Virginian Pilot, the *Raleigh News & Observer*, the *Detroit Free Press*,

the *New York Times*, and the *Philadelphia Inquirer*. As executive

editor, he led the *Inquirer* to seventeen Pulitzer Prizes during an

eighteen-year period, with two gold medals for public service.

In 1994, he interrupted his professorship at the University of

Maryland to return to the *Times* as its managing editor for three

years. Besides *The Race Beat*, he co-authored *The Censors and*

the Schools (1963) and co-edited *Assignment America* (1974). He

delivered this lecture on April 7, 1994.

EUGENE L. ROBERTS, JR.

Writing for the Reader

L et me say with unbecoming immodesty that I have sound credentials for attesting to the writing magic of Red Smith: One, I have no
interest in golf. Two, I've never played a single hole. Three, I plan to
depart this life with my record intact.

In the Red Smith era I searched the sports pages for baseball stories.
My eyes raced to Red's columns to see if he were writing about my favorite
sport, but Smith was a shameless seducer. If he had me for ten seconds, he
had me to the finish—even on his golf stories. To me, golf emerged from his
typewriter not as news from a game but as word from a remote and exotic
world—like Tibet, like Xanadu. I saw the sweating players. I felt the tension
in the crowd. I was transported, dammit, to the last place I ever wanted to
be: the middle of a golf course.

Take, for example, the 1964 match in Houston between Sam Snead and
Ben Hogan:

> Snead was disconsolate because his long irons got him in
> trouble four times, but he scrambled sensationally. The
> seventh hole, for example, is a dogleg to the left around
> a thicket of tall trees. Along the left side behind the
> woods five traps yawn, one behind the other from turn
> to green.
>
> Hogan hit an iron to the knee of the dogleg and had an
> open shot to the green. Sam tried to clear the trees with a
> wood, hit a pine, and his ball bounced back toward the tee.
> It wasn't humanly possible to get home from there, but
> somehow he whistled his second shot through the trees to
> the edge of the green beyond the last trap.
>
> "You dodged a bullet there," said Fred Corcoran after
> Sam got down in two and halved the hole with a four.

"If I'da cleared the trees and drove the green," Sam
said, "it woulda been a great tee shot."

"But I was lousy," he said at the end.

"No, you weren't," a man told him. "I'm so glad I was
able to see this match. I'll remember it along with the War
Admiral–Seabiscuit match race, Graziano–Zale, and Don
Larsen's perfect game."

How do you resist a charmer who writes like that? To this very moment
I couldn't pick a long iron from a lineup of clubs, but for the length of
that column, I enjoyed golf. That, of course, is what the finest writing is all
about: putting the reader on the scene, making him see. Red Smith seems
to have been born knowing this. For ordinary mortals the elementary truths
of good writing come harder. It took a blind man to make *me* see.

I've told this story before, but it seems appropriate for tonight's occasion. My first newspaper job was with the *Goldsboro News-Argus*, which
is the leading newspaper in Wayne County, North Carolina. It then had a
circulation of nine thousand. I wrote its farm column, "Rambling in Rural
Wayne." I wrote about the first farmer of the season to transplant tobacco
plants from the seed bed to the field; about the season's first cotton blos-
som; of picnic tables sagging at family reunions under the weight of banana
sandwiches, banana pudding, chicken pastry, sage sausage, fried chicken,
and collard greens. I wrote of hail storms and drought. I once wrote about
a sweet potato that looked like General Charles de Gaulle.

The editor of the paper was Henry Belk, then in his sixties and sight-
less. This was in the '50s, but he wore battered fedora hats like newsmen
wore in the movies in the '30s and '40s, when he could still see. He was
tall; no, towering. There were no ready-made canes to fit his 6-foot, 7-inch
form, so he tapped with a stretch cane specially made for him out of
aluminum. He cared passionately about the paper, and it was read to him
word for word over the years by a succession of high school students.
In the mornings, his wife, Lucille, once a journalist herself, read him the
newspaper published in the state capital, the *Raleigh News and Observer*.
He was awesomely informed. Most days, at the office, he would call out
from his cubicle and say things such as, "On page 17 of *The News and
Observer* in column three, halfway down the fold, there is a 3-inch story
about Goldsboro under an 18-point head." Then, he would demand, "Why
didn't we have it?"

Mr. Belk was nothing if not demanding. Often when he heard my footfall in the morning he would summon me to his cubicle and criticize the "Rambling in Rural Wayne" column I had written the day before. On too many days, alas, my writing was insufficiently descriptive. "You aren't making me see," Mr. Belk would say. "Make me see." In an effort to force me to be graphic and vivid, he made me end every column with a paragraph labeled "Today's Prettiest Sight." Let me tell you: It's tough to go into a pool room in your hometown for an end-of-the-workday beer known as the guy who writes "Today's Prettiest Sight," but I persevered.

It took me years to appreciate it, but there is no better admonition to the writer than "Make me see." There is no truer blueprint for successful writing than making your readers see. It is the essence of great writing. There are, be assured, many ways to make your reader see, and Red Smith, I am convinced, knew them all.

Mostly, the best way is simple but vivid description. Smith was in the press box for the unprecedented World Series game in 1972 when Reggie Jackson knocked three home runs in a row. "For the third time," Smith wrote, "Reggie hit the first pitch, but this one didn't take the shortest distance between two points. Straight out from the plate the ball streaked, not toward the neighborly stands in right but on a soaring arc toward the unoccupied bleachers in dead center, where the seats are blacked out to give batters a background. Up the white speck climbed, dwindling, diminishing, until it settled at least halfway up those empty stands, probably 450 feet away."

Sometimes making the reader see involves cutting to the heart of things, as when Red called Reggie "this Hamlet in double knits," or when he said in memorializing Babe Ruth, "The man was a boy, simple, artless, genuine, and unabashed. This explains his rapport with children, whom he met as intellectual equals." To craftsmen such as Smith, the right words are to writing as the right tools are to carpentry. Notice that he didn't use a hammer on occasions that called for a sharp chisel.

A few years ago there was a great movement in the newspaper business toward explanatory journalism. Explain things to the reader so that he will understand, we editors implored. We even created awards for explanatory journalism. We were like coaxing parents who cheer and applaud when training their children to go to the potty. Of course, old foxes such as Red Smith knew all along that sometimes you can't make the reader see unless you explain things so well that he or she can't possibly miss the meaning. One of the finest examples of explanatory writing (of journalism, if

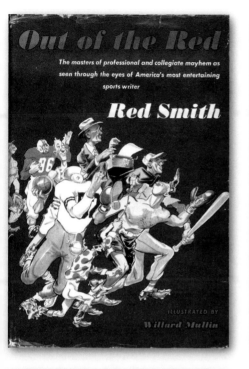

Above: Red Smith's first two collections of columns, *Out of the Red* (1950) and *Views of Sport* (1954), were published by Alfred A. Knopf, and both featured caricatures of the columnist on the dust-jacket covers.

In 1963, *The Best of Red Smith* appeared, with a photo of the author replacing the earlier cartoonlike sketches.

Unless specified otherwise, the photos in this section come from the Red Smith Collection in the Department of Special Collections of the Hesburgh Libraries at the University of Notre Dame.

Near the end of his life, Red Smith selected 182 columns (from approximately 500 possible choices), remembering people who "commanded attention and when they died their deaths touched many." *To Absent Friends* was published a few months after Smith's death on January 15, 1982.

Dave Anderson, a Smith colleague at the *New York Times* and like Smith a Pulitzer Prize–winning columnist, edited *The Red Smith Reader* (1982). In the first sentence of the introduction, Anderson writes: "If you blindfolded yourself, reached into Red Smith's files, and yanked out 130 columns, *any* 130 columns, you would have a good collection."

The recipient of numerous honors during his half-century career in journalism, Red Smith was presented the George Polk Award for sports reporting in May of 1951.

The Smith family aboard the Swedish-American liner *Gripsholm* in the summer of 1952 en route to the Olympic Games in Helsinki, Finland. From left: Catherine Cody (Kay) Smith, daughter Catherine (Kit), Red Smith, and son Terence.

Away from athletic action, Red Smith was often surrounded by the great and the good of sports. Above: Smith signs books with professional golfers Cary Middlecoff (left) and Jimmy Demaret (right). Below: Smith stands between two members of baseball's Hall of Fame, Connie Mack (left) and Jimmie Foxx (right).

Terence Smith graduated from Notre Dame in 1960, when this picture was taken at the university's Morris Inn. With typewriter at the ready, Red Smith filed his column amid commencement activities. *(Photo from the University of Notre Dame Archives)*

Red Smith and his son, Terence, at Masada, Israel, in the fall of 1967. At the time, Terence was a foreign correspondent for the *New York Times*, based in Jerusalem.

In 1968, Red Smith received an honorary doctorate from his alma mater, Notre Dame. Here Rev. Theodore M. Hesburgh, C.S.C., Notre Dame's president, congratulates Smith after the ceremony. *(Photo from the University of Notre Dame Archives)*

Newsweek

ISRAEL Can It Survive Arab Whirlpool?
[SPECIAL INTERNATIONAL REPORT]

U.S.A. Recession Mood at the Grass Roots
[SPECIAL NATIONAL REPORT]

APRIL 21, 1958 25c

Red Smith: Star of the Press Box
SPECIAL PRESS REPORT

This cover of *Newsweek* in 1958 reflects Red Smith's standing in American journalism—and two of his favorite sources of column material: baseball and horse racing.

In his own sporting life, Red Smith was never happier than when he was wading a trout stream with a dry fly on a rod. In 1963, he published a collection of his columns titled *Red Smith on Fishing*, and in 1974, he became outdoor editor of *Argosy*, with the regular feature "Red All Over."

In one of the first pictures of Red Smith as a young reporter, here he is at his desk at the *St. Louis Star*, circa 1930.

Throughout his career, Smith filed many of his columns from press boxes at racetracks and ballparks.

This picture was taken during a football game Smith covered at Notre Dame during the 1960s.

Toward the end of his career as a columnist for the *New York Times*, Smith made the transition from typewriter to video display terminal, one of the earliest computers used by newspapers.

1976

Commentary: Red Smith, for his Sports of The Times column.

Red Smith

How to Get the City Out of Hock

New York City is tapped out like a broken horse player and nobody—not Abe Beame nor the town's smartest bankers nor the best fiscal brains in Albany and Washington—knows what to do about it. This helplessness in high places is mystifying, for there is a simple solution so obvious that it should have occurred to somebody in authority long before this. The city should take over loansharking, prostitution and narcotics traffic just as it has taken over gambling. We are assured by all reliable authorities that there is more than enough profit in these fields to make up the $641-million deficit in next year's budget, and in the unlikely event that Mr. Beame still came up short, why, there are other untapped sources of revenue such as labor racketeering and bank robbery.

Prudery should not stand in the way of solvency for the greatest city in the world. A few years ago when there were moral objections to the city's making book on the races, they were hooted down by Honest John Lindsay, the friendly bookie, and his chief sheet-writer, Howard Samuels. Be realistic, they told us, gambling was a biological urge that legislation could not suppress; therefore, was it not desirable that the profits go to support schools, hospitals and deserving politicians rather than the criminal underworld?

Moreover, we were told, illegal gambling provided the treasury from which the underworld financed such activities as loan-sharking, prostitution and dope-pushing. History tells us that organized crime was starved to death in

On the fifteenth floor of the *New York Times* building, 620 Eighth Avenue, the *Times* has created a display recognizing the Pulitzer Prizes the newspaper and its staff have received. Smith was seventy years old when his award for distinguished commentary was announced in 1976. *(Photo courtesy of Tony Cenicola of the New York Times)*

The courtyard of The Poynter Institute in St. Petersburg, Florida, features classic statements about journalism and writing engraved in stone, including Smith's famous observation about the joys of composition. *(Photo courtesy of Jim Stem of Jim Stem Photography, Tampa, Florida)*

you will) that I've ever read was a Red Smith column in 1981, just months before he died but ahead of the explanatory journalism movement. It was a brilliant lecture on what extraordinary progress had transpired in the mile race in track. Smith summed up the whole history of the sport in about eight hundred readable words. You can find it on page 194 of a remarkable book called *The Red Smith Reader*. This, in part, is what he wrote:

> It doesn't seem possible that 27 years have passed since Roger Bannister broke what has been nicknamed the "4-minute-barrier," yet it was May 6, 1954, when he did the deed.
>
> Since man dropped out of a tree and took off with a saber-toothed tiger on his heels, no pedestrian had traveled 5,280 feet in 4 minutes. In 1864 one Charles Lawes of Great Britain had gone the distance in 4 minutes, 56 seconds, and 90 years later Sweden's Gunder Hägg had lowered the record to 4:01.4.
>
> May 6, 1954, 5 days after Determine won the Kentucky Derby, was gray and drizzly at Oxford, but Bannister knew that if he waited for ideal weather in that blessed plot, that earth, that realm, that England, hardening of the arteries could set in first. So he ran, and the stopwatches read 3:59.4.

In years following, scores ran the mile in under four minutes. In the two weeks before Smith wrote this column, the record changed hands three times. And Smith concluded his column this way:

> Much more interesting than the numbers is the mental attitude involved. It doesn't make sense that scores of milers since 1954 have been faster than all the milers who preceded them in human history. It is obvious now that the barrier was psychological rather than physical.
>
> For a millennium or two, nobody ran a mile in 4 minutes for the excellent reason that it was impossible. . . . Then Roger Bannister showed that it was not impossible, and it was like divine revelation. Suddenly it got to be like this:

Jesse Abramson, covering a Boston track meet for the *New York Herald Tribune,* was in a taxi with a colleague and they were discussing runners and their times. The cabbie spoke up:

"Anything that starts with 4," he said, "is slow."

One of the many important benefits of fine writing on a newspaper is that it often begets more fine writing. It is no accident, I think, that two of the finest writers in all journalism history were to be found on the *New York Herald Tribune* at the same time: Red Smith, who covered sports events; Homer Bigart, who covered wars. The same newsroom climate that nourished one attracted the other. Each looked well scrubbed. Homer stuttered; Red was modest. Both were slow, painstaking writers. Each emitted an earnestness that allowed him to pick almost anyone's pockets for a scrap of news. Each made readers see.

There were, of course, some important differences between the two. Smith liked hyperbole. Bigart favored astringent understatement. Smith labored, if necessary, to avoid "I" or "we" in his copy. Bigart was comfortable with either word if it helped put the reader on the scene. But Red and Homer were as one in making liberal use of simple, vivid, straightforward description. "Generally," Homer wrote from a battlefield in Italy in 1943, "there is no mistaking the dead—their strange contorted posture leaves no room for doubt. But this soldier, his steel helmet tilted over his face, seemed merely resting in the field. We did not know until we came within a few yards and saw a gray hand hanging limply from a sleeve." Later, Bigart transferred from the European theater of war to the Pacific. He wrote the last combat dispatch of World War II. It was datelined: "In a B-29 over Japan, Aug. 15, 1945." This is the opening paragraph of that memorable story: "The radio tells us that the war is over, but from where I sit it looks suspiciously like a rumor. A few minutes ago—at 1:32 A.M.—we firebombed Kumagaya, a small industrial city behind Tokyo near the northern edge of the Kanto Plain. Peace was not official for the Japanese either, for they shot right back at us."

I think Homer and Red would have approved of the way you have arranged academics here at Notre Dame, placing journalism and American studies together in the same department. It is a natural. It combines writing instruction with something worth writing about. Of course, American studies is more than a mere subject. It cultivates a vision, a way of looking at America's people—us. It makes you see.

Some thirty years ago, a young writer graduated from Yale University with a Ph.D. in American studies and made his way onto the staff of the *Herald Tribune* in New York, as Homer and Red had done before him. His name was, and is, Tom Wolfe. Not for him the straightforward description of a Smith or a Bigart. He layered adjectives and nouns into sentences like "Kandy Colored, Tangerine Flake, Streamline Baby." He strung letters, asterisks, and exclamation marks together in an effort to create sound effects on the printed page. He used techniques of fiction, such as foreshadowing, to heighten suspense and increase tension and readership. He tried to crawl into the skins of his subjects. He recreated scenes, events, and episodes. He called all of this new journalism.

He raised the blood pressure of a not inconsiderable number of journalism historians and professors of writing who pointed out that journalists, for decades, had been writing nonfiction that read like short stories and novellas— John Reed's *Ten Days That Shook the World* and John Hersey's *Hiroshima*, for example. Other critics ignored the early writers and accused Wolfe and his followers of—in the name of readability—writing things that they couldn't possibly have known about the moods and thoughts of their subjects. In the furor, not nearly enough attention was paid to how Wolfe was transferring American studies from the classroom to the newsroom so effectively it would become a permanent part of what today we might call "journalistic vision."

When you peered past Wolfe's layered nouns and the snap-crackle-and-pop sound effects, there was this wonderful American studies way of looking at things. He told us about a California subculture, the custom car crazies. He made us see Puerto Rican New York in a different light. How? He spun the story of a Puerto Rican troubadour and folk hero who sold a million records by singing in Spanish of his loneliness and how he wouldn't trade his Puerto Rico, señor, for ten thousand New Yorks. We saw Appalachian America differently after he took us to the racetrack with Junior Johnson, who was then king of stock car races.

Yes, there are many ways to make the reader see. Wolfe, Bigart, and Smith showed us and re-showed us. Wolfe is alive and well. Red Smith and Homer Bigart are not, but for making readers see, they are remembered, and they ought to be remembered as long as good writing is taught in our colleges and universities. They were giants. Most of us, even when we write vividly, will make our contribution by making our readers see: for a minute, an hour, a day. I can cite only one instance in which I am reasonably sure I made an indelible impression.

I learned of it in the Vietnam War when I was a correspondent for the *New York Times*. It was 1968 during the Tet Offensive, more than a decade after I left the *Goldsboro News-Argus*. I heard vague reports of trouble in Hué, the capital city of Annam's puppet emperors during the French colonial era. I made my way there by truck and helicopter and found that the Marines were surrounded and held only two blocks of the city. The Viet Cong and the North Vietnamese forces held on to the rest. Each day after the Marines were reinforced by fresh units, they retook two or three blocks of the city, only to lose most of it again during the night to enemy troops who infiltrated into houses during the darkness.

It took about ten days for the Marines to get ten blocks or so from their headquarters compound. When they did, they found several American advisers who had been hiding under a house since the night the enemy overran the city. They had little water, even less food, and were hanging on by their nerve ends when the Marines broke through.

The Marines took the survivors to the headquarters compound and, to give them a sense of security, put them in the safest place they could find: a bunker dug deep into the center of the compound. I heard about the survivors and went to interview them. I snaked over some sandbags and entered a tunnel. I crawled a bit, rounded a bend, and dimly made out some human forms.

"My name is Gene Roberts," I said. "I'm with the *New York Times*. I've come to get your story."

Out of the darkness came a voice, and it said, "Hey, did you ever write the 'Rambling in Rural Wayne' column for the *Goldsboro News-Argus*?"

Henry Belk, my old editor, would not have been surprised. "Of course that reader remembered you," he would have said. "You made him see."

Questions and Answers

QUESTION: *I was wondering to what extent you would say that this kind of writing—the kind of success that Red Smith and other great journalists achieved—comes from their skill and technique as opposed to the material being written about. Does the material matter in writing good journalism?*

GENE ROBERTS: The material certainly helps. It is essential, in fact. And to do what they did, Red Smith and Homer Bigart worked and worked to come up with the material. Red Smith prided himself on going to every game. He was horrified that someone might actually cover a game by watching TV or listening to radio. He would never do it, because he needed the material, the sense of being there.

The same with Bigart. Bigart put his stutter to good advantage. He would go up to people and stutter and say, "What's going on? I don't know what's goin', going on. I can't understand this. Ex-pl-ai-n it to me." And people would tell him things, thinking he was an idiot, and the next day Homer would have material nobody else had.

The event is important, but most of the time you can look at twenty stories all covering the same event, and one story will leap out above all the rest. And when it leaps out above all the rest, it invariably is because the writer gave you a better sense of being there. He or she puts you on the scene. You see what is transpiring in the story. That makes all the difference and sets apart the great ones from everybody else.

QUESTION: *How do you personally stop yourself from crossing the line between vivid description and verbosity?*

GENE ROBERTS: Newspapers were notorious when I was coming up for almost never letting you write anything longer than a column. And they said, "Anything above one column we'll save for the Second Coming." That was *the* important event, and anything less than that almost by definition was worth a column. So you sort of learned to write tight. Too tight, sometimes, because there do come those events worth more attention, particularly as society has gotten more and more complex.

I happened to be the editor of the newspaper most involved during the Three Mile Island scare. Well, how do you say what went wrong in a human way and in a technical way in a nuclear disaster in one column? The answer is, you can't do it. It takes pages to do it. But unless those pages are well written, unless they give the reader a sense of being there, they don't work and essentially, except here and there, I never have had the luxury of being verbose. I wish I had.

QUESTION: *I'm a former sportswriter, and I think Red Smith, Grantland Rice, and Bob Considine were the three greatest sportswriters who ever lived. What do you think?*

GENE ROBERTS: They were really good, there's no question about that. Bob Considine, you know, went on to other things. One of the great things about Red Smith and Homer Bigart (and one of the reasons they were so good) is that they never tried to be anything other than exactly what they were. They wanted to be the very best in the world at doing what they did. Neither of them tried to write a book. I don't think either of them even wrote very many magazine articles. It wasn't their thing. There was a period in both of their lives when they probably could have gotten very rich by signing book contracts, but they felt strongly that it's better to be good at one thing rather than being a near miss at a lot of things. And both of them felt what they did was absolutely all consuming. That you really couldn't do it right and do anything else.

QUESTION: *Considering all of the major publications you have today, from the* New York Times *in newspapers to magazines like* Newsweek, Time, *and* Sports Illustrated, *who do you think sets the standard in journalism today?*

GENE ROBERTS: Of the three magazines you mentioned, it would be *Sports Illustrated* more than *Time* and *Newsweek,* I think. I wouldn't say that *Sports Illustrated* sets an industry standard exactly, but it certainly fosters good writing.

There are some newspaper writers out there who are just remarkable and as good in their own way as Homer Bigart and Red Smith were in theirs. Professor Schmuhl happens to be an authority on one of those writers who, I think, has set a national standard. He happened to come off my paper, the *Philadelphia Inquirer,* and his name is Richard Ben Cramer. He is a wonderful writer, and he wrote a book about the presidential election before last, the one in 1988, and focused on a half dozen candidates.

The name of the book is *What It Takes*, and he explored the characters and personalities of all of these people who were running for president from the standpoint of what makes them run and what makes them succeed. They are some of the most riveting profiles I have ever read anyplace. I thought that I had read everything about Bob Dole, for example, and I was just amazed to find myself turning page after page in Cramer's book. The same is true about George Bush. You would think that there is absolutely nothing new you could learn about Bush, and yet Cramer told you something new and something insightful on every page. All through the book you had a sense of feeling like you were right there, that you knew these people, that you were witnessing this or that.

I like to think there are some wonderful writers on the *Philadelphia Inquirer*, but I'm not exactly an unbiased witness on that. The writing in the *New York Times* has gotten steadily better over the years. I read the *Washington Post* every day, and there is hardly a day that goes by when I don't see at least one remarkable story. Many, many days there's a writer in there who just knocks your socks off. The *Chicago Tribune* does some fine writing. One of the interesting things that's happened is that good writing is not confined to any magazine or any paper. It is throughout the industry and throughout the country.

QUESTION: *To what do you attribute the apparent success and popularity of* USA Today?

GENE ROBERTS: I attribute it to several things. Interestingly, in copying it (as many papers have done) they have copied the shorts and they have copied the weather maps, but nobody has copied the thing, in my opinion, that makes it work better than any other paper: the most complete sports pages in America. Before *USA Today*, if you were traveling around this country and you wanted to keep up with sports, it drove you crazy. You had to get used to every local paper. Most of them had early deadlines, and you could not—and cannot—depend on them for telling you about the game you were most interested in. *USA Today* has raised a very high standard, I think, in sports coverage.

And I think they summarize a lot of things in shorts that should have been summarized in shorts. And they have blown some of the most important stories that have happened since they were founded.

After I left the *Inquirer,* I took a year off and traveled. I was in the South Pacific when the Gulf War was going on. The only way I could find out anything was to take my shortwave radio to the top of the boat deck and hold it up, and if I were lucky I could get BBC beamed for Africa. It had lots of African news on it and very little about the Gulf War. When I finally got to New Zealand, I was on a plane with people who were starved for news about the war. There was actually a footrace to the newsstand, and the people who got there first were the winners, and they all bought the *International Herald Tribune.* The losers got *USA Today.* Everybody knew there would only be so much in there about the war. This happened to be a big event in which people wanted to know as much as possible.

But I think recently, in the last two years, *USA Today* has become more substantive on the leading story of the day, not on everything or most things, but on the big one or two stories of the day. They are much more competitive than they used to be with the average paper. I think that is probably a direct result of their war coverage, when readers turned their back on them during a critical period.

QUESTION: *Do you know the writings of Ernie Pyle, the great war correspondent?*

GENE ROBERTS: I certainly do and think he was one of the great ones. There was one column in particular that those of you who care about writing should look up and read. It was about a Captain Henry Waskow, who was killed in battle. His troops respected him so much, revered him so much, that they could hardly cope as a result of the loss. Ernie Pyle told the story of this one captain in an unforgettable way. Pyle was remarkable. Like many columnists who wrote every day, he had to do a lot of shoveling just to meet his deadlines. But when he was at the top of his form he was certainly one of the greats.

QUESTION: *We seem to be a nation preoccupied with the sports pages. Are the best writers today writing sports, and regardless of your answer in that respect, who would you read if you were reading sportswriters today?*

GENE ROBERTS: What Red Smith did was unique to Red Smith. I don't think there could ever be another Red Smith. But to me, Tom Boswell, who was a baseball writer on the *Washington Post* and is now a *Post* columnist, is extremely impressive, and Dave Kindred is one of the greats, a master of our craft. I also like George Vecsey, the sports columnist on the *New York Times*. I'm also very partial to several sportswriters on the *Philadelphia Inquirer*. We went around the country looking for good sportswriters, and I thought we collected a good cross-section, and the writing standards there are very high.

QUESTION: *You just mentioned Ernie Pyle and the need to meet the dead-line, to shovel out the work. As an editor, could you describe your approach to a writer who is trying to make the reader see but facing a deadline of daily journalism? How do you balance good writing and speed?*

GENE ROBERTS: That is a very good question and, I think, if you want good writing on a paper and you want the paper to get out you have to do two things almost simultaneously. You build strong structures on the newspaper—so strong that under any circumstances what must be done will be done and the paper will get out on the street.

Then, on the other hand, you set about chiseling into these structures, shoving against these structures, even sometimes declaring war almost on some of the structures, to make sure they don't smother the talent on the newspaper.

We had a rule on the *Inquirer* that anybody could argue about anything with any editor on the paper up until five minutes before the deadline. And then you shut up, made the deadline, and saw the paper come out. Then you could come back and argue all over again. Believe me, the best writers argue and care. If the system takes out a good word, they bleed about it.

Some people I know, thirty years after an event, will be talking and say, "Damn them. They took a sentence out of my story that screwed up that story forever, and today I can't go back and look at that story because the sentence is not in there."

One of the best writers I know, or ever met, is a guy named Roy Reed, who was on the *New York Times* and now teaches at the University of Arkansas. Once he was assigned to cover Hubert Humphrey, when Humphrey was vice president. They went on a two-week trip to Europe, and all this time Roy was filing copy, and he didn't get to read the paper. When they got back to the U.S. and they flew in at Andrews Air Force Base, the vice president was met by this big retinue of people, and they had huge stacks of the *New York Times*, so the vice president could catch up on them, and Roy, too.

Roy grabbed every *Times* he could and he was sitting in the backseat of a car, and by flashlight and what little light came in from the streetlights, he was reading his stories. All the way he was muttering, "They raped my stories, they decimated them, they killed me." As soon as he got home, he went to bed for a week. To restore his soul, he said. Writers are like that, and with the best writers you have to insist on discipline on one hand, but you also have to listen to them and run interference for them in making absolutely sure that they can do what they do best, which is tell the story.

QUESTION: *Can you clarify something for me on the idea of making the reader see? I understand this when you have a feature story. But on a hard news story, how do you walk the line between putting the reader there, or making a reader see, and claims of sensationalism? Is there a place in a story like that for making the reader see?*

GENE ROBERTS: I'll give you an example. If you went back and looked at newspapers for the Japanese surrender in 1945, you would find several versions of the story depending on what papers you looked at. And then after reading what other papers carried, if you went and looked at Homer Bigart's you'd find Homer's was just as newsy. Everybody said, you know, the Japanese today surrendered, and it took place on a ship. But Homer put you on the deck of the ship. He reported that one of the Japanese who signed hobbled in on a cane. The man's hands shook, and Homer said—I can still remember a line—"If the bestialities in the prison camps were not so fresh on one's mind, you would almost feel sorry for him." You could identify with the story, and yet I don't think it in any way crossed the line between objectivity or fairness or unfairness. I think it was a very fair, very objective story and was more fair and more objective because it gave you more of a feel of what the scene was like.

QUESTION: *Years ago when I was an undergraduate student, the school of journalism didn't want me to take its courses. The courses were for journalism majors. Do newspapers today hire students out of journalism school primarily, or do they look for diversity?*

GENE ROBERTS: Interestingly, it is very hard to get hired today whether you're a graduate of a journalism school or not. And, interestingly, the people who get hired today in an industry in which there have been a lot of cutbacks in staff are the people who stay away from the U.S. mail and do not send out their résumés. Instead they go to the local newspapers and bang on the door and insist on getting to talk to someone.

On small papers, the best place to start, you have to remember the editors don't have secretaries. They have to answer their own mail, and if you write them a letter they resent it. They either have to answer it themselves without help, or they have to walk around feeling guilty. And *you* made them feel guilty, and who needs that? But if you show up in their newsroom with examples of your writing in your hand, and you go in at eight o'clock in the morning and you say, "I know you're busy, but I will stick around all day and if you've got five minutes for coffee or anything, I'll come back whenever you say come back."

These are the people in today's market who get hired. Just the fact that you stayed out of the mail and you came to the newsroom is a big plus. The editor knows right away you have initiative and enterprise. He, or she, also had a chance to look at you and knows you don't have two heads. So when he is looking for somebody and maybe he doesn't have an opening right then, he tells himself, "I've already interviewed this person. I don't have to spend money on bringing him in for an interview." Every person I've known, even in the depth of a recession, who got out and visited ten to fifteen or twenty papers and took a day per paper to do it, if a person had anything at all to commend them in the way of writing, they got hired. They found a newspaper.

QUESTION: *Earlier you mentioned Tom Wolfe and the writings done in the mid-1960s. My question is, does "new journalism" still exist today in the 1990s? If it doesn't, what kind of journalism exists, and who would be a good example of journalism in the '90s?*

GENE ROBERTS: Well, there are still a lot of practitioners and people around who pride themselves on being "new journalists." And to some degree, every good writer today, whether he would classify himself as a "new journalist" or not, has been influenced in some way by so-called new journalism. They try to get more of a sense of what the person felt like, re-creating the scene, and I think there can be both an honest and dishonest way of doing that.

The ultimate test, when you're trying to re-create a scene, is if a reader can read it and figure out there's a logical way you could have known that. Then, I think the credibility is high, and I think that is a perfectly acceptable way to write. It is a desirable way to write—if you've really done the reporting and got the detail. But if the reader reads what you wrote and says, "How could he possibly have known that?" then I think you've got a problem.

In the heyday of so-called new journalism, there were people that were pushing it further, I think, than it should be pushed. But you go back and look at John Hersey's *Hiroshima,* and it's a wonderful piece of writing. You feel like you are there; you feel like you have seen the people who survived the A-bomb blast. You identify with them, and yet at no point in this novella-long account of Hiroshima do you feel that he is telling you something that he couldn't possibly have known. So with the best writing, if you can re-create it by asking a thousand questions of a thousand people if you have to, that in my mind is fine journalism and is to be applauded and emulated.

QUESTION: *Could you tell us where the Hersey account on Hiroshima could be found?*

GENE ROBERTS: The library will have it just as *Hiroshima* by John Hersey. The library will also have another wonderful book, called *Here to Stay,* which is a collection of Hersey's writing, most of it from *The New Yorker* right after World War II. Hersey, by the way, followed an interesting path right after World War II. While covering the war he saw concentration camps, he saw human skeletons, he saw piles of dead bodies, and he became preoccupied with the question: What is it in the human spirit that makes you fight to live when you can argue that the world is not worth living in, if it will allow concentration camps and bestialities like that? He pursued these stories. He was the first one to write in a major way, a long time before he became nationally known, about John F. Kennedy and PT 109, because Kennedy swam for miles with a broken back and saved someone in the process. He was interested in what is it that drives someone to survive like this.

One of my favorite John Hersey stories, and it's in *Here to Stay,* is about a wonderful little old lady who's in her eighties, who is trapped in a rooming house in Rhode Island during a flood. The only way she can stay alive is to get out of that house on a steel cable that is attached to the top of the house and runs for the length of several blocks. A steeplejack crosses the cable and helps this little old lady, but nevertheless here's this eighty-some-year-old woman hanging by a wire and doing what you would think is impossible in order to survive. They are wonderful stories, and in every one of them you feel like you are there, and you feel like you know the people.

QUESTION: *I heard the other day on National Public Radio a commentary that before too long we'll be reading our newspapers on TV or computers. In view of modern technology, what do you see as the future of print journalism?*

GENE ROBERTS: I think the only thing print journalism really has to fear is its own owners and managers. I think that if it can survive that it can survive anything. What is happening today in journalism is that people are watering down their newspapers to pick up an additional 5 percent readership. There is nothing wrong with picking up an additional 5 percent readership, and there is everything right about it. But you have to be careful that you don't become superficial and lose the serious reader who has stuck with you through thick and thin.

I just recently talked to a person who is an adviser and consultant to newspapers. She tells me she must have gone into a hundred newspapers in the last few years. At virtually every paper, she finds a certain trauma among the mid-level editors, and the trauma is that they don't have enough resources to do the job. It's driving them crazy. The reason they don't have enough resources is increasingly newspapers have gone public and the ownership has gotten concentrated. Papers have become bigger and bigger, and papers feel under great pressure to meet the expectations of Wall Street. So when you have an economic downturn in what's a very cyclical industry, people start cutting back on the staff and start reducing the quality of material that is going to the reader. I think this weakens the hold on the reader.

I think there will always be readers so long as we give them something to read and make them want to read. You have to remember book publishing is booming like never before. People are reading out there, and definitely the way *not* to satisfy all readers is to serve up everything in increments of two inches or six inches or eight inches. When it's worth only two inches, that is exactly what it ought to be. But when it's worth two columns, it ought to get two columns.

Thank you very much.

Good, Clean Fun

RED SMITH

NEW YORK HERALD TRIBUNE

JULY 29, 1952

HELSINKI—The Lady of the Bath glanced up without curiosity when four gents tottered out of the steam room of the sauna, all naked as jaybirds and broiled like proper sirloins, charred on the outside, medium rare in the middle. The Lady of the Bath, an old doll wearing spectacles and a long rubber apron, was busy soaping and scrubbing the tract of masculine meat on her pine-board table, and the newcomers represented more work on an already crowded day.

The sauna (pronounced *sowna*) is a Finnish bath, and a great deal more. It is a sacred rite, a form of human sacrifice in which the victim is boiled like a missionary in the cannibal islands, then baked to a turn, then beaten with sticks until he flees into the icy sea, then lathered and honed and kneaded and pummeled by the high priestess of this purgatorial pit.

Nothing relaxes a Finn like this ritual of fire worship, water worship, and soap worship. It is an ancient folk custom dating from forgotten times, and it explains why Finland produces so many great marathon runners. Anybody who can survive a sauna can run 26 miles barefoot over broken beer bottles.

The most gracious gesture of hospitality a Finn can make is to bathe with his guest. From an American host, a suggestion that everybody go get washed might imply that the guest was getting a trifle gamy, but Americans don't know everything. Lots of them haven't been bathed by a doll since they were six.

"A foreigner," says a pamphlet on the subject, "who leaves Finland without the intimate acquaintance of a sauna cannot boast of having got into grips with the Finnish mentality. Through it the creature of civilization is enabled to get in touch with the primal forces of nature—earth, fire, and water."

Curious about primal forces, three Americans and Kai Koskimies, their Finnish keeper, had taxied out to Waskiniemi, on the outskirts of Helsinki, where a birch forest meets the blue waters of the Gulf of Finland.

There they stripped to the buff, bowed cordially to the Lady of the Bath, and entered the steam room.

In a murky, low-ceilinged cubicle recognizable by anybody who ever read Dante, several other lost souls attired in sweat sat on benches with faces buried in their hands. The room was heated—an understatement, as ever was—by a sort of Dutch oven in which cobblestones are cooked over a fire of birch logs. A thermometer registered only 130 degrees Fahrenheit, and Kai, making a snoot of disapproval, scooped water onto the hot rocks to get up a head of steam.

The visitors were destined to discover the differences between dry heat and the steamy coziness of this inferno. The steam room is the simple, ancient type of sauna, which is part of the humblest Finnish home. There are four hundred thousand of them in Finland, one for every ten people. "The air gives off a slight but exhilarating aroma of smoke," says the pamphlet. "The effect of the open fireplace feels strong to sensitive people."

Four sensitive people stood it as long as any hickory-smoked ham could have done. Then they oozed out of the cell like melted tallow, and Kai led the way to another room, providing dry heat. There the thermometer outraged him. It registered only 176 degrees, not even warm enough to boil an egg. The sauna proprietor agreed that this was ridiculous.

"This is no sauna," he said, and did something with the fireplace. "In one, two, three minutes it will be warm." In one, two, three minutes the thermometer raced up to 219 degrees. Missionaries are fricasseed at 212.

Bundles of leafy birch branches were provided as knouts so the bathers could beat themselves. Kai splashed water around to cool the wooden floor and benches, but it evaporated instantly. Even with the insulation of a folded Turkish towel, the seats were like stove lids.

Relaxing Finnish-style, everybody sat rocking from cheek to cheek to avoid being fried outright. At the same time, all laid about with the birch, flogging themselves like flagellants. After that came a refreshing dip in the sea.

The Gulf of Finland is colder than an Eskimo spinster. All feeling, however, had been left behind in the stew pot. The instant a guy hit the water he turned numb; he suffered no more than a corpse.

Cleanliness was next on the schedule, and the Lady of the Bath was the babe to provide it. She starts with a shampoo, then works on the subject in sections—just as one eats a lobster, cleaning up one claw, laying it aside, and picking up another. Her powerful fingers probe deep, finding muscles the doctors never have charted. She is skillful, efficient, and thorough. She scrapes the hull with a rough wet towel. The combination massage and scouring process is genuinely relaxing, easing muscles, untying knotted nerves.

That's all there is to a sauna, except for one technicality. The technicality is that as soon as you're finished, you do it all over—the heat, the swim, and the shower. In the winter, when the sea drops 2 degrees in temperature and freezes over, you can't swim. You go outdoors and roll in the snow instead. On the second time around, the temperature in the dry oven had got satisfactorily cozy. It was slightly over 269 degrees. This created some excitement around the sauna. They said it was a world record.

When it's all over, you get a diploma testifying that you are alive and clean. This is partly true.

GEORGIE ANNE GEYER Since her days as a foreign correspondent for the *Chicago Daily News* from 1964 until 1975, Georgie Anne Geyer has put international affairs into perspective for readers in America and abroad. Whether interviewing a world leader or offering analysis after in-depth reporting, she clarifies the complexities and consequences of global change. Currently a columnist for Universal Uclick, she's the author of many books that amplify her research and commentary, including her memoir, *Buying the Night Flight* (1983), *Guerilla Prince: The Untold Story of Fidel Castro* (1991), *Waiting for Winter to End* (1994), and *Americans No More* (1996). She delivered this lecture on September 20, 1995.

GEORGIE ANNE GEYER

Who Killed the Foreign Correspondent?

W ho killed the foreign correspondent? It's a troubling question, because in truth he was a greatly respected fellow. Everybody liked him. Not always the best husband, that's for sure, but always the most loyal comrade and professional companion. One of a special breed—yes, he surely was that. A modest chap, when he paused to consider himself (as, in fact, he often did), he judged himself a blend of Humphrey Bogart, Pope John Paul II, and Zorba the Greek. It is whispered that he went to sleep every night—or so we suspected—humming "One for the Road."

Almost all of the correspondents had more than a slight touch of insanity, of course, or they wouldn't be in such a crazy business.

Covering wars, revolutions, and human frailty in seventeen languages over twenty-three time zones was always a dangerous business, but that gave the edge of excitement that this rare species of human migratory bird needed for survival. Some wit along the way noted that if you have a terrible war with two hundred thousand people struggling desperately to leave and twenty people trying desperately to get in, those twenty are foreign correspondents.

Perhaps the great Ernie Pyle described the war correspondent best. "We correspondents could go anywhere we pleased," he wrote, "being gifted and chosen characters."

Yes, they did feel themselves gifted and chosen, no question about it, but they had to have that self-confidence or they would have gone crazy, seeing the things they saw every day. There was also always a remarkable égalité to the foreign correspondent corps. This is because there is no other profession where so many are able to go across often forbidden borders in such a privileged—and yet equal—way.

Among them, there were only a few rules for acceptance, but these were certain ones. You had to be honest, you didn't undercut a friend, and you always—always—paid for your round of the drinks. Not helping a colleague in trouble would get you ostracized forever.

And those are not really a bad set of rules for life, when you think about it.

So why would anyone *kill* the foreign correspondent?

Yes, there was truly something remarkable about him. There he was—and, now, often, *she* was—out there, in a strange land, perhaps speaking the language, perhaps not, more than likely in a war and in extreme danger. And just *loving it*: loving the dark and isolated nights, the purity of the work, the total control over every aspect of one's existence. He was—we'll just use "he," or this tentative obituary will go on into the next war—in love with the world and with his ability to conquer it, not through military might but through knowing it. He was also in love with the word, which was his weapon for conquering and his vehicle for knowing the world.

In fact, he was *our* representative abroad—he never ceased being one of us, for he was a kind of international everyman. He hated bureaucracy as much as other men fear experience. As one correspondent in Vietnam put it, "There's only one thing better than being 5,000 miles away from the office—and that's being 10,000 miles away from it."

And—just think about it—nearly all of the information we get about the world comes from these crazy, creative, obsessed, diligent, fun-loving people. They are our couriers between cultures, carrying messages from people to people. I would actually dare to suggest to you that in no other profession is responsibility for what we know centered in such a small and fragile group.

And you know something else? Despite the dangers and despite the discomforts, the correspondents could get damned angry and enraged with the world, but they very seldom grew pessimistic; they didn't in general feel it was all for nothing or that mankind was no good. Given the kinds of events they had to witness constantly and somehow live through and abide, this always struck me as very strange indeed—and rather wondrous, too!

I came to my own conclusions about this. I decided that this was mainly because the correspondents were "there." They were experiencing things first-hand just as all of us do at those times and moments when our lives are most authentic and most worth living.

And although the men in the field would have vociferously denied this—angrily denied it—"macho," you know—the fact is that, you scratch any good foreign correspondent, and you find a man or woman with a mission. The best ones never believed in journalism as any "search for truth"—they left that to the poets and the theologians (not to speak of those phony, self-inflated journalists), who have enough trouble with it. The real foreign correspondents were too realistic for that. With their experience of the world, they knew that journalism was the search for the "little relative truths that at best keep us sane" in this, our brief journey here on Earth.

But who actually *killed* the foreign correspondent? And *why* would anyone kill such a splendid fellow? As the King of Siam said in *The King and I*, "It is a puzzlement."

For the body was never found. What's more, while word got out around the world that he had died, there were various stories—all romantic, all plausible (particularly given the extent to which he would go to dramatize himself). Some said he died in Rwanda trying to cover the awful carnage there. Another said he had died in a plane crash in the Sea of Japan (that would be the worst—the greatest fear of the crazy foreign correspondent is that of dying in some such mundane and humiliatingly "normal" way after taking so many ridiculous chances). Still others remain convinced he had been taking an Aeroflot plane from Bishkek to Baku, and that the pilot's three-year-old son was flying the plane with his little dog on his lap when it crashed.

At any rate, we shall miss him terribly. It is at times like this that one remembers the words of the great French writer and early aviator Antoine de Saint-Exupéry, in himself the very exemplar of the character of our foreign correspondent. Writing of these kinds of people, he wrote in one of his superb romantic books, "They land alone at scattered and remote airports, isolated from each other in the manner of sentinels between whom no words can be spoken. It needs the accident of journeyings to bring together here or there the dispersed members of this great professional family." And I'll bet on his tombstone, he'll have inscribed, "I did it my way."

We all have our memories. He did; I did:

Meeting Fidel Castro in Havana in July of 1966. In those early years, my beloved male colleagues kept telling me that I must take these "great interviews" with "great leaders" seriously. I did until that night.

The interview with history's great "barbudo" began at midnight. Actually, it is rather easy to interview Castro—you don't need to ask any questions. He starts talking, and about nine hours later, he stops talking! So I was listening, listening, listening, until, at precisely 1:30 A.M., he stopped talking (you notice this). He looked at me, very serious and not joking, and said soberly, "It's time to get the ice cream."

Having no idea whatsoever what he meant, I immediately retorted with, "Oh, that's very nice."

He picked up with, "We now have twenty-eight flavors."

I came back with, "Oh, that's very nice."

He moved on to, "That's more than Howard Johnson's has."

I waded right back with a more spirited, "Oh, that's very nice."

Then he rather revealed himself. "Before the Cuban Revolution, the Cuban people loved Howard Johnson's ice cream. This is our way of showing we can do everything better than you Americans."

This saga of our time did not end there. I put the little story at the end of my long interview with Castro, and the next week I got a cable from my paper, the *Chicago Daily News*. "Howard Johnson's has responded!" they wrote. "They now have thirty-two flavors."

Then there was the time I was traveling overnight from Washington to Paris. It was December 1978, and it was cold and snowy. I was going out to this small French village to interview that great friend of humanity and of children, the Ayatollah Khomeini.

When I got to the village, the young Westernized Persians around Khomeini immediately put a black scarf over my head with just my eyes showing. I really didn't mind it, but it is hard to work with just your eyes showing. And in a way I could even understand it: Being as enticing as I am, a man of his years, he had to be protected against himself.

Soon, two of us were sitting on a Persian rug in a little French summer house, when in swept Khomeini. I had the feeling of a great black apparition floating to the floor; and during the hour that I was there, he never looked at either of us but just stared between us as though at some vision that we could not see. I had the strangest feeling, as I sat there, of waves of evil emanating from him.

He had his answers well rehearsed: The Iran that he would take over from the Shah within only three months would be "a democracy," and women would have full rights. Then he swept out again.

Because I read history, I knew very well what was going on. The Persian Shiites believe in the tenet of "dissimulation." This means it is incumbent upon you to lie to protect the faith, and it arises historically out of their centuries of defeat from outside. But how to translate this knowledge into everyday journalism?

I finally decided to be very fair; and so I quoted what he said, mentioned dissimulation, and in effect said that he was lying. It was a singularly unsatisfactory way of dealing with a very difficult subject.

In those same weeks, a friend of mine, an Afghan-American scholar, was also there in the village. The Persians did not know about his Afghan background, and so he overheard them say in Farsi, which he understood, "Tell him that the Ayatollah wants democracy and women's rights—that's what the Americans like to hear."

And then there was December of 1987.

You have to realize that the Cold War had defined all of our lives. So when I was invited to the White House that December, as Mikhail Gorbachev visited Washington and five thousand journalists from all over the world crowded the city, I was ecstatic. Four of us columnists were invited to meet with President Ronald Reagan.

There we were at 2 P.M., right on the dot, and the president came into the Oval Office looking like the proverbial million bucks. He was slim, dressed in an elegant silk suit, and looking happy as any creature on Earth could possibly be. I immediately looked at his hair—mine was dyed, his was not. Then we began to ask questions.

One of the men soon asked, "What about the 'evil empire'? How long will we fight with the Soviets?"

"Oh, that's all over," the president said. "We get along just fine now." Then he wagged a finger at us. "They no longer believe in one-world Marxian domination."

We asked him three times; he answered the same way three times. At first, we thought he didn't know what he was saying; by the time we left, we knew that we had heard the announcement of the end of the Cold War.

Ah, but I digress. I have been thinking so much about my friend's death—about the *foreign correspondent's death*—that I have got off on my own journey. I'm sorry. I didn't mean to, because we have some very serious matters to discuss here tonight.

For two new developments define what is indeed killing the foreign correspondent today—and both are exceedingly dangerous developments.

The first: Gradually but persistently, the foreign correspondent of the old, traditional style is dying out. A whole congeries of trends and tendencies, of malign influences and benign intentions, have come together to diminish, if not destroy, the profession as we know it, and those tendencies are bound to get worse unless and until something is done.

I am talking, of course, about the old-style foreign correspondent, the one who was sent abroad by his paper to live for usually three to six years—and sometimes a lifetime—in one area. He learned the language, the history, the culture, so that when something big happened (which was every day) he was immediately and supremely able to put it into historic context.

Although I tried very hard, I was unable to get exact figures about how many American correspondents there are representing the United States overseas today, but all of the foreign editors tell me that the numbers are way, way down. In Beijing this summer, I had long talks with many of the correspondents, and they regaled me with sad stories of how their numbers were diminishing as papers merged. Computers (ironically designed supposedly to free reporters by making their work proceed faster through technology) were tying them down to every breaking story because they feared missing any minor story. Funds to support any of the old-type adventuresome travels, which distinguished the foreign correspondent in balmier times, had literally dried up.

The second is the fact that, at every turn, there are incomparable new perils for the foreign correspondent, thus further weakening this very crucial but fragile arm of the profession.

Danger, for instance. Foreign correspondence has always been dangerous, but now it is becoming *unspeakably* dangerous. Nineteen ninety-four, for instance, had the dubious distinction of being the bloodiest year for the profession in history. According to the International Federation of Journalists, the list of correspondents killed worldwide in that single year went up to an all-time high of 115. It was a "year of media slaughter," spokesmen gravely averred. What's more, they were now being killed in the most primitive and savage of ways—by knife or by axe, not by gun or by bomb—and, even more important, they were being deliberately targeted.

But, let us go back for just a moment in history—for, like most correspondents, I depend upon history for my guidelines and indicators.

Actually, the earliest I can trace back this grand fellow, the foreign correspondent, was during the Crimean War of 1854. Before that time, British editors simply took news from foreign newspapers or depended upon letters from the battlefront; after this, the British papers began actually *hiring* men to go out to the warfront. So was the war correspondent born.

By the time I became a foreign correspondent, beginning in 1964, the pattern was quite clear. Major papers across the country, as well as television and sometimes radio, sent correspondents abroad. There were many voices. We cost a lot—$200,000 a year when I was with the *Chicago Daily News*. And there was great cachet to being a foreign correspondent; it was the glamour job of newspapering.

But there was something else: We were "protected" (or at least felt we were, which is really the same thing). In part, this was due to the fact that the world respected American power; in part, it was because of guidelines laid down by groups such as the International Committee of the Red Cross, which declared, in various accords gradually accepted over the years, crazy independent people like foreign correspondents to be noncombatants.

Now, this may not sound very important, but the fact is that it is very important. This amazingly civilized idea—that the foreign correspondent was out there to be respected by all mankind for doing an important job and thus should be considered as standing outside of the warfare—actually took root. We were privileged observers, like the clergy, like the Red Cross, like the nongovernmental organizations.

And then, ladies and gentlemen, I watched while it all suddenly changed. People think it changed in Vietnam, but it didn't.

In Vietnam, even the Viet Cong respected the rules of noncombatancy. In Cambodia, they did not—and record numbers of reporters were killed. At almost the same time, the terrible civil war in Lebanon was beginning. Suddenly we were seeing not war but the absence of traditional warfare. Lebanon was the first warning, in our times, of a world approaching anarchy, or what I have called since the late 1970s a state of permanent disintegration.

And so, there, all of the rules of noncombatancy, of neutrality, were no longer observed in that world that had been taken over by what I called the irregulars: the guerrillas, the commandos, the terrorists, the militiamen. And in these conflicts, the foreign correspondents had no protection at all.

Sometimes we were the "new diplomats," as when, for instance, I would attempt to explain American policy—futilely, I might add—to someone like Yasser Arafat in his back alley office in Beirut. More often, we were the "new targets," and the numbers of journalists killed soon bore that fact out.

We were everyman caught up in the whole process of disintegration and anarchy that began to smite the world in the 1970s.

But, meanwhile, changes were also coming at home that were cutting back the sheer *numbers* of foreign correspondents.

I remember in the late '70s, sitting with the late Phil Foisie, the wonderful foreign editor of the *Washington Post* who had done so much to dignify foreign news, and we argued over our business. He had come by then—as had many other editors—to believe that reporters and foreign correspondents were essentially interchangeable. You could take any good street reporter and put him or her on the streets of Cairo or Karachi or Rio de Janeiro and get a good story.

But you can't: The foreign correspondent is a person with a special, manic, valiant temperament, someone who can best work alone in the strangest of places and put out simply superb copy. But, most importantly, good foreign coverage makes very different demands on a journalist than does local coverage. It demands a far more scholarly and even holistic approach to coverage. Indeed, perhaps Alistair Cooke once described the specialness of the work of the good foreign correspondent best when he wrote,

> It is the stimulating duty of a foreign correspondent to cover everything. Whereas a domestic reporter, even at his best, graduates from general reporting and hops up the ladder to success towards a single specialty, a foreign correspondent is required to act on the preposterous but exhilarating assumption that he takes all knowledge for his province.

Cooke also answers well the nagging—and calculably incorrect—claim that no one can ever really know another society in a short span of time, particularly as an outsider. "The best stuff ever written on the Constitution was by Bryce, a Scotsman," he pointed out, "and the best thing on Peru is by a Bostonian. But, of course, you start from scratch. You don't take things for granted you don't think you know. That's an important thing. The resident of a country thinks he knows. The foreign correspondent has to go back to the origins of things every day. You can't write about a violation of interstate commerce without explaining to the British where the whole concept started so you teach yourself."

And so, although some newspaper editors still maintain that regular street reporters are the same as—and can be interchangeable for—foreign correspondents, the truth is that, temperamentally and intellectually, they are really two very different types of people.

Still, today's journalism is more and more characterized by the attitudes which have led to "parachute journalism." Here, the innocent reporter is literally "parachuted" into El Salvador one day, into the Falklands war the next, into Bosnia the next. It is not surprising, of course, that no one could do any in-depth job in such a frivolous way. This development of "parachutism" also fed directly into the infantilizing of foreign news—and particularly into the inexperienced correspondent sensationalizing everything to death. Indeed, what else *could* they do? Usually, they hardly knew where they were.

Then there were the changes in the staffs, two-career families, journalists wanting not adventure but to move up the management ladder. Many of us couldn't believe what we were seeing. The result is that staffs all over are being trimmed back and that papers with foreign staffs are closing left and right.

And then came the Gulf War, still another totally new and different experience for the foreign correspondent.

Now, I had attended Vietnam military press seminars at the various war colleges ever since the Vietnam War. The military, having been so traumatized by Vietnam, were analyzing, watching, planning. The press was not. And so, when the Gulf War came, there were some sixteen hundred young reporters sent out there; they didn't know the military and they didn't know the area. There you could really see—on CNN in living color—how we were throwing away the traditional foreign field, for when there are that many correspondents, you give the military the power to restrict coverage in any way they please.

When *Saturday Night Live* had a bit on the naive journalists in the Gulf War asking the poised and savvy military briefer, "What is the password to get through to Iraqi lines?" you knew that, as the editor of the *Dallas Morning News* said to me at the time, "We lost that one."

Meanwhile, the numbers of foreign correspondents kept going down. I would calculate that there are now no more than sixty or seventy overseas from major newspapers, where there used to be four hundred and up (again, in the absence of real figures, I am calculating, but reliably). And the papers kept cutting back.

Moreover, at the same time, we saw still another phenomenon, that of *countries in which foreign correspondents could simply no longer work.* I call to your attention, particularly, Algeria. There you have today the most rabid of Islamic fundamentalists battling the old military government.

Foreign and local journalists are particularly targeted. There were twenty-six Algerian journalists and a French one killed in 1994 in a deliberate death campaign. Robert Ménard, director of the international professional group Reporters Without Borders, said, "Going there is like playing Russian roulette."

And so, in Algeria, we do really see something totally new: a country so dangerous, with correspondents so deliberately pinpointed for death, that no one will go there, and no editor will send anybody to go there.

In eerie words that could prophesy the age that is coming, the leading French media expert on Algeria, Jose Garcon, said, "The Algerian war has become a story without images. No one is there to record them." I am not exaggerating when I say that many of our worlds could become "stories without images." It is only the foreign correspondents who give the stories palpable form and who act as the couriers, carrying those images through the night.

Ahh, but I can hear some of you whispering in the back row, "My, she does go on, doesn't she? And you would think that she never even heard about CNN. Do you think she has any understanding at all of the fact that we are no longer living in her beloved, precious, wondrous Chicago? (She's from the South Side too, you know, the tough side, primitive side, maybe that explains it!)"

I can hear you thinking, "But what about Marshall McLuhan's *global village*? What about the Information Age that is going to make us all brothers and bring peace on Earth? (And why *does* she go on so about some friend; was he just killed in some strange place or something?)"

Ladies and gentlemen, let me proclaim it now and for all time: There *is* no global village, and there *is* no information revolution (maybe there is for the top 2 percent of international elites, but surely not for the masses of the populations of the world).

You want examples? I will give you the Serbian one:

I went to Yugoslavia—to Serbia—in 1989 because I knew that, with the end of the central hold of communism, Yugoslavia was going to split apart. It was almost a scientific observation, it was so inevitable. I watched Serbian president Slobodan Milošević orchestrating, planning, and plotting these wars: He was arming the militias, forming them, propagandizing the people through television.

But perhaps the strangest thing is not even that the Serbs have fallen for his rabid propaganda; so have many Americans of Serbian descent, who have every access to good and free information but massively shun it in favor of the cynical propaganda of a mass murderer.

A memory: One day several years ago, I was sitting in Kosovo, the Albanian area in the south which is simply a police state ruled by Serbia. There, I watched with the oppressed Kosovars while Serbian television showed their version of Bosnians *thanking* their Serb oppressors for "liberating" them! This is the world we are living in.

Perhaps Dean Peter Krogh of the prestigious Georgetown School of Foreign Service best characterized the CNN Generation—and what it *can* and what it *cannot* do—and why the person on the ground, be it the foreign correspondent or the diplomat, is of such supreme importance, indeed today more than ever.

I quote here from his speech at his twenty-fifth anniversary at Georgetown the spring of 1995.

First he recalled how CNN's Ted Turner, upon receiving an award from the school several years ago, actually suggested that the school change its name to something like a "school of world affairs" or of "global togetherness."

Why? "Because nothing is foreign anymore."

Well, ex-cuse me! The real world out there is getting more foreign all the time. The world I see—and know—is *not* coming together in that wondrous, popular, nonexistent global village; to the contrary, as the center of communism broke down and as the United States has reneged its leadership role in the world, peoples, tribes, ethnic groups, are everywhere breaking apart—and breaking down. To most peoples of the world, the world outside is more foreign than ever.

Dean Krogh put it brilliantly, saying, "In an age of real-time, multimedia, interactive forms of communication, there is a tendency to declare obsolete (or at least dispensable) the diplomat and the foreign correspondent in the field. We will do so at our peril. The myriad forms of instantaneous communication threaten to substitute immediacy for insight, reaction for reflection, sentiment for judgment, hyperbole for reality and deniability for integrity."

He went on, "Over the past twenty-five years, the numbers of foreign bureaus and foreign correspondents have declined. Deeply informed individual insight from the field is fast disappearing. News and media services compound the problem by making news more homogeneous. The media increasingly are reduced to establishing a fleeting physical presence only after CNN announces there is a crisis abroad. . . . Yet, CNN itself is, by its very nature, flawed. It provides unevaluated and sometimes exaggerated reports of developments abroad which drive a domestic rush to judgment and a correlated reaction."

So, yes, CNN is wonderful—for what it does—but it has really very little to do with the foreign correspondent on the ground, with his or her grounding in history, trying to explain the context and meaning of the story and not just the soundbites. And, of course, on the CNNs of the world there is no correction of mistakes, no context, no real coherence.

Yet—Peter Krogh again: "As the world gets bigger, the foreign policy agenda simultaneously grows longer. Replacing the set agenda of the Cold War is a veritable avalanche of pressing international issues. Our diplomats and journalists need to inhabit these issues where they reside in a far-flung world."

I was in Russia just last week. I saw what had never happened before in world history: a superpower that had collapsed, and without being defeated in war and with its armies intact. I saw a country that is going down, down, down, and will almost surely end up in some sort of nationalistic dictatorship. I saw a country that cannot adapt to the modern age because it simply does not have the principles to do so.

Those are the things that good foreign correspondents tell us.

And this week, I am here with you—on this magnificent campus, with its superb history. I am deeply honored to be here to give the Red Smith Lecture—but, then, that is only natural.

I'm the "perfect" person. I don't know a quarterback from a quarterhorse, or second base from second fiddle. But I do cover the Game of Nations.

At any rate, thank you from the bottom of my heart!

Well, forgive me, but I was just thinking about my friend again—you know, the foreign correspondent—who just died. (Or I think he did.) You remember, I told you about him when we started this pleasant evening.

We still don't know where he died, or how, or where he is buried, if he is. He was always pretty romantic about the whole profession—told me once that he wanted on his tombstone the words "My God, it was fun!" That was typical of all the foreign correspondents. I do hope someday I'll know what happened to him—and be able to place those words on his tombstone.

Meanwhile, you know, something interesting has happened. Even while the numbers are going down and even while the foreign correspondence corps is dangerously threatened, there *are* some young correspondents out there—in some of the most dangerous places in the world, like Bosnia, like Rwanda, like Chechnya—who continue to do a superb job.

Think of Sarajevo and the journalists, often unsung and unnamed, who have stayed there throughout the siege. It was they, every time one of the Western governments or the U.N. lied, who were there to say what was really happening; two young *New York Times* correspondents reported on how the Bosnian Serb missiles were all hooked up to Belgrade, for instance, and a *Christian Science Monitor* correspondent discovered the massive Serb massacres.

And so, once again, and now again on the peripheries of Europe, diplomats are preening, dictators are falsifying, and men of power are ignoring the victims. And, once again, it is only the correspondents on the ground—those odd lone sentinels, those courageous misfits, those representatives of all of us, those searching souls—who are bringing us the little and sometimes big truths of politics and warfare, of ambition and human pride.

We need many more of them—and we shall need many, many more of them in the future. We need to train young people not only to climb the ladders of journalistic ambition—city editor this year, managing editor the next—but also to have the romantic commitment to know the world, so that we may all know it. We need to give them—and *to insist upon their getting*—in-depth training in language, in history, in cultural anthropology.

I believe that schools like Notre Dame are uniquely equipped to turn this trend around. We shall certainly all lose if you do not.

I am sure my friend, the foreign correspondent, would agree—wherever he is tonight!

Questions and Answers

QUESTION: *I was wondering what you think about the parallel Dean Peter Krogh of Georgetown University drew between foreign correspondents and diplomats. That strikes me as an interesting parallel, and I wonder what you think.*

GEORGIE ANNE GEYER: That is a very interesting parallel. It is not usually made. I think the parallel is right because what we are talking about are people who are out there individually using their intelligence but also using their instinct. Good diplomats and good correspondents have an instinct for countries. They learn about the countries, but then they know the feel of them like a good street reporter does.

It is no accident that a lot of my friends are diplomats because they were in the embassy doing one part of the work, and we were out in the streets doing another part. But we foreign correspondents always had the advantage because we could go everywhere. Of course, their advantage was that they were in the diplomatic meetings with leaders. But they would tell us what happened, so we had that advantage, too. The comparison is the lone individuals out there doing the job.

What I was trying to say tonight was that this is the only way, despite all of the technological advancement, that we are going to know things. This will come from the courageous, lone individual, whether it is the diplomat or the correspondent. Now, increasingly, the businessman is also becoming important. In Moscow and most of the world now, the international businessmen are all over the place, and a lot of them are extremely well informed, and I notice that there's change in my own behavior. I'm using them much more as sources. I go to them more than I used to, because they just weren't that important before.

Yes, technology is wonderful. I use it to help myself; but if it doesn't help me, I don't want it. I don't know if the president and vice president of my syndicate know this, but when I am overseas I write longhand on white paper and fax it. Everybody else is like a packhorse carrying all this stuff around, and I am there happily in the coffee shops, writing longhand. It works fine. My editor at the syndicate says it is fine. She can read it, and we have no problems at all.

QUESTION: *From the story you told about interviewing Ronald Reagan and from many of your other remarks, I get a sense that men are more involved in foreign correspondence. Could you talk about this situation?*

GEORGIE ANNE GEYER: Was it a very male-dominated profession? Yes, it was when I started, but a lot of women came in, and I certainly encouraged them. When I started there were about sixty men and me, always. At that age I thought that was about the right ratio. Later I decided that thirty men and me was quite all right.

I really welcomed other women, and they came in and did very, very well. But they haven't stayed—that's the difference. They tend to get married and move on to positions in the States, which of course is fine. They tend to stay in journalism, but they don't stay in the foreign field. There are some overseas who tend to be with their husbands in capitals where both work, and that sometimes works out pretty well.

When I started in 1964, the *Chicago Daily News* had probably the greatest foreign staff in the country. It was very famous for that. I was just a kid out of Northwestern covering Chicago and loving it. I was having a grand time, but I did want to go overseas, and all of our correspondents were not only men but they were older men. They covered World War II, they swam the Bosporus, they got Count Ciano's diaries. They were icons.

Well, here was this little, plump, blonde kid from the South Side of Chicago. I got this little grant that allowed me to go overseas, and I went to Latin America. I remember Larry Fanning, our wonderful editor at the time, said, "Well, Gee Gee, you go overseas for six months." I didn't burden him with the knowledge that it was going to be for years. He said, "You don't want to go to South America. That's dangerous." I said, "Larry, it's not very dangerous, and besides, anywhere you go is dangerous." He said, "No, no, no. Those are street wars. You will be in danger in South America. They're street wars." He then said, "I will send you to Vietnam." I said, "But, Larry, listen to yourself. This is insane." He said, "No, no, I've got it figured out. You can stay in Saigon. There are no street wars there. You just stay in Saigon." I said, "Larry, I am going to Peru."

Well, he thought I was absolutely crazy, but I loved Latin America. I wanted to be in Latin America, so I kept extending the time six months. Two years later, when I was in Chile, I got a cable saying, "Congratulations. You have been named our South American correspondent." So I met the guys in the bar, as we did in those days. (It was great in those days. We all helped one another; we were great pals. That kind of camaraderie you don't see much anymore.) I showed them the cable, and they were all in hysterics. They said, "Well, you know your editor is the only person in the hemisphere who hasn't known that you have been their correspondent for two years."

At first it was hard. I was very young. I was plump. I was blonde. I was from the South Side of Chicago. No Latin American man believed I was a serious correspondent. They had just never seen a woman correspondent. That was the problem. They just didn't take me seriously. Later it became, I think, a real advantage. In the Middle East, for instance, it was an advantage.

But for about my first year in Latin America, I'd finally get an interview with the president or vice president or a general. If something important was happening, they wanted to talk to the men. If nothing was happening, they wanted to take me for lunch, dinner, and dancing for starters. I am very finicky about my moral status, and I keep my personal life very separate. But I didn't know what to do about this. I never lie, I hate lies, but I did start telling them that I was married. But it didn't work, and my beloved mother would have said, "See, you lied and it didn't work." I can hear it. But immediately I would say, "Well, I am so sorry, General, but I'm married. I can't go dancing with you." He would say, "I'm married, too." It was like some bond between us!

So then I went back to my little apartment in Lima, perfectly chastised and chagrined, and I thought, "Well, Gee Gee, why don't you just tell them the truth. Tell them you are madly in love with someone." And most of the time I was. It worked fine until one day in Chile in the early '70s. The Latin men, God bless them, don't mind getting involved with a married woman, but someone who's in love—that's sacred. I was going to interview one of the leaders of the military junta in Chile. Very charming man, very intellectual, more on the liberal side.

I went over on Saturday to his big house. There were a couple of hundred troops there. I went into the big garden, with lots of family members, dogs, children around. We had a Pisco sour, talked for a couple hours, and at the end he said, "Well, this has been so interesting, why don't you come back tomorrow for lunch?" I said, "Oh, Sunday lunch, that's nice." Great source, very charming man. So there I was at noon on Sunday, thinking this is all just fine. I got to the house, and there were just two soldiers outside. I went into the garden, there was nobody there except the general and his servants. So, I said to myself, "Gee Gee, how did you get yourself into this one with all your South Side plotting?"

We sat down to have the Pisco sour and I said, "General, where's your family?" He said, "Oh, they have all gone to the beach." I said, "Oh, oh." So we had this Pisco sour, and immediately his hand reached for mine. I said, "General, there seems to be a misunderstanding. You know, you are such a charming man, but you know I am madly in love with someone." And I was at that time. But instead of the usual response, he looked at me very calculatingly, and he said, "Where is he?" and I said honestly, "Well, he is in Chicago." He said, "How long has it been since you have seen him?" And I said honestly, "Well, it's been about three weeks." He said, "Do you really think he is being faithful?" I was kind of miffed at that, because we didn't talk like that in those days. I knew my mother wouldn't like that—at all. I said, "I am certain that he is." And he looked at me very calculatingly and said, "Aha! It has been scientifically proven that a man can only be faithful for eight days. So he's not being faithful to you. Why should you be faithful to him?"

I have to tell you I was almost filled with admiration. I had never heard such a good line. And then we got into this absurd argument about where it had been scientifically proven. So I am happy to report to you that I did stay for lunch—but I left immediately afterwards, thus disproving the old adage that there are no free lunches.

I'm sorry. I can't help looking at everything with a kind of funny twist. Even when it was difficult, it was just so much fun, and the men in the field were wonderful. I think there is more competition now between men and women in the field. At that point there was so few of us, women were sort of like mascots. It was more leisurely then. We worked like dogs, yet we never took ourselves so terribly seriously. There seemed to be enough happening in the world for all of us to cover. I never understood why we should be so terribly competitive with our fellow correspondents.

QUESTION: *You said there has been a decline in foreign news for the past several years. What does this mean to public knowledge, especially for young people of college age?*

GEORGIE ANNE GEYER: That's the $64,000 question. If there is indeed a whole generation out there that does not have the benefit of knowing what happens to us as a people, what happens to us? Well, first of all, in terms of foreign news, if you read some of the big papers in this country—the *Washington Post*, the *Washington Times*, the *Baltimore Sun*, the *New York Times*, *Chicago Tribune*, *Los Angeles Times*, the *Dallas Morning News*, and many more—they have a full roster of foreign news. You can still get it. It's just the numbers feeding into it are much smaller, and papers that used to have full foreign bureaus do not have them anymore.

What seems very serious to me is the lack of civics training in our schools and the lack of historical background in our country. I depend upon history for everything. I don't mean to sound immodest, but I always know what is going to happen because I know what people did before. In Iran, when I was sitting with Khomeini, I knew exactly that he was dissimulating, how dissimulation is a tenet of Persian Shiism. It started for very good reasons. They were being overrun by enemies all the time, and they lied to defend the faith.

Young people always ask me, "How do you control your interviews?" It comes up all the time. My answer always is I control my interviews by knowing more about the subject than the person I am interviewing. And it's true. I need to know the history of the countries I'm covering. If, say, I didn't know the history of Anwar Sadat, how could I know what he was telling me, whether it was true or whether it was not true or whether it was self-serving or whether it was only self-gratifying? How could I possibly even be an intelligent or honest reporter of what a person was saying?

But even worse than that, I think, is if I don't know myself, I can hardly do anything in the foreign field, let alone in our own country. If I don't know what my system is, if I don't know what our history is, if I don't know what our great works are, I can't even begin to understand what their great works are. I have just the opposite view of the whole idea of multiculturalism. I am the real multiculturalist. You can't understand anybody else without knowing first who you are. I am a Western, Christian woman from the South Side of Chicago. And knowing that, then, I can work with and really understand and appreciate other people. Otherwise it is all falsity; it's all emptiness.

That also always stood me in good stead because they knew who I was. I am very anti-totalitarian, but I get along fine with the communists. In June, I faxed China. I was leaving for Japan in five days, but I asked if I could visit China in a couple weeks. They faxed back quickly: "Oh, Miss Geyer, we are so happy to have you come again." They knew how anti-communist I am. I write three columns a week—and that is a rather revealing process. But they like me because they know who I am. They don't want people who don't know who they are. I see that phenomenon all over the world.

Now, the problem within our own country is even more serious. If we don't know what our system is, if we don't know what our history is, how can we make informed decisions? My friend Milton Rosenberg, the great radio talk show host in Chicago who is professor of psychology at the University of Chicago, was telling me a couple weeks ago, "I have a little test that I give to incoming students. One question is when did the Civil War occur?" He said most of them don't know what century it was in.

I don't know where you even start with that. How can you then understand Egyptian history? You have no context. You have no discipline in your mind. I don't know if that is really the answer, but those are the things that are terribly important to me.

QUESTION: *I'm intrigued by what you said about your business contacts in foreign countries. Could you explain more fully how American businesspeople deal with cultural circumstances so different from our own?*

GEORGIE ANNE GEYER: I really hadn't said that about businesspeople until just now. I have been doing it instinctively, and now I realize that suddenly a lot of my sources are business. Of course, there weren't businesspeople before, because there was no business in China or Russia. I was stunned going into Moscow ten days ago. The last time I was there was four years ago, when I went to Central Asia, which was a real adventure trip. But there are all kinds of new buildings, and the old buildings are now painted. I mean, there are pastel-colored buildings in Moscow, which kind of stuns you! And there are cafes and there are nice restaurants, and everything costs so much now. I had a scotch at the Slavanskaya Hotel, and it cost $11! Believe me, that focuses your mind. I went back to the second-rate hotel where I was staying, and I didn't have any more scotch. I had vodka.

I don't know if this is the answer to your question, but more and more I see the businesspeople as becoming the cultural sophisticates, whereas the diplomats have less importance because diplomacy is done more by telephone and by special envoy than by embassy. And the foreign correspondents: While they still have their important role, there are just so many fewer of them that there is much less diversity. It's the businesspeople who have gotten very sophisticated culturally, particularly the oil people. Of course, there is this big looming fight about oil in the Caspian Sea, which

I have been writing about. The oil men and women are extremely savvy culturally; they know how to deal with people, and they know what they are dealing with.

One of the figures I got in Moscow this time is the fact that 80 percent of the banks in Moscow are now controlled by organized crime. So a lot of the businesspeople's time is taken just dealing with the criminalization that is happening in many parts of the world. In China, as well. I do think, in fairness to our business men and women, that they are getting much more sophisticated about dealing with other cultures; they are not expecting anymore that everybody operates the way we do. On the other hand, you know, we have laws that stop companies from giving payoffs. We want to be understanding about other cultures without abandoning our own values and principles.

QUESTION: *It must be very frustrating for you to turn on CNN, seeing them interviewing world leaders and taking everything at face value. How do you react when you see such programs?*

GEORGIE ANNE GEYER: Actually, I don't watch CNN except when I am overseas. I do watch it in my hotel rooms overseas, because in Russia, for example, it's not easy to get foreign papers, even the *International Herald Tribune*—and in Beijing too. So it's easy to just snap it on. What you are saying just really exemplifies the point that Peter Krogh is making, which is they are doing valuable work and I personally use it. It keeps me up on things, but there is also no corrective there. There's no analysis; there's no way to come back and say, as with my Khomeini story, "Yes, he said that, but he doesn't mean it. He doesn't mean it in our terms, or he means to say this." I was not happy with my way of doing it, but I still don't know any better way to do it. But CNN never says that. And they can't. It's not their medium. They don't have that capacity.

Think of it this way: I have the smartest cat probably in the whole world. He is really intelligent and very clever, but he can't bark. No matter what he does. CNN doesn't bark. You can't ask them to do more than they do, but my reasoning there is that, in addition to the CNN syndrome, we need more people out there who are doing the in-depth reporting and analysis.

QUESTION: *Are all the foreign correspondents necessarily viewed as writers? What about speakers, for example, some of the reporters for National Public Radio, who have ten or even fifteen minutes for reports?*

GEORGIE ANNE GEYER: I don't put National Public Radio in the CNN category. (I like CNN. I don't want that to be misunderstood.) But in fact just the night before last, I was listening to a long interview on NPR with Roger Cohen from the *New York Times* on the Bosnian war, and it was just brilliant. I mean it renewed my faith, because he has been one of the ones covering the war. It was a half-hour program, and he put everything together so coherently and so cogently. I think NPR is one of the bright spots.

QUESTION: *I speak for myself and perhaps for others when I say thank you for your work. Although we haven't known you, we've known your name, and we do know your friend, the foreign correspondent. You and your friend keep us in touch with the world through your reports. I, for one, try to keep up with all of these friends I've never met. I follow them around the world. Although they haven't a clue about me, I think they're writing for me. And I thank you, and your brothers and sisters.*

GEORGIE ANNE GEYER: That makes it all worth it. Thank you all very much.

Red Trotsky Talks to Red Smith

RED SMITH

PHILADELPHIA RECORD

MARCH 18, 1937

MEXICO CITY—The red fire of revolution which forged the reputation of Leon Trotsky and was to become a worldwide conflagration is flickering out in the oldest, sleepiest village of the Western Hemisphere.

Today the arch-plotter of modern time sits in the study of a borrowed home in Mexico City's suburban Coyoacan, a mild and amiable and aimless old man pottering with old ideas.

The Great Revolutionist is somewhat bigger than a growler of beer and somewhat less fiery. Fumbling with the writings by which he earns a living, he exhibits all the wild-eyed revolutionary fervor, all the sinister aspect, all the mastery of men, all the compelling powers of oratory, all the irresistible ardor and magnetism of an elderly and not very successful delicatessen keeper in the Bronx, inking his fingertips over the month-end statements.

Leon Trotsky does not admit he is through any more than he says in so many words that he will return to the Soviet Union someday to lead Russia and the workers of the world.

But the latter obviously is what he means when he says,

Stalin's biggest mistake was in exiling me. He thought if he sent me out of the country, he could ruin me by reviling and libeling me in the press, in all the agencies of propaganda which he controls.

But outside of Russia I have gathered a new group around myself. I still do harm. My writings, my books, what I say, they penetrate into Russia. I do harm.

Harm. He says it like a small boy insisting, "I'm tough. I carry matches."

It was mid-afternoon when word came to the Athletics training camp that Trotsky would see the Philadelphia newspapermen. Probably he had not been told these newspapermen worked only in the children's department, the sports staff.

Probably, too, it was the first time in his life any group of interviewers met him on a completely equal footing of understanding; they knew precisely as much about communism as he did about baseball.

The suburb in which the exiled war minister of Lenin is holed up became the first permanent white settlement on the continent when Hernando Cortez made it his headquarters for the assault upon the Aztec capital of Mexico City. Today it is the quiet, characterless sort of middle-class residential district you might notice as your train pulls out of Des Moines.

Its placidity emphasizes the incongruity of the squad of armed Mexican police lounging in the dusty, half-paved street that leads to a house owned by Señora Frieda Rivera, wife of the revolutionary artist Diego Rivera, who collects so many capitalist dollars for painting murals lampooning the capitalist system.

Behind the tall gate of heavy oak, kept closed and barred, live Rivera's guests: Trotsky and his wife; an American secretary, Bernard Wolfe, former instructor of political science at Yale and Bryn Mawr; a French-Dutch secretary; a Czech secretary. The Riveras live elsewhere.

Wolfe admitted the newspapermen. A pistol butt protruded from his waistband. An ornament, he said, as Trotsky had no fear of violence.

Wolfe ushered the visitors through a tiny patio, knobby with stone Aztec gargoyles, across the narrow brick veranda which makes a promenade along the bright azure wall of the house, and into the study.

No stage setting in this room, a rather bare rectangular chamber containing a half-dozen leather-backed chairs, a long table cluttered with papers, a few shelves of books, three crystal balls suspended from the ceiling.

Trotsky entered briskly, almost, but not quite, dapper in dark gray pin-striped suit without a vest, soft striped shirt with attached collar, dark tie. His mustache and goatee are gray, his pompadour white. He seems older than his fifty-seven years, possibly because, like the very young and very old, he talks only of himself.

"Any Hearst papers?" he inquired as introductions were made. None. He seated himself at the desk, exchanged shell-rimmed glasses for pince-nez, showed flashing white teeth in a smile.

"That is a great advantage."

Hearst papers are to him the "fascist press." How could he keep them from getting his statements? Possibly they got them through the Mexican papers.

"When the next trials start I shall not give statements to the Mexican papers," he continued. "Not through unfriendliness, but because the reactionary interests and the Soviet try to use them to make it appear I am meddling in politics here.

It was so in Norway. Although I kept aloof from politics, the Stalin government kept trying to entangle me, and succeeded, until the Norwegian elections revolved about my personality."

He spread his hands in a deprecatory gesture that said, "Innocent little me in Norwegian politics!"

His English is fairly fluent, heavily accented. Now and then he gropes for an Americanism, turns quickly to Wolfe for prompting or assurance that he has used the right word.

Mention of the next trials sent him off pell-mell into his favorite subject, the conspiracy trials in Russia, which he contends are pure fake, trumped up for propagandist purposes.

How long does he expect such trials to follow one another?

"Until world opinion has become finally convinced either of the truth or falsity of the Gaypayoo's charges and the alleged 'confessions.'

You see, each trial has left doubts. In the recent Radek trial it was mentioned that I had a meeting, a friendly conversation in Berlin, with Rudolf Hess, the Vice Führer. Many people wondered how I could be on friendly terms with Hess.

I predict the next trial, of the Germans accused of sabotage, will purport to give details of that meeting."

Does he believe Kamenev and Zinoviev and other convicted "plotters" have been shot?

"Yes. Keeping such men in prison would be too dangerous, like storing up bombs. There were, for example, two political adversaries of mine who were arrested and 'confessed' to conspiracies. When I read the confessions, it did not seem possible they could be false, for I knew the honesty of these men.

Later I heard their story. They had been promised freedom for confessing, but were not given their freedom. So they began to stir up trouble in prison. Then they were shot."

Why do men continue to "confess" if they are shot anyway?

"Common sense would tell them to refuse, to say, 'No, it is not true. I will not compromise my memory, the memory of my children so.'"

But a man is in a row of cells. Now and then one is taken out and shot. The Gaypayoo comes and says, 'You see what happened to your friend. Confess and you will live.'

"Those who confessed are dead, too,' the man says, but the Gaypayoo says, 'No. Radek, he is not dead. Others are not dead. You have a chance."

So for a hope, for a straw to grasp, this man confesses to what he did not plot. And the infernal conveyor, the endless belt of trials by which the Stalin bureaucracy justifies itself before the world, moves on."

What of Stalin, the man?

"He is the complete bureaucrat. He could exist only in a bureaucracy. He did not build the machine; he is a product of the machine. Separate him from the machine and he is nothing."

Why does the Soviet feel the need of making Trotsky the archvillain, the man behind the plots in all these trials?

A shrug. "Because I am their adversary."

Then do they still fear him so much?

This pleased him. He smiled broadly. "I, too, am astounded, but so it is."

He closed the interview on that note, his blue eyes sparkling with what seemed a juvenile exultation over being considered a very tough party.

Departing, the newspapermen surveyed the premises briefly, found the single-story house slightly cramped, inquired as to how the Great Revolutionist spends his day.

Seems he arises about 7:30 A.M., walks in the patio, eats, writes some, dictates some. Mostly, it seems, he just putters.

DAVID REMNICK David Remnick became editor of *The New Yorker* in 1998, after six years as a staff writer at that magazine. Winner of the Pulitzer Prize for general nonfiction for the book *Lenin's Tomb* (1993), Remnick spent a decade as a correspondent for the *Washington Post*, with a stint in sports, before being assigned to the Moscow bureau in 1988. Besides *Lenin's Tomb*, his other books include *The Devil Problem* (1996), *Resurrection: The Struggle for a New Russia* (1997), *King of the World: Muhammad Ali and the Rise of an American Hero* (1998), and *Reporting: Writings from The New Yorker* (2006)—which proves editorial responsibilities don't prevent a journalist from telling compelling stories. He delivered this lecture on March 25, 1998.

DAVID REMNICK

How Muhammad Ali Changed the Press

I n the later acts of his career, Muhammad Ali would take his place in the television firmament, and his Boswell would be Howard Cosell, he of the marvelous adenoids. But in the days preceding his fight with Sonny Liston in Miami in February 1964, Cassius Clay was not yet Muhammad Ali, and Howard Cosell was a bald, nasal guy on the radio who annoyed his colleagues with his portentous questions and his bulky tape recorder, which he was forever bashing into someone's giblets. Newspapers were still the dominant force in sports; columnists—*white* columnists—were the dominant voices; and Jimmy Cannon, late of the *New York Post* and, since 1959, of the *New York Journal-American*, was the king of the columnists. Cannon was the first thousand-dollar-a-week man, Hemingway's favorite, Joe DiMaggio's buddy, and Joe Louis's iconographer. Red Smith, who wrote gloriously for the *Herald Tribune*, employed an elegant restraint in his prose that put him ahead of the game with more high-minded readers; Cannon was the popular favorite, a world-weary voice of the city. Cannon was king, and Cannon had no sympathy for Cassius Clay. He did not even think he could fight.

Cannon was an honest man in a gamey world. Throughout the '30s, '40s, and '50s, boxing beat writers would line up at Madison Square Garden on Saturday mornings for a weekly envelope filled with cash—not a fortune, but just enough so that the promoter could be reasonably confident that the reporters would talk up and cover his bouts, just enough to keep them from asking the wrong questions. On some fight nights, the same beat writers might find an envelope on their assigned seats at ringside, too. The practice of organized graft was not limited to boxing, nor was it considered particularly wrong. It was just part of the business. Ball teams paid for writers to travel with them on the road; owners of racetracks and arenas sent around Christmas presents: televisions, washing machines, tea services. At big events, like a championship fight, publicists and promoters offered up a selection of prostitutes: no charge for the columnists, discounts for reporters. Columnists (Cannon included) would routinely accept free food and drink at nightspots like 21, Toots Shor's, and the Stork Club. With arenas and teams and promoters doling out such loot, was it so unreasonable to expect favorable notice? A stray promotional line in a column?

Predictably, not all the voices in the press were convinced that full-scale congressional hearings on boxing were necessary. "Outside the routine business of running the country," Red Smith wrote in December 1959, "the United States Senate has nothing to worry about except the space race, atomic warfare, spiraling living costs, the world march of communism, Fidel Castro, Bishop Pike's views on birth control, the national debt, unrest in steel, and the 1960 elections. In the circumstances, anybody can understand why Sen. Estes Kefauver, a restless spirit, deems it necessary to relieve his boredom by investigating fist fighting." Smith described Frankie Carbo, the mobster who ran the sport, as "the more or less benevolent despot of boxing's Invisible Empire."

So that was the world of boxing even as it overlapped with the rise of Cassius Clay. One afternoon shortly before the Clay–Liston fight, Cannon was sitting with George Plimpton at the Fifth Street Gym watching Clay spar. Clay glided around the ring, a feather in the slipstream, and every so often he popped a jab into his sparring partner's face. Plimpton was completely taken with Clay's movement, his ease, but Cannon could not bear to watch.

"Look at that!" Cannon said. "I mean, that's terrible. He can't get away with that. Not possibly." It was just unthinkable that Clay could beat Liston by running, carrying his hands at his hip, and defending himself simply by leaning away.

"Perhaps his speed will make up for it," Plimpton put in hopefully.

"He's the fifth Beatle," Cannon said. "Except that's not right. The Beatles have no hokum to them."

"It's a good name," Plimpton said. "The fifth Beatle."

"Not accurate," Cannon said. "He's all pretense and gas, that fellow. No honesty."

Clay offended Cannon's sense of rightness the way flying machines offended his father's generation. It threw his universe off kilter.

"In a way, Clay is a freak," he wrote before the fight. "He is a bantamweight who weighs more than two hundred pounds."

Cannon's objections went beyond the ring. His hero was Joe Louis, and for Joe Louis he composed the immortal line that he was a "credit to his race—the human race." He admired Louis's "barbaric majesty," his quiet in suffering, his silent satisfaction in victory. And when Louis finally went on too long and fought Rocky Marciano long past his peak, he eulogized the broken-down old fighter as the metaphysical poets would a slain mistress: "The heart, beating inside the body like a fierce bird, blinded and caged, seemed incapable of moving the cold blood through the arteries of Joe Louis's rebellious body. His thirty-seven years were a disease which paralyzed him."

Cannon was born in 1910 in what he called "the unfreaky part of Greenwich Village." His father was a minor, if kindly, servant of Tammany Hall. The family lived in cold-water flats in the Village, and Cannon got to know the neighborhood and its workmen, the ice men, the coal delivery boys. Cannon dropped out of school after the ninth grade and caught on as a copy boy at the *Daily News* and never left the newspaper business. As a young reporter he caught the eye of Damon Runyon when he wrote dispatches on the Lindbergh kidnapping trial for the International News Service.

"The best way to be a bum and earn a living is to write sports," Runyon told Cannon and then helped him get a job at a Hearst paper, the *New York American*. Like his heroes, Runyon and the Broadway columnist Mark Hellinger, Cannon gravitated to the world of the "delicatessen nobility," to the bookmakers and touts, the horse-players and talent agents, who hung out at Toots Shor's and Lindy's, the Stork Club and El Morocco. When Cannon went off to Europe in the mid-'40s to write battle dispatches for *Stars and Stripes*, he developed what would become his signature style: florid, sentimental prose with an underpinning of hard-bitten wisdom, an urban style that he had picked up in candy stores and nightclubs and from Runyon, Ben Hecht, and Westbrook Pegler. After having been attached to George Patton's Third Army, Cannon came home newly attached to the *Post*. His sports column, which would be the city's most popular for a quarter century, began in 1946 and was dubbed "Jimmy Cannon Says."

Cannon was an obsessive worker, a former boozer who drank more coffee than Balzac. He lived alone—first at the Edison Hotel, then on Central Park West, and, finally, on 55th Street. He was a cranky egomaniac whose ego only grew with age. He sweated every column. When he wasn't at a ball game or at his desk, he was out all night, wandering from nightclub to nightclub, listening always for tips, for stray bits of talk that could make their way into his column. "His column is his whole life," said one of his colleagues, W. C. Heinz of the *New York Sun*. "He has no family, no games he plays, no other activities. When he writes it's the concentration of his whole being. He goes through the emotional wringer. I have no idea what Jimmy would do if he weren't writing that column, he'd be so lonesome."

For his time, Cannon was considered enlightened on the subject of race. That is to say that unlike many other columnists he did not make fun of the black athletes he covered, he did not transform their speech into *Amos 'n' Andy* routines. He gave them their due. As much as he adored DiMaggio, a fighter like Archie Moore captured his *schmaltz*-clogged heart just as easily:

> Someone should write a song about Archie Moore who in the Polo Grounds knocked out Bobo Olson in three rounds. I don't mean big composers such as Harold Arlen or Duke Ellington. It should be a song that comes out of the backroom of sloughed saloons on night-drowned streets in morning-worried parts of bad towns. The guy who writes this one must be a piano player who can be dignified when he picks a quarter out of the marsh of a sawdust floor. They're dead, most of those piano players, their mouths full of dust instead of songs. But I'll bet Archie could dig one up in any town he ever made.

Cannon would begin other columns by putting the reader inside the skull and uniform of a ballplayer ("You're Eddie Stanky. You ran slower than the other guy") and elsewhere, in that voice of El Morocco at three in the morning, he would dispense wisdom on the subject he seemed to know the least about—women: "Any man is in difficulty if he falls in love with a woman he can't knock down with the first punch." Or, "You can tell when a broad starts in managing a fighter. What makes a dumb broad smart all of a sudden? They don't even let broads in a joint like Yale. But they're all wised up once a fighter starts making a few."

There are precious few writers of any sort who do not date quickly, and journalistic writing, with rare exceptions, dates as quickly as the newsprint it's written on. Even Mencken dates, and Cannon was no Mencken. Without making excuses, Cannon's wised-up one-liners and the maudlin sentiment were of a time and a place, and as Cannon aged, he gruffly resisted the new trends in sportswriting and athletic behavior. In the press box, he encountered a new generation of beat writers and columnists, men like Maury Allen and Leonard Schecter on the *Post*. He didn't much like the sound of them. Cannon called the younger men Chipmunks because they were always chattering away in the press box. He hated their impudence, their irreverence, their striving to get beyond the game and into the heads of the people they covered. Cannon had always said that his intention as a sportswriter was to bring the "world in over the bleacher wall," but he failed to see that this generation was trying to do much the same thing. He could not bear their lack of respect for the old verities. "They go up and challenge guys with rude questions," Cannon once said of the Chipmunks. "They think they're big if they walk up to an athlete and insult him with a question. They regard this as a sort of bravery."

Part of Cannon's anxiety was sheer competitiveness. There were seven newspapers in those days in New York, and there was terrific competition to stay on top, to be original, to get a scoop, an extra detail. But the Chipmunks knew they were in competition now not so much with each other as with the growing power of television. Unlike Cannon, who was almost entirely self-educated, these were young men (and they were all men) who had gone to college in the age of Freud. They became interested in the psychology of an athlete ("The Hidden Fears of Kenny Sears" was one of Milton Gross's longer pieces). In time, this, too, would no longer seem especially voguish—soon just about every *schnook* with a microphone would be asking the day's goat, "What were you *thinking* when you missed that ball?"—but for the moment, the Chipmunks were the coming wave, and Cannon's purple sentences, once so pleasurable, were beginning to feel less vibrant, a little antique.

Part of Cannon's generational anxiety was that he wrote about ballplayers in an elegiac voice. He had plenty of scorn for the scoundrels of sport—Jim Norris, Frankie Carbo, Fat Tony Salerno—but you would never learn from Cannon that DiMaggio was perhaps the most imperious personality in sport or that Joe Louis, in retirement, was going slowly mad with drugs, that to guard himself against imagined predators from the IRS and the CIA he clogged the air-conditioning vents with cotton and smeared his windows with Vaseline.

The new generation, men like Pete Hamill and Jack Newfield, Jerry Izenberg, and Gay Talese, all admired Cannon's immediacy, but Cannon begrudged them their new outlook, their middle-class upbringings, their educations, their youth. In the late '50s, Gay Talese came along and wrote countless elegant features for the *Times* and then, even more impressive, a series of profiles in the '60s for *Esquire* on Floyd Patterson, Louis, DiMaggio, Frank Sinatra, the theater director Joshua Logan. None of the pieces were what writers would call "trash jobs"—they were filled with affection for the person and admiration for the craft—but they also delved into Patterson's fears, Louis's terrible decline, DiMaggio's loneliness, Sinatra's nastiness, and Logan's mental breakdowns. Talese combined the techniques of reporting and fiction; he filled his notebooks with facts, interviews, and observations but structured his pieces like short stories.

When Talese left the paper in 1965 to write books and longer magazine articles, he had one inheritor in place, a reporter in his mid-twenties named Robert Lipsyte. Like Cannon, Lipsyte grew up in New York, but he was a middle-class Jew from the Rego Park neighborhood in Queens. He went from his junior year at Forest Hills High School straight to Columbia University, from which he graduated in 1957. Lipsyte wrote about high school basketball players like Connie Hawkins and Roger Brown. He helped cover the 1962 Mets with Louis Effrat, a *Times* man who had lost the Dodgers beat when they moved out of Brooklyn. Effrat's admiration for his younger colleague was, to say the least, grudging: "Kid, they say in New York you can really write but you don't know what the fuck you're writing about."

If there was one subject that Lipsyte made it a point to learn about, it was race. In 1963, he met Dick Gregory, one of the funniest comics in the country and a constant presence in the civil rights movement. The two men became close friends and eventually Lipsyte helped Gregory write *Nigger*, his autobiography. Even as a sports reporter, Lipsyte contrived ways to write about race. He wrote about the Blackstone Rangers gang, he got to know Malcolm X and Elijah Muhammad. He covered rallies at which black protesters expressed their outrage against a country that would celebrate blacks only when they carried a football or boxed in a 20-foot ring.

In the winter of 1963–1964, the *Times'* regular boxing writer, Joe Nichols, declared that the Liston–Clay fight was a dog and that he was going off to spend the season covering racing at Hialeah. The assignment went to Lipsyte.

Unlike Jimmy Cannon, Red Smith, and the other village elders, Lipsyte found himself entranced with Clay. Here was this funny, beautiful, skilled young man who could fill your notebook in fifteen minutes.

"Clay was unique, but it wasn't as if he were some sort of creature from outer space for me," Lipsyte said. "For Jimmy Cannon, he was, pardon the expression, an uppity nigger and he could never handle that. The blacks he liked were the blacks of the thirties and the forties, they knew their place. Joe Louis called Jimmy Cannon 'Mr. Cannon' for a long time. He was a humble kid. Now here comes Cassius Clay popping off and abrasive and loud and it was a jolt for a lot of sportswriters, like Cannon. That was a transition period. What Ali did was make guys stand up and decide which side of the fence they were on.

"Clay upset the natural order of things at two levels," Lipsyte said. "The idea that he was a loud braggart brought disrespect to this noble sport. Or so the Cannon people said. Never mind that Rocky Marciano was a slob who would show up at events in a T-shirt so that the locals would buy him good clothes. They said that Clay 'lacked dignity.' Clay combined Little Richard and Gorgeous George. He was not the sort of sweet dumb pet that writers were accustomed to. Clay also did not need the sportswriters as a prism to find his way. He transcended the sports press. Jimmy Cannon and Red Smith were appalled. They didn't see the fun in it. And, above all, it was fun."

As the fight approached, Lipsyte heard that the Beatles would be dropping by the Fifth Street Gym. The visit had been arranged, of course, by the eternally hip P.R. man Harold Conrad, who was publicizing the fight for Bill Macdonald. The Beatles were in Miami to do the *Ed Sullivan Show*. Lipsyte was twenty-six, a card-carrying member of the rock 'n' roll generation, and he saw that for all its phoniness, a meeting between the Beatles and Clay was a meeting of the new, two acts that would mark the '60s. The older columnists passed, but he saw a story: the future of music and the future of sports in one room.

The younger writers, like Lipsyte, saw Clay as the "fifth Beatle," parallel players in the great social and generational shift in American society. For some of the older columnists, the scene was representative of all that was going wrong in the world. "Clay is part of the Beatle movement," Jimmy Cannon would write famously a few years later. "He fits in with the famous singers no one can hear and the punks riding motorcycles with iron crosses pinned to their leather jackets and Batman and the boys with their long dirty hair and the girls with the unwashed look and the college kids dancing naked at secret proms held in apartments and the revolt of students who get a check from Dad every first of the month and the painters who copy the labels off soup cans and the surf bums who refuse to work and the whole pampered stylemaking cult of the bored young."

After Clay beat Liston, the greatest upset in boxing history, and became heavyweight champion, he gave a morning-after press conference at the Veterans Room of Convention Hall. He answered all the traditional questions about how he felt, about which fighter he might take on next, about whether Liston was tougher than expected, less tough than expected, or *precisely* as tough as expected. The session was, by Clay's standards, remarkably subdued. There was no verse, no monologues, no taunts. "All I want now is to be a nice, clean gentleman," he said. "I've proved my point. Now I'm going to set an example for all the nice boys and girls. I'm through talking."

Loud, ironic applause greeted that declaration, and even Clay had to smile. But the thing about Clay was that he never really lied to the press; he believed what he was saying at the moment he was saying it. And at this moment he saw his career as a limited venture.

"I only fight to make a living, and when I have enough money I won't fight anymore," he went on.

Finally, a reporter interrupted. Wasn't it true, he wanted to know, that Clay was a "card-carrying member of the Black Muslims"?

Clay recoiled not so much from the idea of breaking news—he had assumed by now that everyone knew he was a convert to the Nation of Islam—but rather from the terminology. "Card-carrying" had the ring of McCarthyism, and "Black Muslim" was a term repugnant to members of the Nation.

"'Card-carrying.' What does that mean?" Clay said. "I believe in Allah and in peace. I don't try to move into white neighborhoods. I don't want to marry a white woman. I was baptized when I was twelve, but I didn't know what I was doing. I'm not a Christian anymore. I know where I'm going and I know the truth, and I don't have to be what you want me to be. I'm free to be what I want."

That was enough to confirm all the hints that had been dropped in the press: Clay was a member of the Nation of Islam. But whether the press understood it or not, he had also forsaken the image of the unthreatening black fighter established by Joe Louis and then imitated by Jersey Joe Walcott and Floyd Patterson and dozens of others. Clay was declaring that he would not fit any stereotypes not of his own making, he would not follow any set standard of behavior. And while Liston had also declared his independence from convention (through sheer don't-give-a-damn truculence), Clay's message was political. He, and not Jimmy Cannon or the NAACP, would define his blackness, his religion, his history. He was a vocal member of an American fringe group, and America would soon be learning about it.

The sporting press, which barely knew a thing about the Nation of Islam, required more details, and so the next morning some reporters descended on Clay and Malcolm X as they were eating breakfast at the Hampton House Motel. If any of the reporters thought Clay would back off from his previous day's statements, they were mistaken.

"A rooster crows only when it sees the light," Clay said. "Put him in the dark and he'll never crow. I have seen the light, and I'm crowing. I'm the heavyweight champion, but right now there are some neighborhoods I can't move into. I know how to dodge booby traps and dogs. I dodge them by staying in my own neighborhood. I'm no troublemaker. I don't believe in forced integration. I know where I belong. I'm not going to force myself into anybody's house. . . . People brand us a hate group. They say we want to take over the country. They say we're communists. That is not true. Followers of Allah are the sweetest people in the world. They don't carry knives. They don't tote weapons. They pray five times a day. The women wear dresses that come all the way to the floor, and they don't commit adultery. All they want to do is live in peace."

Just about the only people to react to the news of Clay's conversion with a shrug were the men in his corner. "What's in a name?" Angelo Dundee said by way of Shakespeare. "To me he's still the same individual, same guy. Actually, I didn't know what Muslim was, really, because I thought it was a piece of cloth."

But outside of that small circle of handlers, Clay's conversion was a shock. The leading columnists reacted with outrage.

"The fight racket, since its rotten beginnings, has been the red-light district of sports. But this is the first time it has been turned into an instrument of hate," Jimmy Cannon wrote. "It has maimed the bodies of numerous men and ruined their minds but now, as one of Elijah Muhammad's missionaries, Clay is using it as a weapon of wickedness in an attack on the spirit. I pity Clay and abhor what he represents. In the years of hunger during the Depression, the Communists used famous people the way the Black Muslims are exploiting Clay. This is a sect that deforms the beautiful purpose of religion." Cannon's point of racial orientation would always be Joe Louis. Clay's association with the Nation of Islam, Cannon declared, "was a more pernicious hate symbol than Schmeling and Nazism."

Bob Lipsyte's coverage in the *Times* was of a different order, partly because the paper's news columns did not allow for much opinion, but also because he was of a different generation and possessed of a far different set of experiences, not least his close friendship with Dick Gregory. "It's true that I wasn't freaked out about the conversion the way Cannon or Smith were," he said, "but you have to remember how scary Malcolm X was to some people, and not just white people. The *New York Times*, for one, never really knew how many people he could put on the street for a revolution."

Malcolm appreciated the depth and restraint of Lipsyte's coverage and told him so. Back at the newsroom on West 43rd Street, Lipsyte recounted the compliment to one of his editors.

"Well, that's great," the editor said. "Maybe we should put huge ads on the side of all our trucks saying, 'Malcolm X Likes Bob Lipsyte!'"

A couple of years later, after Ali had beaten Liston a second time and then beat Floyd Patterson in a sadistic exhibition of resentment, Bob Lipsyte came down to Miami to do some feature stories on Ali. "I remember waking up that morning in my hotel and watching a session of the Senate Foreign Relations Committee on TV, of the first really sharp debates on Vietnam," Lipsyte recalled. "William Fulbright was chairman and Maxwell Taylor and Senator Wayne Morse were really going at it. Taylor had that jock certainty that generals had. Now this was early 1966. The mood in the country was still antipeacenik, pro-war. The tide had not yet turned. But with this debate you could feel the pulse of something happening."

In the early afternoon, Lipsyte drove over to Ali's house, a low-slung house in a black neighborhood. The two men sat outside in plastic lawn chairs. School had just let out, and Ali watched the high school girls go by, commenting on each one in a harmless, pass-the-afternoon sort of way. Several of Ali's Muslim friends were around, and one came out and told Ali he was wanted on the phone. It was one of the wire services. The reporter told Ali that in the midst of escalating its troop levels in Vietnam, the Army had changed its mind: His score on the military qualifying exam was now good enough. Ali had been reclassified once more. He was 1-A. He could soon expect a call from his draft board. Did he have any comment?

"Ali came back out and his mood had changed completely. He was fuming," Lipsyte said. "Until that moment, I was thinking how wonderful this was, how you could step into this sanctuary, this time-warp, where nothing has anything to do with the war.

"Ali knew even less about the war than I did, it wasn't on his radar screen at all," Lipsyte went on. "As he kept going back inside for more phone calls and the TV trucks started appearing, the Muslim chorus was chortling. They had all been in the Army. They came to the Muslims after hard times, after jail, after the Army, and they started telling Ali, 'Of course, the Man is gonna do whatever the fuck he wants to do with you.' They started telling him how the cracker sergeant would drop a hand grenade in his pants."

The calls were nonstop. This was a big story, evoking memories of other young athletes and pop stars drafted at the peak of their careers: Joe Louis, Ted Williams, Elvis Presley. But this was different, this was Vietnam. Ali was getting accustomed to being asked about racial politics, but now he was hearing new questions: What do you think of L.B.J.? What's your view of the draft? What do you think about the war? What about the Vietcong?

"And all of a sudden he hit the note," Lipsyte remembered.

"Man," Ali said, "I ain't got no quarrel with them Vietcong."

The line came and went so quickly that Lipsyte missed it. "No question that I blew that story." But enough papers and television stations did pick up the quote. Eventually, so did the *New York Times*. As he had been before and as he would be again and again, Ali was acting as a mirror to American society. He may not have been able to locate Vietnam on a map, he knew very little about the war, but he was thrust into the midst of the national agony and reacted with a moment of intuition and speed. *I ain't got no quarrel with them Vietcong.* "It was the moment for Ali," Lipsyte said. "For the rest of his life he would be loved and hated for what seemed like a declarative statement, but what was, at the time, a moment of blurted madness."

From then on, Ali took a political stand, insisting that his religion did not permit him to participate in war. Since that afternoon in Miami, he learned more about the war and deepened his understanding of what was happening both to the country and to himself. But he didn't waver. The members of the Louisville Sponsoring Group knew they were on their way out as Ali's business management team, but, all the same, they quickly helped line up cushy ways for Ali to get credit for Army service: the reserves, National Guard duty. If worse came to worst, they figured, the Army would have Ali put on boxing exhibitions for the troops. This way, they figured, Ali, like Louis before him, could enhance his public image without risking his life and untold millions of dollars.

Ali was instantly denounced by Jimmy Cannon, Red Smith, Arthur Daley, all the columnists whose notions of how a heavyweight champion must behave were formed in the Louis years. "Cassius makes himself as sorry a spectacle as those unwashed punks who picket and demonstrate against the war," Red Smith wrote. Various senators and congressmen declared Ali a traitor and a pariah. Even his hometown legislature, the Kentucky State Senate, felt compelled to issue a proclamation saying he brought "discredit to all loyal Kentuckians and to the names of the thousands who gave their lives for this country during his lifetime."

As time passed and the government put pressure on him, Ali made his stance clearer. He would not fight exhibitions. He would not move abroad. "Why should they ask me to put on a uniform and go 10,000 miles from home and drop bombs and bullets on brown people in Vietnam while so-called Negro people in Louisville are treated like dogs?" he said to a reporter for *Sports Illustrated*. "If I thought going to war would bring freedom and equality to 22 million of my people, they wouldn't have to draft me. I'd join tomorrow. But I either have to obey the laws of the land or the laws of Allah. I have nothing to lose by standing up and following my beliefs. We've been in jail for 400 years."

With time, the columnists changed with Ali, not least Red Smith. By 1968, like so many other people in the country, Smith had turned around on the war, his views on race evolved. Cannon, too, came to see the world in a slightly different way. A young man, Muhammad Ali, was, in large part, responsible for their new view of the American scene.

Questions and Answers

QUESTION: *Every now and then I go to the Johnson Library in Austin, Texas. What was the relationship between Muhammad Ali and Lyndon Johnson?*

DAVID REMNICK: L.B.J. wasn't very happy with Muhammad Ali. Remember who went to Vietnam in large proportions: black men, young black men from the cities. To see a role model, a huge public figure like the heavyweight champion of the world, aligned with Malcolm X for a while and then certainly with the Nation of Islam, was troubling to many at the time. It was very discomforting, not only for the president of the United States but also for a large proportion of whites and also for a lot of middle-class blacks. So L.B.J. was the least of it, but it was bad propaganda for a war that was heating up. Remember, the war was accelerating. It was at a low burn in the early '60s, but by 1965–1967 it was beginning to peak.

QUESTION: *Why did you decide to write a book about Ali?*

DAVID REMNICK: Why this subject? Well, it's a funny thing. My greatest fault as a journalist—and I hope sometimes a virtue—is this notion about writing about different things. The fastest way to make a name in journalism is to have one subject and beat the brains out of it. You turn on the TV and there is Robert Novak, and it's like he is playing Hamlet or some role on TV. You know what you are getting. He is going to be wearing a black suit and he is going to be conservative. He'll be talking about Washington politics.

I spent a lot of time in Russia. I've written about different sorts of things. Ali interested me because, first of all, he scared the hell out of most people thirty years ago. It is very hard to explain even to people my age—I'm in my late thirties—much less college students how scary he was. If you were liberal, you were for integration. You were for all of us living together. Now this is sadly a kind of dying dream.

Well, along comes this guy who says, "I don't want to get beaten up and have dogs tearing at me in Birmingham. You don't want us, I don't want you." That was the politics of Malcolm X, crudely stated as I'm saying here. That interested me enormously—the way the intersection of high politics and pop culture, which is so much a part of the American story, was going on. It's about how a boxer both reflected what was going on in

America, especially racially, and also influenced it in some way. Ali is now like Paul Bunyon—we all love him—he lights the torch at the Olympics. Strom Thurmond probably sheds a tear, but thirty odd years ago he scared the hell out of a lot of people.

QUESTION: *A recent documentary,* When We Were Kings, *with Ali and George Foreman in Zaire, was really a fantastic film showing live footage at the time there. In it Ali seems to view himself as a prophet for all African Americans in the country and around the world. Could you comment on this?*

DAVID REMNICK: Some of this is hype and some of it he took seriously. Remember one quality about Muhammad Ali: He is extremely funny. And the funniest scene in *When We Were Kings* is when he goes into the cockpit of the plane as they are flying into Zaire and he starts riffing about the black pilot and talking about how all the white passengers must be terrified 'cause they had never seen a black pilot before. He's playing the dozens, as they say on the streets. Riffing. He's very, very funny. What saved Ali from alienating the nation is that he finally always undercut himself with humor, and in the rare instance when people didn't get the joke it backfired.

Joe Frazier never got the joke. Joe Frazier always resented it. I don't blame him in some ways. Joe Frazier was a poor kid from South Carolina and in much tougher circumstances even than Ali, who grew up in Louisville in sort of semi-middle-class circumstances. Ali was trying to make Joe Frazier out to be an Uncle Tom, and he was kidding, and he was doing it for promotional purposes, but Frazier never got the joke. He hated it and resented it. Most fighters figured, "I'm fighting Muhammad Ali. This is the best thing that's ever going to happen to me." Win, lose, or draw, for all the obvious reasons they went along for the ride.

QUESTION: *What do you think of the argument that you sometimes hear that tries to account for the decline of newspapers by saying that journalism used to be a job for ordinary guys, the same people who would be cops or firemen, and therefore journalists were writing for an audience that shared their values in the 1930s, 1940s, and the 1950s? But when the 1960s came along a sort of college-educated journalistic elite started writing for each other, and this has resulted in losing their readers in some sense?*

DAVID REMNICK: In due respect, I don't agree with it. And maybe I'm not agreeing with it for all of the obvious reasons and baggage I bring to the podium. I think it is very important that we have some papers that are in fact for an elite audience. I think this word *elite* as a bad word is ridiculous. What *elite* means at the *New York Times*, the *Washington Post*, the *Wall Street Journal*, is that they have the values that even though it is not cost-effective we are going to have twenty-five foreign bureaus. It costs a lot of money to have a reporter, driver, secretary, and an office in Moscow—and to know in your heart that the readers don't give a damn about it. They just don't, very few do.

The *Washington Post* is a different kind of paper from the *New York Times* in that the *New York Times* is a paper of the top layer in terms of education, income, and so on. It is basically an elite paper, and it is not even a city paper now. Of its roughly 950,000 daily circulation, 300,000 is in New York City proper. The suburbs dominate, and then there is the national distribution. The *Washington Post* is something different. It is also an elite paper, but it has what is called a very high penetration because it's a monopoly paper. Everybody who is going to read a paper in Washington reads the *Washington Post*. There are no tabloids and no equivalents to the *New York Post* or *New York Daily News*, and so you have this high–low aspect to the *Washington Post*. You have these foreign bureaus, you have high-minded columnists, endless feature stories on Peruvian poets, and so forth, but you also have tons of comic strips in the *Washington Post* and advice columns and "Hints from Heloise" and other stuff. I think if you were to go back to this much-romanticized version of what newspapers were and you got that as your *New York Times* in the morning, you would be appalled. The *Washington Post* before Ben Bradlee came along had one foreign bureau, and that person was half-time with *Newsweek*. I don't want to go back to that. To be a foreign correspondent, it might be nice to know a language or history or something like that. I see no virtue in less education. I just see a virtue of being able to write in such a way that you're communicating with more than just yourself.

QUESTION: *You've written extensively about Russia. Are you opposed to Yeltsin in Russia?*

DAVID REMNICK: Opposed to Yeltsin in Russia? Who would have thought of a Yeltsin Russia? I think they are going to be all right. I'm sort of the little voice in the wilderness thinking that the big beast has been slain and the rest is commentary, as they say in the Talmud. They'll be okay. When the United States became the United States, we went through a lot of things that the Russians are going through now. I don't want to grossly exaggerate the similarities, but we had robber barons, we had gross inequities in income, we still do, which got only worse in the 1980s. We had all kinds of violence in this country, and still do. So I think the Russians, having unburdened themselves of empire and of the most foolish and brutal political system of the century, are way ahead of the game. I don't have any nostalgia for pre-1991 Russia. Are there lots of problems? Yes. And I hope I have written about them at some extent, as so many others have.

QUESTION: *What impact did the assassination of Malcolm X and its association with the Black Muslim faith have upon Ali and his Muslim belief?*

DAVID REMNICK: That is an interesting story. Malcolm X befriended then–Cassius Clay. Clay invited Malcolm X to come to Florida to be with him while he was preparing for his championship fight. Malcolm X was essentially chased out of town by the promoter, who said, "Get out of here. I don't want anybody to see you around because you are such a threatening figure and you're jeopardizing the fight." Malcolm X did that, and he came back on fight night to watch it. They then spent the next two weeks together at the Theresa in Harlem, a famous hotel frequented by most black celebrities at the time. They were the best of friends. But what happened at the very same time is that Malcolm X was in a battle with Elijah Muhammad. They were splitting, and Elijah Muhammad, seeing Ali becoming champion, wanted Ali on his side, although before he had no real interest in him. Now you have the heavyweight championship—this is money, this is prestige, this is the greatest recruitment poster he can imagine. So Elijah Muhammad then seduced Ali, gave him his name, and Ali, in not the most attractive fashion imaginable, basically jettisoned Malcolm X as a friend. When Malcolm X was assassinated in 1965, Ali did not exactly go overboard expressing his regret. Nowadays it's different. One of the first things Ali showed me when I went to see him—you know he lives twenty minutes from here in Berrien Springs, Michigan—he very slowly took out of his briefcase a picture of himself with Malcolm X. This is clearly something he looks back on with enormous pride and affection.

QUESTION: *Recently it was said that Ali was the greatest athlete, maybe the greatest figure, of this century. Do you agree with that?*

DAVID REMNICK: I think it's exaggerating his role to say he is the greatest figure of the century. I think he is the most electric sporting figure of the century. I can't imagine who else it would be. But, of course, that is my generation. I'm talking out of my childhood. Maybe for someone twenty-five years older than me, Joe Louis, Joe DiMaggio, or Willie Mays would be. I have no idea. That seems very reasonable. I think what you are referring to is on the cover of *GQ* magazine. Ali is called sportsman of the century.

QUESTION: *Tell us about Ali now.*

DAVID REMNICK: He is not well, to phony baloney about that would be a disservice. He has Parkinson's disease. He's at a young age to have it. The progression of that disease, as I know from personal experience of my own father, can be terrible, plus the fact that he was hit in the head over and over and over again by the best heavyweights of his time. In the first part of his career he succeeded by being fast. He never got hit, essentially. When he came back after his exile of over three years, he was still very, very good, but his legs were not what they were. It will happen to you. But he discovered he could take a punch. A very useful discovery in the short run and a very bad one over time. If you have ever seen a tape of the Joe Frazier–Ali fight in Manila, the third of their fights—Ali called it the closest thing to death, and it was just brutal, and he survived it and won the fight. Have you ever been hit in the head? Have you ever been punched in the face? Imagine being punched in the face over and over again. The glove doesn't do anything to soften the blow, it only prevents your bones and your hands from breaking. That's all a glove does, it doesn't soften the blow. There are literally thousands of pounds of pressure in a blow delivered by a heavyweight. It's quite something. But Ali took it all—and won.

I'm the Greatest

RED SMITH

NEW YORK HERALD TRIBUNE

FEBRUARY 26, 1964

MIAMI BEACH—Cassius Marcellus Clay fought his way out of the horde that swarmed and leaped and shouted in the ring, climbed like a squirrel onto the red velvet ropes, and brandished his still-gloved hand aloft.

"Eat your words." He howled to the working press rows. "Eat your words."

Nobody ever had a better right. In a mouth still dry from the excitement of the most astounding upset in many roaring years, the words don't taste good, but they taste better than they read. The words, written here and practically everywhere else until the impossible became unbelievable truth, said Sonny Liston would squash Cassius Clay like a bug when the boy braggart challenged for the heavyweight championship of the world.

The boy braggart is the new champion, and not only because Liston quit in his corner after the sixth round. This incredible kid of twenty-two, only nineteen fights away from the amateurs and altogether untested on boxing's topmost level, was winning going away when Liston gave up with what appeared to be a dislocated shoulder.

He might have been nailed if the bout had continued, but on the evidence of eighteen frenzied minutes, Cassius was entitled to crow, as he did at the top of his voice before Liston retired: "I'm the greatest. I'm gonna upset the world."

"That's right," his camp followers howled. "That's what you're doin'."

And he was.

On this score, Clay won four of the six rounds, and in one of the two he lost he was blinded. Apart from the unforeseen ending, that was perhaps the most extraordinary part of the whole wild evening.

It started between the fourth and fifth rounds. "Floating like a butterfly and stinging like a bee," as he and his stooges had predicted, Cassius had made Liston look like a bull moose plodding through a swamp.

Dancing, running, jabbing, ducking, stopping now and then to pepper the champion's head with potshots in swift combinations, he had won the first, third, and fourth rounds and opened an angry cut under Liston's left eye.

Handlers were swabbing his face in the corner when suddenly he broke into an excited jabber, pushed the sponge away, and pawed at his eyes. As the bell rang he sprang up waving a glove aloft as though forgetting that a man can't call a time-out in a prize fight. In the corner, frantic seconds sniffed the sponge suspiciously.

Cassius couldn't fight at all in the fifth, but he could and did show a quality he had never before been asked for. He showed he could take the sternest hooks and heaviest rights Liston could throw—or at least this Liston, whose corner said later that the shoulder had slipped in the first round.

Just pawing feebly at the oncoming champion, Clay rocked under smacking hooks, ducked, rolled, grabbed, and caught one brutal right in the throat. He rode it out, though, and at the end of the round he had ceased to blink.

"You eyes okay, champ?" they were screaming from his corner as the round drew to a close. "Everything okay?"

He didn't confirm that until the bell rang for the sixth. Then, getting up from his stool, he looked across the ring, nodded with assurance, and went out to enjoy one of his best rounds, pumping both hands to the head, circling, dancing.

"Get mad, baby," his corner pleaded. "He's retreatin', champ."

It was at the end of this heat that he came back crowing about upsetting the world. Yet he couldn't have known how quickly his words would be confirmed.

Just before the bell for the seventh, Cassius sprang up and waved both hands overhead in a showoff salute to the crowd. He took a step or so forward, as the gong clanged, then leaped high in a war dance of unconfined glee. He had seen what scarcely anybody else in Convention Hall had noticed.

Liston wasn't getting up. Willie Reddish, Sonny's trainer, had his hands spread palms up in a gesture of helplessness. Jack Nilon, the manager, swung his arm in a horizontal sweep, palm down. The fight was over, the championship gone.

Dr. Robert C. Bennett of Detroit, who has treated Liston in the past, hastened into the ring and taped Liston's shoulder. The former champion told him he had felt the shoulder go midway in the first round, and the left hand had grown progressively numb from then on.

They'll fight again to answer the prodding question of what might have been, and it will be a big one. Although return bout clauses are frowned upon these days, Bob and Jimmy Nilon,

Jack's brothers, have an independent contract with Clay entitling them to name the time, place, and opponent for his first defense.

As Bob Nilon explained this, Clay rode the ropes. "Eat your words," he bawled.

TED KOPPEL A forty-two-year veteran of ABC News, Ted Koppel served as anchor and managing editor of *ABC News Nightline* from 1980 to 2005. One of the most honored programs in the history of broadcast journalism, *Nightline* established new standards in television news by examining subjects in depth, principally through Koppel's intrepid reporting and interviewing. A member of the Broadcasting Hall of Fame, he's won forty Emmy Awards, ten duPont–Columbia Awards, ten Overseas Press Club Awards, and eight Peabody Awards. In 2006, Koppel joined the Discovery Channel to produce documentaries on global affairs, and the same year he became a senior news analyst for National Public Radio. He's the author of *Nightline: History in the Making and the Making of Television* (1996) and *Off Camera: Private Thoughts Made Public* (2000). He delivered this lecture on September 16, 1999.

TED KOPPEL

Journalism:
It's as Easy as ABC

I t's funny how lives brush up against one another in the most random and unexpected ways. Thirty years ago, I was Southeast Asian bureau chief for ABC News, based in Hong Kong. My wife, Grace Anne, was pregnant with our third child, and I had just rushed back from Malaysia, where I'd been covering race riots in Kuala Lumpur. I was in the waiting room at Canossa Hospital in Hong Kong, smoking one cigarette after another, and worrying a lot because there was some trouble with the delivery. There was another man, about my age, in the waiting room. His wife was having some problems with the delivery of their baby, too. Far more serious problems, as it turned out, than ours. Their baby was stillborn. The son who was born to us that day is now a staff attorney for the Legal Aid Society in New York. That other man in the waiting room was Terence Smith, then Saigon bureau chief for the *New York Times* and now media correspondent and senior producer for *The NewsHour with Jim Lehrer* on PBS. The little baby that died that morning would've been Red Smith's grandchild.

Beyond reading his wonderful columns, that's as close as I ever came to the legendary Red Smith. Until this evening.

It's a source of great pride to me that you've invited me to deliver the Red Smith Lecture in Journalism. But, I must confess, I also had an ulterior motive for accepting. My father-in-law, Eugene Patrick Dorney (as Irish and as Catholic as those names suggest), has, with reasonably good humor, put up with me for the thirty-six years that his daughter and I have been married. He has rarely, if ever, given vent to the disappointment he must occasionally feel at having a son-in-law who is not a Catholic and who was born in England. It has been a little more than flesh and blood can bear that his daughter and I met at—and still root for—Stanford when it plays Notre Dame.

Gene Dorney, who is rolling with style and grace toward his eighty-fifth birthday next May, is as ardent a Notre Dame subway alumnus as any you have ever spawned. You have just made his day. And if those puny little fellows on your football team can brush Michigan State out of the way on Saturday afternoon, you will have made his year.

It will probably also improve the humor of my good friend Tom Bettag, who is now executive producer of *Nightline* and tries not to leave me out alone in public too often. Tom reached the peak of his journalistic aspirations as sports editor of *Scholastic* some thirty-odd years ago, when he was an undergraduate here. His son, Andy, who's with us too, also takes a casual interest in Notre Dame football.

But let's spend a few minutes now talking about the nature of journalism in this country. It's a moving target, a changing phenomenon; something that is already a far cry from what Red Smith knew; and is evolving, quickly, into something that will soon be very different from what I've known throughout the better part of my career.

Some basics first. I don't know how many of you have ever paused to think about this, but journalism is one of the very few professions that requires no training whatsoever. Clearly you cannot become a doctor or a lawyer without training. You need training to become a carpenter or a plumber. But to be a journalist in America requires nothing more than your assertion that you are one. You don't need a license. You don't have to belong to a union. No permit is necessary. It is a privilege implicitly granted to every American by the First Amendment to the Constitution. Every one of you in this hall here this evening has as much right to call himself a journalist as I do. Until fairly recently, though, that privilege was largely theoretical.

Sure, you've always been able to write anything you wanted, and for most of this century at least, you could've cranked out a few hundred copies of your screed on a mimeograph machine and then passed them out on a street corner. But if you wanted to reach a somewhat wider audience, you still needed to work for the man (and it almost always was)—the man who owned the printing press.

When I joined ABC News in 1963, there were three networks, and of all the people who watched television on any given day, at any given time, over 90 percent of them were watching ABC, NBC, and CBS. If you wanted to work as a television correspondent and reach a national audience, you had to go to work for someone who owned a network.

So it's all well and good, in theory, to talk about every American's right to be a journalist; but for most of the past 223 years, that's all it's been: a theoretical right. That is in the process of undergoing a revolutionary change.

The average U.S. household now receives fifty-seven television channels. That actually sounds more impressive than it is. A lot of those channels are simply reprocessing the programs that used to be on ABC, NBC, and CBS twenty or thirty years ago. But there's Fox, there's CNN, there's MSNBC, ESPN, HBO, Showtime, Nickelodeon—all kinds of options that simply did not exist thirty years ago. And they are merely the tip of the iceberg.

The fact is that communicating with a national audience, indeed with a global audience, is now technically within the reach of anyone who can log on to the Internet. And the poster boy of that new reality—indeed, a seminal figure in the new journalism—is Matt Drudge. Matt Drudge embodies the realization of that historic promise that truly anyone in America can be a journalist.

It's not, as I've already suggested, that we lacked the freedom in years past. Most of the time, most American citizens could write or say whatever they wanted. The problem—setting aside, for the moment, political or civil rights considerations—the problem was one of distribution. What difference did it make if I had the freedom to say whatever I wished, if no one was willing to publish or broadcast it? It was journalism's analogue to that old philosophical chestnut about the falling tree in the forest.

Without the capacity to distribute, you could say whatever you wanted, but no one was going to hear it. Now, anyone with access to a computer and a Web site can literally reach anyone in the world who has the capacity to log on. And that's about as technical as this discussion is going to get. Except to add that what any intellectual or idiot can now do in print, either person will soon also be able to commit in living color and on video.

We can already transmit color video over the Internet, and soon that capacity will be routine and nearly universal, which is both a blessing and a curse. But since we're going to have to live with both, I'd like to spend the next few minutes talking to you about consequences: Moral, practical, ethical consequences.

To understand the world we're about to enter, you have to know something about the one we're leaving behind. Cambodia, 1970. I want to call my wife in Hong Kong, to find out how she and the new baby are doing. You can't call from the hotel, so I hire a cyclo driver to take me down to the PTT, the Post, Telephone, and Telegraph. I hand in a written form ordering the phone call; and then I wait for two and a half hours. When the call goes through, I'm directed to a numbered booth, and when I pick up the phone and say "Hello," I can hear my wife, through a cloud of cotton wool, crackling with static: "Honey, I'm just giving the baby a bath. Call me back in ten minutes." There is, of course, in those days no way on Earth to call back in ten minutes.

Kosovo, 1999. We are driving, God only knows where, in our armored Land Rover, some miles outside Pristina, and we want to let the office in Washington know what direction we're thinking of taking on a script that hasn't even begun to take shape. This is not an urgent call. This is not a call that must be made. But each of us is equipped with a cell phone that can reach Washington or London in a matter of seconds. We can call our office, we can call our wives, we can call our brokers, we can call to see what's playing at the multiplex on Saturday night. We are linked by an infinite web of strands to a jungle of mostly unessential options.

A beach on the South China Sea, 1970. We've just completed an amphibious assault with the Marines a few miles below the demilitarized zone that separates North and South Vietnam, and by the end of that day, I have some sort of a story to tell, about a colonel who insists on water discipline and how, by mid-afternoon, 40 percent of his battalion have been knocked out of action by heat exhaustion because each man was limited to three canteens of water. Anyway, I have this story and it's pretty good, and now I'm trying to hitch a ride back to Da Nang aboard a medevac helicopter. By the time I make it to Da Nang, there are no more flights south that day; but I find a colleague who's flying out first thing in the morning, and he'll pigeon the film back to Tan Son Nhut airbase in Saigon for me. Now I spend the next hour trying to reach our office there so that I can tell the bureau chief to have someone meet the flight and transship my film to Tokyo, where it can be transshipped to Los Angeles, where it can be transshipped to New York. There, it'll be cleared through customs by a film expediter, who'll give it to a motorcycle courier, who'll bring it into the lab where the film will be developed. From there it'll be brought into an editing room to be cut and married to the narration that I recorded under a tree, about a mile from the beach where we landed with the Marines about three days earlier. And then it'll be screened by one or more producers, who'll decide whether they want to use it and when.

The nature of time has changed over these last thirty years; and with it a wide range of expectations. These days, we would have the capacity to set up a portable ground station on the beach along the South China Sea, and that story of mine that took three days to ship back to the United States could be satellited back to New York in minutes and on the air as soon as an engineer rewinds the tape.

But frequently, these days, we do things merely because we can. The ability to broadcast live creates an imperative that simply did not exist thirty years ago. It produces a rush to be first with the obvious; a tendency to focus on events because they just happened rather than because of their actual importance. When we knew that a story had to survive for two or three days before it got on the air, we tried to give a broader context to what we wrote. It was pure self-preservation, of course; but our stories had to have a somewhat larger meaning than a simple recitation of the latest events. In fact, we learned to leave out the most time-sensitive references because they would date a story, which used to be the surest way to get a story killed.

All too often these days, news is defined as whatever has happened in the last half hour. And the live coverage that is the mainstay of our twenty-four-hour news networks seems to require a constant updating of whatever that day's main story may be, no matter how trivial the latest developments may be. You might think that the accumulation of updates would eventually provide some sort of depth, but it rarely, if ever, does. Unless, of course, the main story involves the death of a princess or a Kennedy, the inappropriate-and-absolutely-inexcusable-but-definitely-not-sexual activities of a president, or the progress, along a California freeway, of a white Bronco carrying a Heisman Trophy winner who, it turns out, did not murder his wife. On those kinds of stories, we not only provide depth—there is no end to the depths that we will provide.

What's happened in television news over the last thirty years is completely counterintuitive. Back then, the news divisions had relatively little money (because news wasn't supposed to be profitable), and satellites were few, and renting time on them was very expensive. Still, the network news divisions had bureaus all over the world, and foreign news was one of the main ingredients of a network newscast. Now, satellites are ubiquitous and relatively cheap, each network news division has an annual budget in excess of half a billion dollars, and we've closed most of our foreign news bureaus for budgetary reasons. What I'm saying here is applicable to so many different aspects of our lives.

Thirty years ago no one would have bothered trying to reach me on a phone in my car because car phones barely existed. That may mean that I missed three or four important messages over the course of a year. It also means that I neither received nor made the hundreds of irrelevant phone calls that were never placed because the technology was not yet in place. Now, all too often we do it not because we must but simply because we can.

I understand and even appreciate the miracle of e-mail. I have a friend, a doctor, who has given up his practice in orthopedic medicine so that he can satisfy a lifelong dream to sail around the world. No matter where in the world he is, we can reach one another as easily by e-mail as if he were still in his Richmond, Virginia, office. But I am also reached daily, sometimes hourly, by people who feel that simply because they have communicated some banality to me by e-mail (that is to say, instantaneously) I am under some sort of obligation to reply immediately. I can, therefore I must.

I'm limiting myself this evening to a discussion of communication, and for the most part I'll be talking about mass communication, but you know what I mean. It applies to almost every aspect of our lives. Hundreds of time-saving devices that should, in theory, have produced a contemplative culture in which we relish the luxury of all those freshly acquired hours. We should be refining the quality of our existence, gravitating toward philosophy and poetry. Instead, "How do I love thee?" I don't have time to count the ways. My beeper's going off. I have electronic mail to answer. My cell phone keeps fading in and out. Direct TV gives me too many options and not enough choices, and television news is becoming a real pain in the butt.

Yes, if a tornado is heading for our community, I am immensely grateful for a television station's capacity to get the very latest information on the air, instantly. But most news stories don't fall into that category. I would prefer, more often than not, that reporters and producers have adequate time to gather their facts, weigh their importance, check their accuracy, align them clearly and elegantly against the video that's been shot.

Journalism is so much more than simply training a live camera on an event. Satelliting back to the United States live video of Iraqi anti-aircraft tracers firing into the night sky over Baghdad is a triumph of technology, but it is almost bereft of anything to do with journalism. It is, essentially, a sound and light show, without context. The reporter, attached to his ground station, is required to babble on endlessly, sandwiching guesses between assumptions and seasoning it all with speculation. He could be off gathering information from resident diplomats or even driving through the streets of Baghdad, collecting whatever little nuggets of information can be observed. Instead he is answering desperate and silly questions from Atlanta, or Washington, or New York, from anchor people whose primary responsibility is to keep the machine running.

Our scientists and engineers have performed brilliantly. They have delivered to us capabilities undreamed of throughout the span of human existence. Where we have failed is in the creation of material worthy of our new media, in the intelligent application of disciplines and standards that acknowledge old verities, even as they adapt to the new realities of an interactive world. A couple of generations ago, T. S. Eliot warned us against the confusion of information, knowledge, and wisdom. "Where is the wisdom we have lost in knowledge?" he asked. "Where is the knowledge we have lost in information?" We are, these days, drowning in information, very little of which is translated into knowledge, almost none of which evolves into wisdom.

What Tom Bettag and I have in common with Red Smith is that we all grew up in a world of gatekeepers, a relatively small community of writers and editors who sifted through the universe of available information and then chose for its audiences of readers and listeners and viewers what was important or relevant, amusing or entertaining. Not all of these gatekeepers applied the best or highest standards, but many did. And among those who did there was a sense of obligation. They had access to information that was, quite simply, beyond the reach of most other people in the world. Competition still gave the process its momentum; the need to boost circulation or attract an audience provided a constant reminder that they were operating in a marketplace of ideas. It was always a money-making operation, but there was an editorial process. It was expected that information would pass through several sets of hands, each of which applied commonly accepted standards. Journalism has always been a rough-and-tumble world, but there were certain rules of sourcing and cross-checking, standards of editing, language, and grammar that always distinguished establishment from tabloid journalism. And somewhere, in all of this, there was an acknowledgment of the need for context.

So what does that say about the expanding world of journalists now operating on cable or satellite TV and soon to be operating on HDTV or broadband or on the Internet? The glory of those new technologies is precisely that they make the acquisition and the dissemination of information a truly democratic process. As I said at the outset, everyone has always had the right; now nearly everyone also has the reach and the opportunity.

I couldn't possibly reconcile a lifetime spent demanding access to information and the right to disseminate it with now arguing that we should place restrictions on the rights of others to do the same. And anyway, the Internet, in particular, was designed to be immune to precisely that or any other sort of interference. Whether or not Matt Drudge uses two sources or one (or none, for that matter) is—and should remain—beyond my power to influence.

What I do believe is that the community of professional journalists has a greater obligation than ever before to lead by example. Information on all the media is now so voluminous that it tends toward the chaotic. We can still serve a critical function in bringing order to information.

The new technologies are all geared toward speed. Speed has always been an important part of journalism; but not to the exclusion of other standards. Traditional journalism requires a sorting out of good information from bad, of the important from the trivial. That sort of commitment and expertise may be out of fashion, but the need for it is greater than ever before.

There are at least two kinds of extreme ignorance. For centuries we have been familiar with the first kind, an ignorance that covered most of the world like a dark cloud, an ignorance that exists in a vacuum, where no information is available. The second kind is a more recent phenomenon, one which presents itself in the form of a paradox. This second form of ignorance exists in a world of electronic anarchy, where so much information abounds that the mind doesn't know what to believe. Information does not always lead to knowledge, and knowledge is rarely enough to produce wisdom.

Which pretty much describes the challenge confronting our world as we move into the third millennium. In such a world there is a greater need for the processors of words than for word processors. There is a need for editors. There is more of a need for good journalists than ever before.

And on the off chance that some of you may choose to make your careers in journalism, I'd like to leave you with a few random thoughts to help you on your way. The technologies of delivering information have changed, but the fundamentals of honest reporting haven't. There's nothing new about deadlines; even quarterly journals have them. Although we now live in a world in which immediacy is valued so highly, never publish or broadcast a story before you're comfortable with its accuracy. Remember that some things seem important and other things are important. It's easy to write about the first batch. Try to reserve some of your energy for the second lot, too. Establish a set of guiding principles for yourselves—reasonable ones, this is not the priesthood—but stick to them. Emphasize honesty, fairness, decency. Don't be afraid of questioning authority. Skepticism is all right, but try not to lapse into cynicism. Provide a voice to the powerless. Never lose your curiosity. You have this incredible license to talk to anyone, to go anywhere. Make it interesting. Journalism is not a solitary exercise. It requires an audience. The central purpose of journalism is the communication of ideas. The gathering of facts, the shaping and editing of a story, all these only amount to half the process. You need readers and viewers to complete the process, and remember, if you bore people they won't hear what you have to say.

Try not to be afraid. There are many places in the world where writing the truth can cost you your freedom or even your life. It is very difficult to be a good journalist in such places. For most of us, though, what do we have to fear? A loss in circulation or ratings? A drop in advertising revenue? Losing our jobs?

Well, don't ever be afraid of losing your job. You'll find another one. And even if you don't, you can take comfort in the fact that times have changed. These days, you can actually go out and start your own newspaper—or your own network.

Oh, and one more thing. Go, Irish!

Questions and Answers

QUESTION: *In recent years, there has been a blending of news and enter-tainment, and some programs (such as* Politically Incorrect*) blur the line between the two. What is your reaction to this kind of thing?*

TED KOPPEL: I actually have no problem at all with a program like *Politically Incorrect,* because I think it falls into an old and sometimes honorable, sometimes dishonorable category which is in a sense no different from Dorothy Parker back in the 1920s. It's a bunch of smart-ass people sitting around making comments about events that are going on. That's not news; it is entertainment.

As I suggested in my prepared remarks, I don't have a problem with news being entertaining, at least in the sense that part of the process is that we have to grab your attention, and it is more difficult than ever before for us to do that with so many different voices competing for your attention. I'm less worried about entertainment programs like *Politically Incorrect* delving into the area of news than I am about news programs delving into the area of entertainment.

I don't mean reporting on entertainment. I mean trying to be so en-tertaining that they ignore the really important events and just focus on things that they think will seize your attention and grab you and hold you to the television set. News you can use, that kind of thing. News about your health, not because it is not perfectly legitimate to report on health issues, but because these are the kinds of health issues that have less to do with what's really important than with just grabbing your attention. Again, I think news is less serious these days than it needs to be. But you can be serious and entertaining at the same time.

QUESTION: *While press freedoms in the U.S. are probably greater than they are anywhere else in the world, I travel a lot to London and Toronto, and it's my impression that the news coverage in these cities tends to be of a higher quality. I would much rather read* The Economist *than* Time *or* Newsweek *and wonder what it is about our marketplace that has cre-ated this sort of lesser brand of news. Do you accept this notion?*

TED KOPPEL: I caution you to be careful about judging the industry as a whole, the media as a whole, by what is best or worst in any community.

The freedom that you acknowledge—but then sort of shunt aside—is ultimately the important part of that package. If we don't take advantage of that freedom by putting out good material, that's our problem.

But if you are not finding good material in American journalism, you're not looking hard enough. It's there. I don't necessarily accept that *Time* and *Newsweek* are the equivalent of *The Economist*, but I think there are some very fine journals out there which may have smaller distribution lists than *Time* and *Newsweek* do, which are every bit the equal of *The Economist*.

Part of our problem in this country is that the babble of voices is so great that you tend to confuse the best and the worst and the mediocre. They all come out at the end of the sausage-making machine, as though we are all part of exactly the same process. We are part of the same process, but what comes out of the other end is not the same.

What you will never find in a country where the freedoms are less is what the U.S. is capable of producing in journalism. The finest British journalism at the best of times did a lousy job of covering "the troubles," as they were known in Northern Ireland. Why? Because reporters weren't allowed to. Any time you get a high-security issue that the government or the Home Office doesn't want covered in Great Britain, they slap a "D" notice on it, and that means that it cannot be published. At those times, no matter how good *The Economist* is, it's doing a lousy job of covering that particular story.

QUESTION: *How do you feel about being politically correct and the importance of being politically correct, which keeps you from reporting certain stories certain ways? A journalist may be on the air and cannot make a reference to a particular racial group because it can offend that racial group, or certain stories cannot be covered because they might be deemed offensive.*

TED KOPPEL: I don't accept the premise. We can cover anything. We can say anything, even that offensive word that you were thinking about in your head, if we say it in the right context. If you say it just for the sake of saying "Wow, look at us, we can say this word on the air," that's a terrible thing to do. But if you say it because a public figure has used that word and it is important that everybody know what that word is, I don't have any problem with saying it on the air and frequently have.

If you want to get into it—and, forgive me, but I think this is a group of adults; we don't have any children here—when Tom Bettag and I were in Kosovo a few months ago, I sat there interviewing a couple of Serbs, and one of them was insisting that not only were Kosovar Albanians well treated by the Serbs who were then controlling Kosovo, but that, in fact, if a Serb as much as slapped an Albanian, he would go to prison for six years. And I said what was on my mind at the time, "Bullshit."

Because we did this on videotape Tom and I could easily have edited it out. But we decided not to because that summarized for both of us exactly what we felt. I think it is a question of where and when. We're on at 11:30 at night. In that context was it okay? Yes, I got a few letters of complaints, even some e-mails of complaint. I didn't feel bad about it afterwards.

What was going through my head, quite frankly, was if I had been sitting in Berlin in 1941 and some German had been telling me that all of these outrageous stories we are hearing about what's happening to the Jews is just so much nonsense, and that, in fact, if a German were to even slap a Jew he would go to prison for six years, what would I have said? I'm not sure that I would have limited myself to that word. It's a question of how you do it. It's a question of when you do it. Again, it's a question of context.

QUESTION: *What kind of impact do your emotions have on your interviews?*

TED KOPPEL: I try not to let that happen. One of the great strengths of *Nightline* is that it is a partnership. At the top of the program's hierarchical structure is Tom Bettag, then me, and the two of us have a very close relationship. I count on him very heavily to tell me when he thinks I am stepping over the line. I know he would.

It's not as difficult as you may think. The day is twenty-four hours long, and I'm free to express and vent my emotions for twenty-three and a half hours of the day. I'm supposed to try and be a professional for a half hour a day.

It's always struck me as kind of strange that these sorts of questions are rarely directed toward surgeons or lawyers. "Tell me, as you are making that first incision, does your personal dislike for the patient ever enter your mind?" Or, as your brilliant summation that you have prepared is about to emerge from your lips, do you think, "I really hate that SOB." We're professionals. Occasionally we all slip, and when we do, it's good to have colleagues working with us who make sure it doesn't happen too often.

QUESTION: *As a Jewish American, do you sometimes have difficulties dealing with the Middle East, and how do you feel about the fact that the Secretary of State, the Secretary of Defense, the spokesperson for the Secretary of State, the National Security Advisor, and the new ambassador to the United Nations are all Jewish?*

TED KOPPEL: You are right in four out of five. William Cohen, despite his last name, is not Jewish. But the point is well taken. I will answer your question by answering it in terms of how I deal with the issue. You're right. There are going to be many times when my own religion and the sympathy that I may feel, for example, for the state of Israel have the potential of interfering with my objectivity. I have curiously enough had to deal with that most often from Jewish groups complaining to me that they felt I was not sympathetic enough to the Israeli point of view.

My answer to them, and it will be my answer to you, is I have always believed and have always insisted that any American professional who does his or her job properly not only has the right but the capacity to do so without allowing his or her personal religion or race to get in the way. When a Jewish organization calls me or writes to me and says, "Why aren't you more sympathetic?" my answer is, "You are playing right into the hands of the anti-Semites who would say it is not possible for a Jew to be objective in the role of reporter, Secretary of State, spokesman, or National Security Advisor."

I rather suspect that if any one of these people were to show uncommon or inappropriate partiality to Israel, there would be many people, not simply Arab Americans but many other Americans, who would rush to point that out. I'm not aware of Sandy Berger having shown any particular partiality, or James Rubin at the State Department, or Madeleine Albright. If anything, Madeleine Albright has to deal with the same kind of thing I'm talking about, where people feel she is bending over backwards to be too partial to the Arab position. I think you've got to give people a chance to do their jobs cleanly and professionally, and if you catch us doing it any other way, nail us to the wall. I think that is perfectly fair. And would be fair of any other group.

QUESTION: *Do you have any ideas to offer in terms of the American voting public getting enough information to make intelligent choices in the election process?*

TED KOPPEL: Two things. In a sense it comes back to one of the earlier questions. No one in America can argue that information is not available. You may be too lazy or not technically confident enough to find it, but it's there. There is no country in the world that has more information available than the United States.

I don't know if any of you are sailors; I'm sort of a novice sailor and fascinated by the analogy between sailing and journalism. In sailing if you want to find a point (and these days we find it with the help of satellites), you can do it with two points, but preferably three. If you have three points and they intersect, they will tell you precisely where you are.

In a curious way the same thing is true in journalism. If I have three sources who are not connected directly to one another and they give me quantities of information and there are certain points on which all three agree, that's about the best way in a very quick process that I can hope to find the truth.

That's what reporters are supposed to have been doing and are still supposed to be doing to this day. These days you, as consumers, are going to have to start doing the same thing. Using the outlets, using what you see on network TV, or what you see on CNN, or what you hear on National Public Radio, or what you read in *The Economist*, or what you read in the *New York Times* or another newspaper. It doesn't make any difference where you get it.

When you find that there are points of convergence about information, chances are pretty good that the information is accurate. It's not a question of the information not being out there. It's out there.

What you have to be very careful about in this day and age, of course, is that we all start using the same information, and you see it popping up in the *New York Times* and the *Washington Post* and ABC and *The Economist*, and we all got it from Matt Drudge. I mean, that's the danger. But you can do it if you work this thing properly. You can do it.

QUESTION: *In your reference earlier to reporting on the death of Princess Diana and the death of John F. Kennedy, Jr., what are your thoughts on the conflict between the rights of the press to report something and the rights of privacy?*

TED KOPPEL: It's sort of a sliding scale. Forgive me if I should know you, I don't. I'm assuming you are a private person and that you are not a public figure. You have a greater right to privacy than I do. I have a greater right to privacy than a politician who is running for public office.

In other words, if other reporters want to come after me because of something I have done, that's perfectly legitimate. I would feel that they have less right to be interested in what my family does. I don't even have a whole lot of sympathy for reporters who believe that they have a great deal of right to pursue the families of politicians. In some rare instances they do. When politicians make their families part of the process of becoming elected, when they use the family to gain sympathy with the voters, let's say, then I think at that point reporters begin to have a greater right to delve into whether this ideal family life that we see presented to us is, in fact, quite as ideal as it seems.

Public figures have less privacy than private figures do. People who run for public office or people who hold public trust have less of a right to privacy than people who do not.

QUESTION: *As someone who is a well-established journalist who works for a huge media organization, a huge network, to what degree are you influenced by the views of the company for which you work?*

TED KOPPEL: I honestly don't think there's influence. Tom Bettag and I, again, are in this wonderful position in that we are both old enough and have been in this business long enough that we are not going to allow anyone to destroy what we have spent a professional lifetime building up. The advice I gave to all of you—of not being afraid to lose your job—holds true. I'm ready to walk out at a moment's notice rather than do what the company tells me I ought to be doing. I don't feel that is a real issue. I don't feel that's a problem.

QUESTION: *What are your views on journalist celebrities and, more to the point, celebrity journalists, like Sam Donaldson, making a pile of money giving lectures? ABC used to permit that.*

TED KOPPEL: In point of fact, they still do under certain circumstances. I used to make a pile of money giving lectures. In fact, I arrived at a point a long time ago—about twelve, thirteen, fourteen years ago—when I was offered so much money to do one lecture—it's going to drive you nuts, isn't it, trying to figure how much it was. It was a pile of money. It was so much money that I went home and talked to my wife and said there is no way that anyone who hears that I made that much money for essentially a couple hours' work will ever believe there's not influence—even though in my heart I knew that this was not going to influence me one way or another in regard to the group that offered that amount.

And so, at that point, I just stopped and said I am not going to do lectures for money anymore, and I haven't, and I don't. But having said that I ask you to focus more on what my feelings were. You cited Sam Donaldson in particular. I assure you that Sam is as honest as the day is long. He really is. He's an old and dear friend, and I'm clearly giving you my own bias on him.

I don't know of an instance of influence, and there are a few hundred of you here this evening, and if any one of you does, hit me with it. I don't know of an instance of where a journalist, one of my ABC colleagues, has given a lecture for a pile of money for a group that then benefited beyond that evening's performance or information. I'll pause for a second while you think about that. Honestly, I don't.

I can understand that people say, wow, $10,000, $15,000, $20,000, $30,000 for a few hours of work. It is the closest thing to legitimized stealing I have ever heard of, but it is rarely, if ever, given by groups that don't get their money's worth. If you go to a dinner where some group charges the people who come to the dinner $250 a person and they can get five hundred people there and they pay the journalist who draws that kind of crowd $25,000 or $30,000, I don't have any problem with that.

I thought it was a little inappropriate when, without mentioning particular presidents, ex-presidents started doing that for a million dollars a crack or a couple million dollars a crack. But again, I can't imagine they were giving anything away. I assure you the speeches weren't worth that.

QUESTION: *Would you talk about how it came about that networks have closed so many of their foreign news bureaus?*

TED KOPPEL: As I said before, it's a tremendous irony. It's a real paradox. It came about because news divisions became money-making operations. It's probably fair to say that the really huge money-making operation for a network was *60 Minutes* at CBS.

Suddenly there was this realization that you could make money from events, in other words, things that happen naturally. You don't have to hire a Hollywood screenwriter to write this hour. You don't have to hire a director or a producer to put it together. It just happens, and all you have to do is cover it. And if you cover the right kinds of stories, you can actually put together an hour of television for a lot less money than it costs to produce an hour of entertainment. You can sell it for pretty much the same money you sell the hourly entertainment. Now that's a great deal.

For a few years there was a sort of coexistence between these magazine programs that were making a pile of money and the fact that we certainly also have a moral responsibility to keep the hard news-gathering part of the news division going—you know, the *CBS Evening News*, the *NBC Nightly News*, and *World News Tonight* at ABC.

The dangerous issue that you weren't asking about is that large corporations take over networks, which in turn have their own news organizations. These large corporations tend to look at their television news organizations as being just another cost center, another profit center. They say, "Wait a second. Refrigerators brought in $200 million last year, and the news cost center only brought in $75 million. But the news cost center costs more to operate than the refrigerator cost center does. You accountants go back and take a look at that and see why that is."

Then they come back and say, "Well, we've been looking at this, and we've got this bureau in Moscow and we have fourteen people in Moscow, and it is costing us $1.63 million a year to keep them there. We have been looking, and in point of fact, *World News Tonight* used only seventeen spots out of Moscow last year, *Nightline* used five, *20/20* did one, and that is pretty much it. We looked at this and amortized it and it works out to $76,000 a spot. That's really not worth it." Then, someone up the line says, "Boy, you're right about that. Let's cut five jobs in Moscow." And they do.

It's a quick way of saving money. The problem is that the news division has just eviscerated or come close to eviscerating one of its most important bureaus in the world. That's dangerous. Here we are, looking for more and more information, worrying more and more about the interrelationships and interdependence of the world, and here we are, having less international information than we had thirty years ago.

QUESTION: *After all you have observed and experienced in the political realm, are you not tempted to say, "I can do this better," and run for office yourself?*

TED KOPPEL: No.

QUESTION: *How about the "I can do this better" part?*

TED KOPPEL: No. I really don't. I do not belong to the bash-the-politicians club. I know a lot of people in office, particularly senators in Washington, who I think are just fantastic human beings and trying like hell to do a really great job. I have a lot of admiration for many of these people, and the process is awful.

Christine Todd Whitman, the governor of New Jersey, decided not to run for the U.S. Senate because she figured she would have to raise some incredible amount of money every day. I think it was $50,000 or $70,000 a day. Fund-raising is a sort of hands-on job. You can try to send other people out to do it for you, but if you are wealthy and you have the capacity to give a lot of money to a campaign, you probably want the putative senator to call herself.

What an ugly part of the job that is. At the same time to be able to be chief executive of the state, that's pretty tough going. Or at the same time to be a senator. There are so many good people—like Jack Danforth, for example, who is now running the Waco investigation—who quit the Senate because they just couldn't handle that garbage anymore. There are good people. I think the process needs tweaking and fine-tuning, but that is for another night.

QUESTION: *What helped you develop your style as you began? Did you watch your competition, or were there journals that you read?*

TED KOPPEL: I guess, to a certain extent, all of those things. I remember when I was nineteen taking a trip to Moscow and standing in front of the Kremlin—this was at a time when I hadn't decided yet (the older among you will know instantly what I am talking about, and the younger may not) whether I would be Ted Koppel or Edward J. Koppel.

There was a very, very famous journalist by the name of Edward R. Murrow, who sort of set the standard for all of us and to a larger extent still does set the standard for all of us. I did a piece out of Moscow. I was freelancing and trying to sell something to NBC radio. I remember standing there in front of the Kremlin saying, "This is Edward J. Koppel in Moscow." Murrow was *sui generis*.

Style comes after a while for good or ill. Whatever it is, it can be terribly annoying, or it can be good, or it can be whatever. Style is something that is a reflection of who and what you have become over the years. It's kind of like your face. They say after forty you have the face you deserve, which is pretty depressing for some of us.

QUESTION: *Do you think we can ever elect a president in three months, which is sort of in line with a British election campaign in picking a prime minister?*

TED KOPPEL: Of course we could. Are we likely to? I don't know. I honestly don't. I think one of these days enough people are going to say this process is really bad. It's not broken, but it's limping along, and we need to do some fairly dramatic things to fix it. Shortening the campaign time would certainly be one of those reforms—because if you shorten the time, you will also reduce the costs. But it's going to take more than that.

QUESTION: *During the Vietnam War the press reported a lot of material that was controlled by the government. Do you feel the same kind of thing happened during Desert Storm, and are there many instances when the government controls the output of information from the media?*

TED KOPPEL: Actually, we were freer to report in Vietnam than journalists have ever been before or since. I say that as someone who spent a year in Vietnam in 1967 and then was in and out of Vietnam for the better part of three more years in 1969, 1970, and 1971.

Part of the effort to control the information that the American media got in Desert Storm was the consequence of the young lieutenants, captains, and majors who were in Vietnam and who were now colonels, generals, and admirals having such a visceral resentment to the freedom of the media during the Vietnam War—that they really tried to control it a great deal.

There is no question that governments have always tried to control information. If you went back to World War II, you would know the dispatches during the Second World War were censored. If you were a reporter, a war correspondent, a combat correspondent during the Second World War, for one thing you wore the uniform, you wore a U.S. Army uniform, you had a patch that said "combat correspondent" or whatever it said. Then before you could file your story, it had to go through a military censor. Censorship was far more complete during the Second World War than it was in Desert Storm, but no doubt the government and the Pentagon in particular tried to control what we got and how we got it.

They have learned that one of the biggest failings of most journalists is that we are naturally lazy. Many of us. If you throw food in our direction, we probably won't go out hunting and foraging for our own.

QUESTION: *Do you feel the U.S. government tries to control a lot of the coverage, particularly coverage in the Middle East, that tends to be more favorable toward the Israelis and therefore very negative toward countries like Iraq despite the fact that there is a great deal of international opposition to U.S. policies in Iraq?*

TED KOPPEL: Let me say that I used to get that kind of question a great deal fifteen or twenty years ago. Fifteen or twenty years ago, I think it was probably fair to say that U.S. policy toward Israel was very much biased in favor of Israel and anti-Arab for reasons of great power diplomacy. The Arab states tended to be aligned with the Soviet Union, and therefore Israel was seen as a very valuable ally in the Middle East, not just valuable in terms of its location, but also valuable in terms of its military prowess.

All the billions of dollars that were given to the Israelis and the billions of dollars in military sales that were made to the Israelis were seen as a very cheap way of stopping Soviet expansion. You say it still is happening today, and you are quite right. We still give more money to Israel than we give, I believe, to any other foreign country, although I think we give almost as much to the Egyptians as we give to the Israelis.

The point that I am making, though, is that your question and the thrust of it, of a natural bias, would have been a more accurate question twenty years ago than it is today. I think you are really going to see an evolution or a devolution over the next few years in which assistance to Israel probably declines, probably because the great power confrontation with the Soviet Union no longer exists.

QUESTION: *Do you think that the power exerted in terms of giving more time to one political candidate than another candidate strengthens or weakens our democracy?*

TED KOPPEL: What did they used to call that kind of question in Logic 101? The question has a certain loaded quality to it. It asks me to accept the supposition that you make and then respond to it. I half accept the proposition that you make.

We tend to go after interesting candidates, and we do a miserable job of representing the positions of substantive but boring candidates. That means, for example, that a Pat Buchanan will always get a load of coverage, sometimes good, sometimes bad, because he is interesting. He's a hot personality, whereas someone like Steve Forbes tends to get a lot less coverage and has to use his money, which obviously is considerable, to buy himself exposure. If you will accept the framing or the reframing of your question in that context, do I think that is good or bad for American democracy? It's probably more bad than good.

After Fifty Years

RED SMITH
NEW YORK HERALD TRIBUNE
APRIL 1, 1956

On March 31, 1931, a farmer near the village of Bazaar, Kansas, looked up from his plowing when he heard the motor of a transport plane faltering. Then he broke into a run. Within hours, headlines shouted the news across the land: "KNUTE ROCKNE KILLED IN CRASH."

For a few days the papers were full of it—obituaries, tributes, feature stories, some painfully sentimental, like the one about the Atlanta newsboy shouting the news to passing crowds while tears rolled down his face. Then other and timelier matters took precedence, and you might have expected that Rockne would have been forgotten, as were the names of the seven who died with him.

After twenty-five years, that hasn't begun to happen. The name of Rockne is recognized as readily today as in 1930, when his last Notre Dame football team was barreling over Southern Methodist, and Navy, Pittsburgh and Pennsylvania, Army, and Southern California to the national championship. His photograph would be known instantly, with the small, sharp blue eyes and the bent and flattened nose.

The nose, incidentally, had been remodeled by a baseball bat, and twelve-year-old Knute exhibited it triumphantly at home to parents, who had forbidden him to play football. "You think football is rough," he told them, "look what I got in baseball."

This broke down parental objections to football, and when Rock was an end and captain of the Notre Dame team, his mother went the whole way and attended a game against South Dakota. Rock had a spectacular day, and his mother was impressed.

"Who," she asked, "was that boy who turned the cartwheel? He was wonderful." Her son never again was able to feel any special warmth for cheerleaders.

Knute Rockne was a great football coach, but there have been many. He was a great man who happened to choose football as a career. It is likely that he would have had exceptional success in almost any other field, for he had exceptional qualities: an agile and original and keenly analytical mind, a quick wit, one of those incredibly retentive memories, and a tremendous gift for influencing people. He could address an assembly of middle-aged, pot-bellied automobile salesmen—this is eyewitness testimony—and, pretending this was a football dressing room, lift them shouting out of their chairs with an old-style fight talk. He would soar to a screaming crescendo and break it off there without warning, looking on mischievously while abashed listeners discovered that they were on their feet.

Tom Conley, captain of Rock's last team, and Herb Jones, the business manager of athletics who was Rock's secretary, spoke at a breakfast following a memorial mass at Notre Dame. If they said that in his forty-three years Rock did as much as any man to influence American youth, personally and through the men he sent out across the country as coaches and through the legends still told about him, then they did not exaggerate. After fifty years, his influence has not ended.

JIM LEHRER Jim Lehrer spent his first decade in journalism as a reporter, columnist, and editor at the *Dallas Morning News* and at the *Dallas Times-Herald*. In 1970, he switched to broadcast news on public television in Dallas, later moving to Washington for PBS. He joined Robert MacNeil for coverage of the Watergate hearings on PBS and then became Washington correspondent of the *Robert MacNeil Report* in 1975. The next year *The MacNeil/Lehrer Report* began, evolving into *The MacNeil/Lehrer NewsHour* in 1983, *The NewsHour with Jim Lehrer* in 1995, and the *PBS NewsHour* in December 2009. Recipient of the National Humanities Medal and a member of the Television Hall of Fame, he's also won two Emmy Awards. Besides his journalistic work, Lehrer is a prolific writer, including more than twenty novels and plays as well as two memoirs, *We Were Dreamers* (1975) and *A Bus of My Own* (1992). He delivered this lecture on March 19, 2002.

JIM LEHRER

Returning
to Our Roots

I am delighted to be here at what could be called a celebration of all
things having to do with Smith.

There is not only Red Smith. There is also Terence Smith, son of
Red Smith, like his father, also a graduate of Notre Dame. Like his father,
Terry has spent a distinguished career in journalism, laboring for obscure
organizations such as the *New York Times* and CBS before landing on his
feet at the terrific place where he works now.

It is my and my colleagues' way of honoring Red Smith. We believe the
least we can do for the memory of Red Smith is to give honest, meaningful
work to his wayward son. And we are happy to do so.

But, seriously, to be a part of an event with Red Smith's name on it is
truly an honor for me, as it would be for anyone who has or does practice
journalism, or who has or does try to arrange words in such a way as to
make sense, to report the news, to tell a story.

Walter Wellesley (Red) Smith was the best there was at all of that—
from his first job as a reporter on the *Milwaukee Sentinel*, and then with
the *St. Louis Star-Times*, *Philadelphia Record*, and then the *New York
Herald Tribune*, and, finally, the *New York Times*. He was a writer about
sports who was known for his literary craftsmanship, for having shaped the
way daily journalists cover and write about everything, not just sports.

As the *Encyclopaedia Britannica* says, "Red Smith's natural and precise use of the English language was so superior he was made a consultant
on usage to a variety of dictionaries and encyclopedias."

That is hard to imagine in the present world of journalism. There are, in
fact, a lot of things that are hard to imagine in the present world of journalism, and I, for one, think it is most appropriate that Terry Smith, Red's son,
makes his living now covering the world of journalism, the media world,
the way information is transmitted today. Nobody does it better than
Terry—and nobody ever will.

I have a rather strong hunch that Red Smith wouldn't be very happy about some of the present-day practices in American journalism. I share some of this unhappiness.

In fact, I have in recent years made a small point of knocking some of the trends and practices in my line of work called journalism. Going from speech to speech, street corner to street corner, door to door, sometimes, it seems, spreading words of alarm, explaining why (I believe) journalists have fallen in the public esteem opinion polls down there with the Congress, the lawyers, and now even with the accountants. No offense to any member of those groups present here tonight.

I wish that I could change the tune a bit today for you and report that journalism has been born again, and suddenly all is well. There are some hopeful signs, but journalism continues at times to embarrass me, to annoy me, and to anger me occasionally.

The causes of my concern are out there for all to see, and I'm sure you know what I'm talking about. There's a tendency of journalism at times to be something more akin to professional wrestling—something to watch rather than to believe.

The savagery of some of the so-called new journalism, marked by predatory stakeouts, coarse invasions of privacy, talk show shouting, no-source reporting, and other popular techniques. The stunning new blurring of the old lines between straight news, analysis, and opinion.

A most unjustified arrogance that seems to have afflicted some of my colleagues. It can be seen in the stench of contempt in their approach, words, sneers, and body language that say loud and clear, "Only the journalists of America are pure enough to judge all others."

A new and growing confusion about the need to be entertaining rather than informing—a tendency to see news as an entertainment commodity rather than as information.

And on and on the list goes.

I have recently added some new things to my list.

One of them is something going on now that you nonjournalists of the world should know about—and that is the most unusual and growing influence of the cable news networks: CNN, of course, but also MSNBC and the Fox News Channel.

It has nothing to do with the sizes of their audiences, which are small when compared to the commercial television networks and even to us.

When we're on the air our audience is larger than MSNBC, CNN, and Fox News Channel combined.

But it's the kind and type of people who are watching and listening. People like me are watching them—people in their offices engaged in the practice of journalism in newsrooms, of all sizes, of newspapers, magazines, television and radio stations, and networks, in all kinds of cities, towns, and markets.

Walk into any of them and you'll immediately notice that there are television sets most everywhere, and they are turned on, constantly, permanently, to one or more of the cable news channels. The significance of that, I have concluded, is enormous—not necessarily bad or evil, simply enormous.

Because the sounds and news judgments flowing constantly from those television sets have replaced those earlier clackety-clacks and news judgments that came from the old ticker machines of the wire services, the Associated Press and the United Press and the International News Service machines. Later to become the AP, UPI, and Reuters machines, they had an enormous effect on coverage of news throughout the world. The way a story was played by the wires led to similar play in newspapers, television newscasts, and so on.

Now, it's the cable news coverage that is having that same influence. My concern is not yet a red flag, but it is a yellow one of caution. Here's why:

The cable news operations have airtime to fill, excitement to generate, that may not always be tied directly to the true value and weight of a particular story. Two obvious examples from fairly recent news history are the O. J. Simpson matter and the intricate details of the Monica Lewinsky story. I believe the gavel-to-gavel, wall-to-wall coverage of those two stories on cable drove the mainstream coverage as well.

An unconscious process of osmosis was at work. Gosh, CNN or MSNBC or Fox ran that as "breaking news" with bells and whistles all day or ran the trial all day. That means it's important, and we here on the *Sumter Daily Item* or the *Wichita Eagle*, or the *Washington Post*, or the *Los Angeles Times*, or the *CBS Evening News*, or *The NewsHour* on PBS should see it that way, too. And because it's television, there's a companion assumption—that the whole world is watching along with all of us in our newsroom.

That's not so. Most people are at school, at work, or at play and are not glued to their favorite cable television news outlet all day any more than the average nonjournalist American was glued to the sounds and stories of the old wire machines.

I am not advocating shutting down the cable news operations or removing all television sets from newsrooms. I'm merely commenting on a development in our business that could lead to profound consequences for all of us who either dispense or consume the news. And, as I see it, that covers all of us here tonight and most everyone else somewhere else this evening.

It matters because at a time of consolidation and amalgamation in the news and information business, I believe it is more important than ever that each of us in journalism make our own independent judgments about what is news and how it should be reported and displayed. It is that difference in judgments that make up a fully blossomed and functioning free press.

If I had been talking to you six months ago, before September 11, I would have left it here on a rather sour, down note about my line of work, journalism.

But September 11 did come, and it brought tragedy to the lives of thousands of Americans, fears to millions, and God knows what else to us and to the rest of the world before it's over. But amidst the horror and the awfulness, there have been some heartening things happen. And one of them is what it has done to American journalism.

I believe that, for the most part, the story and its many pieces and tentacles have been responsibly covered by the mainstream news organizations, electronic as well as print. But, more importantly, it has brought home a message loud and clear (I hope) to some of my sister and fellow practitioners—that there is, and has been, a serious world out there that deserves to be covered seriously.

Now, as all of us have learned about Afghanistan and the Taliban and Pakistan and Uzbekistan and countless other places and people, and as we discuss and debate the power of the United States and how it should be exercised, and the threats to our peace and to our way of life, I am finding more and more journalists saying, "Thank God." It's taken a tragedy of enormous proportions, but maybe, just maybe, we are returning to our roots, and those roots are in the business of information—not entertainment.

If you want to be entertained, go to the circus. If you want to be informed, read my newspaper or magazine, watch or listen to my television or radio broadcast.

We'll see how long it lasts, but I am hopeful. And I also must say the coverage, even more recently, of the Enron story and its many parts also shows an additional glimmer of hope.

Although coming to it late, I think, again, most of the press that I have observed have gone at the story with a seriousness the story deserves. It has also, I think, jarred a few in business journalism into realizing that cheerleading for particular stocks and companies isn't going to be tolerated anymore. It ain't journalism. Covering business means covering its annual reports and various deals and accounting practices as well. Here, again, we will see how long my hope lasts and how justified it is.

Then, along comes the David Letterman and Ted Koppel story. I think it would be a mistake to overstate what all of that means for the practice of journalism in America. Forget David Letterman and Ted Koppel and their specific situations.

What matters, I believe, is what—if anything—it says about the future of serious journalism, as practiced, at least, on television in large organizations with needs that are not exclusively journalistic.

The fact is, the possible moving of one late-night thirty-minute television program does not mean the possible or sure end of television news as we know it. There are now more ways to receive news than ever before, from the two C-SPAN channels and the cable news channels and the growing number of news Web sites.

There are more outlets for news and information now than there have ever been. The issue may be only one of transition.

Maybe we are moving to a time when the major commercial broadcast networks, CBS and NBC as well as ABC, get out of the news business altogether.

They might go about the business of entertaining and leave the informing to others.

That may be a huge tragedy, if and when it happens, or it could be only another of those important milestones called change and tomorrow.

And, as they say in journalism, only time will tell.

For the record—and speaking of change—a few years ago, I was asked by the sponsors of an Aspen Institute seminar on journalism if I had personal guidelines I used in my own practice of journalism and, if so, would I mind sharing them.

Here is part of what I sent them:

- Do nothing I cannot defend.

- Cover, write, and present every story with the care I would want if the story were about me.

- Assume there is at least one other side or version to every story.

- Assume the viewer is as smart and caring and good a person as I am.

- Assume the same about all people on whom I report.

- Assume personal lives are a private matter until a legitimate turn in the story absolutely mandates otherwise.

- Carefully separate opinion and analysis from straight news stories, and clearly label everything.

- Do not use anonymous sources or blind quotes except on rare and monumental occasions; no one should ever be allowed to attack another anonymously.

- And, finally, I am not in the entertainment business.

Those guidelines for me—and for all of us at *The NewsHour*—will never change.

Thank you.

And now your questions. Ask me anything, but with two guidelines: I'm not a pundit, and I don't take criticism well.

Questions and Answers

QUESTION: *If the Federal Communications Commission allows multiple ownership of news outlets in the same market, and even more so, large numbers of TV stations and radio stations, do you see that as a danger?*

JIM LEHRER: I don't really know enough about the subject to give you an informed answer. I can tell you that there are some people who believe it's awful, and that the more you consolidate, the fewer people you have making news judgments, and that the fewer people you have collecting news is a bad thing.

There are some who would argue that you will get more news better covered because you will have journalism organizations that will have the resources that will really cover a story in depth. And yes, they may be able to do it on radio and on television and in print at the same time. You can look at it in both ways. But I don't have an informed opinion, to tell you the truth.

QUESTION: *With all the decisions, all the news every day, how do we go about deciding what's news?*

JIM LEHRER: I have learned in all these years that a journalism organization truly is known internally and maybe eventually externally by what it throws away more than it is by what it does. As Terry said and I just gave you my guidelines, we don't have to remake ourselves every day on *The NewsHour*. We have a major commitment, for instance, to foreign news. About one quarter of what we do is foreign affairs. We have some built-in interests. We don't do the weather, and unless the thunderstorm comes in the studio, we don't cover weather. We very seldom do sports stories. We don't do personality stories. We're old-fashioned in this very fundamental respect.

What we believe the average person wants and expects from journalism is to go to the places you can't go to because you're too busy, because you have other things to do. You can't go to the courthouse every day. You can't go to city hall every day. You can't go to the White House, you can't go to Congress, you can't go to the FCC. You can't do all these things. So we go on your behalf, report back, and then you decide whether it's good, bad, or indifferent. That's how we see our job. If we load our decision making a certain way, it's toward the most inaccessible, the least covered of the inaccessible.

We have one hour of airtime every night. We don't have a page 33-B like a newspaper. A newspaper can throw it inside. We don't have any inside. It's all front page. So we have to balance all these things.

We're set up on the beat system, like Terry's thing is the media. Terry is held responsible for, produces ideas, reports, and then produces the end product in his area. We have people in the economics and business area and in politics and all of that.

It's kind of an ongoing discussion about what's the main story of the day. How important is it? How much time should we devote to it? What kinds of resources can we bring to it?

We have all kinds of silly rules. I invented a rule many years ago called the Carter–Brezhnev rule. Remember, Jimmy Carter used to be president, and a guy named Leonid Brezhnev used to run the Soviet Union? One morning there was a development in nuclear arms control, and I said, "Well, let's see if we can get President Carter. Let's get Carter in the Oval Office and Brezhnev in the Kremlin and interconnect them and work it out." Then I said, "In case we can't do that, we ought to have a backup."

But the Carter–Brezhnev rule is you always go for the number one cast, and then you go down from there. But there's no scientific answer to your question. We've made mistakes. We make mistakes all the time. It's a daily news program. There are times when I think, "Oh my God, what are we doing this for? Why are we devoting so much time to this particular story?" Then there are times when I realize, "Oh my God, we should have done this instead of that." It is a business that is fraught with the potential to be wrong, and we seize it. But on those magic nights I think, "Oh my God, we've got it absolutely right tonight." And those days happen.

QUESTION: *Do you see a resurgence in foreign news reporting as a good thing after September 11?*

JIM LEHRER: Well, I heard some interesting information earlier this evening about a project trying to get local newspapers to cover more foreign news. It ain't working. To me it's an outrage, and it's an outrage on so many levels. It's also good business. You cannot tell the American people the world is getting smaller and smaller and smaller, and then ignore the rest of the world.

To me there is an untapped interest of the average American in what's going on in the rest of the world. September 11 has awakened it in a way that not only should be capitalized on for all kinds of journalistic reasons but for self-interest reasons, the self-interest of individuals and also the self-interest of the news business.

I think we now know that you cannot ignore anything. We cannot say, "Oh well, that's the old—in fact, the old term used to be 'Afghanistanism.'" In fact, when I started in the newspaper business, "Afghanistanism" meant something totally irrelevant to the people of Texas. You could make a case that there is very little that happens anywhere in the world that is irrelevant to anybody anymore. I think journalism is missing a huge opportunity to cover these stories. I'm worried that my hope that I spoke of earlier is not going to bear fruit, to tell you the truth. I don't understand it. It doesn't make sense to me.

QUESTION: *Is there a movement afoot to increase ratings in public broadcasting, and how would that affect you?*

JIM LEHRER: Robert MacNeil used to say, "Ratings do not matter to us unless they're very high." Ratings and the audience size are a very interesting question for folks like us, the people in public broadcasting. As MacNeil and I used to say, "If nobody is going to watch us, why bother putting on a tie? Why don't we just call each other every evening and talk about it on the telephone? Why go to all this trouble and expense?"

In all of television, not just commercial television, not just public broadcasting, there has been a flattening out of the audience, and cable is part of the reason. But that's not the main reason. The main reason is VCRs and so many other things. People can pick and choose what they do with their time very readily and very easily. The technology is what's doing it as well as other things.

Public broadcasting in prime time—and that doesn't include us—is having some audience problems. And people, obviously and understandably, would want to do something about it. In our case, our audience is four and five times the size of cable programs they are writing about all the time in the television news columns.

I'm not putting anybody down, but they have a couple hundred thousand people watching MSNBC on average most of the time. That's just an example. CNN is higher than that. In prime time Fox News has more. But in public broadcasting there has been nothing said to me directly or indirectly. I've picked up nothing like, "Oh my gosh, if your ratings don't go up, you're going to be in trouble." Quite the contrary. The support for our program is as high as it's ever been. We've held our audience pretty well. I wish it were higher.

One of the things we have never had any opportunity to do is advertising. We never had any money to advertise. I am trying to do something about that now because there are a lot of people who don't know about us. If you know about us and don't watch us, that's one thing. But if you've never heard of us, that's another matter. So I think we could increase our audience considerably if we were able to advertise, and we may try to do that. But there is no overt pressure to juice it up or any of that sort of stuff to try to get higher ratings.

QUESTION: *About the 2000 presidential candidate debates, what have you brought from that experience?*

JIM LEHRER: Well, I lost 15 pounds and gained five years in the course of those three debates. It was a very difficult experience. I'd done a lot of earlier ones, but the ones in 2000 were really difficult because the race was so close, and it came down to those three debates.

The candidates were very, very uptight, and their people were very combative. There was no sense of camaraderie, "Isn't this a wonderful world in this democratic process together?" No way. So it was extremely difficult.

I don't know what to say beyond that other than from my point of view, I had a bottom line. I had several bottom lines. I didn't want anybody ever to be able to say that I had been unfair to either one of them. Second bottom line, I didn't want anybody to say afterward, "Oh well, Bush won or Gore won because Lehrer did such and such a thing in the presidential debates."

My job was to let them debate if they would. If they chose not to, that was their problem. That was between them and the voters. It was not my job. It would have been entirely different if they had been appearing on our program and I was running a discussion between them. For a presidential debate, it's kind of a civic duty. It's not functioning as a journalist. I know it sounds weird, but it's a function to facilitate these two candidates or three candidates. In 1992, I did a couple with Ross Perot, Bill Clinton, and George Bush, the father. But it's just to facilitate the exchange. That's what I felt my job was. As I say, in 2000 my mind was seared when that was over with, and so was my soul a little bit. It took me a long time to recover, to tell you the truth of the matter. It was very difficult.

QUESTION: *Can you tap into sources of National Public Radio with your program?*

JIM LEHRER: Yes. We've done some things with National Public Radio. Most commercial radio has given up the news business. So most of the news on radio now is on National Public Radio. There used to be a requirement. If you had a license to have a radio station, you had to do a certain amount of news and public affairs. That is no longer the case. And as a consequence, locally, at a regional level, and at a national level, public radio has become the leading resource for news on radio.

QUESTION: *Will commercial broadcasting ever offer corrections?*

JIM LEHRER: Well, they don't have the need. You see, they don't make mistakes. Seriously, I don't know. I really believe in doing that. When you make a mistake, correct it. It gives you credibility.

When I started in the newspaper business, they never corrected anything. I remember one time we got something really wrong on the newspaper I was working on in Texas. I went to the city editor with another reporter and said, "You know, we really got this wrong." He said, "Hey, you can't correct that." I said, "Well, why not?" He said, "Well, because if the reader starts thinking that we get things wrong, they won't believe anything we do."

QUESTION: *Can you tell us about the bus you own?*

JIM LEHRER: We keep the bus at a place up in the panhandle of West Virginia. It's a 1946 Flxible Clipper. I painted it in the colors of the Kansas Central Lines, which is the bus line that Terry mentioned that opened for business in June 1946 and closed down in July of 1947. My dad filed for bankruptcy. It was a bad situation. It was great for my brother and me. It was great fun, but my dad never got over it, having to file bankruptcy.

The bus that I have is one of those things that makes me believe that there may be a superior being of some kind out there, because I found a bus in pristine condition, and it is exactly like the one my dad could not afford to buy. Had he been able to have bought it, instead of two or three old junk buses, he might have been able to stay in business and wouldn't have gone broke. I bought this bus ten years ago. I painted it in his colors, and my grandsons and I drive it around.

QUESTION: *How did you deal with the pressure from the parties and the candidates before the presidential debates?*

JIM LEHRER: I had no trouble dealing with the candidates and the parties. It's an unwritten rule: No contact of any kind whatsoever. A lot of interest groups sent me information and all of that. But I was able to isolate myself. And, in fact, because I was the only moderator, a few days before each debate I isolated myself even from our own staff at *The NewsHour*.

Nobody knew what the questions were going to be. Only I did. I did talk to my wife, Kate, about them when I finally got them all set. I just wanted to make sure that there was no way for anything to get out. But I felt no pressure at all to ask a particular question or not ask a particular question. I made a decision, right or wrong, that I was not going to introduce any new issues, that that was not my job as the moderator. But I was moderating between these two candidates on issues that had already arisen. There was nothing in terms of what I should ask or any of that.

QUESTION: *Did any of your three daughters go into journalism?*

JIM LEHRER: One daughter is editor-in-chief of one of the Scholastic magazines for children, and she is a journalist. She was with NBC before that. Another daughter was a professional journalist and then edited a literary magazine. She lives overseas. She has three children and became a freelance fiction editor while she was overseas and now writes children's books. The third daughter, the youngest daughter, has done some writing. She worked at the Children's Defense Fund until she got married and started having children. Right now she is a freelance writer. My wife is a novelist, and the joke in the family is that you have to be careful when you bring up an idea around the house because you then have to fight your own family to use it. We are all a very wordy group.

QUESTION: *What's the difference between covering a baseball game and a presidential race?*

JIM LEHRER: It's a good question. In some ways they are absolutely the same—who won, who lost, why? It's who, what, when, where, why, and how, whether it's a baseball game or a presidential election. You could argue that there's a little less at stake in the baseball game than in the presidential election. But for the people playing the game, they'd probably disagree with that, at least at the time they are playing the game. As a journalist, it's all the same. You have obligations to people to get it right.

The basic function of a journalist is the same, it seems to me, whether you're covering a baseball game or covering a presidential election.

QUESTION: *Do you think it might be useful to find new ways to present the news that might be more entertaining to bring new audiences to it?*

JIM LEHRER: I agree with you, but the purpose isn't to entertain; the purpose is to inform. You may use an entertaining way to do it. Good point. If it's an entertaining way to present the news, fine, as long as you present the news. The bottom line is you are presenting the news, and your purpose is to inform rather than to entertain. It seems like a small point, but it's major to me.

If you use the news to entertain, I don't like that. But if you use entertainment techniques to inform, that's fine. If you're trying to make the news entertaining to some more people, younger people, or different kinds of people who are not used to watching news, fine. As long as the news is about something serious.

My point is that if you put on something just because it's entertaining and there is no serious issue to it, that to me is the problem. But if you want to say, "I think there is a way to present the Middle East crisis in a way that would attract a larger audience," I think that's terrific. I think that's fabulous. It's using different techniques. In fact, I would love to try to do some experimental news using techniques like music and sit-coms and try to get some of those people involved in using their expertise for serious purpose. I'm with you on that.

QUESTION: *Because of the murder of journalist Daniel Pearl and other threats to journalists, what's going to happen to foreign reporting?*

JIM LEHRER: Well, it's a serious question whether or not people will back off because of that. There's been no evidence of it thus far; in fact, quite the contrary. There has been more protection for journalists functioning in

Afghanistan, Pakistan, places like that on security measures. But in terms of backing off of the journalistic part of that, there has been no sign of that. It could happen, but I don't think there is anybody who has ever gone into journalism, particularly overseas, that has not been aware of the fact that there are dangers involved. I think it goes with the territory. I interviewed Mariane Pearl, and she herself said that there is a danger in the air. But thus far I am not aware of any slacking off of vigorous, serious journalism because of the Daniel Pearl case and the other threats.

QUESTION: *Do we have an objectivity problem here, as opposed to journalism overseas?*

JIM LEHRER: Most people from abroad would argue they are the ones with the objectivity problem, not us. In fact, most journalists come over here and say, "My God, I'd give anything to function in a cleaner environment." The French newspapers, the British newspapers, they all have a point of view. It is part of their journalism, and the people who read them understand that, and the news broadcasts are the same. The BBC is an exception. Some people would even argue it is not. We get a lot of pieces from various news organizations overseas that do not meet our standards for objectivity and fairness.

I have always heard it just the opposite from the way you presented it. We are usually criticized for going too far the other way. We say, "On the one hand this, on the other hand that." There are people within America who would argue that there are left-wing newspapers and there are right-wing outlets, but nothing like what exists in the rest of the world.

Everybody knows *Le Monde* is a liberal newspaper. It is and it always will be. And so is the *Guardian.* Everybody knows that all the Murdoch papers abroad are right-wing newspapers. That's not necessarily the case here in the United States. There is no straighter news service than the Associated Press. I can't imagine somebody saying they would get straighter news from somebody other than the Associated Press or Reuters. They are about as clean as it could possibly ever be. They have rules that are stringent.

QUESTION: *Why isn't there more news about Latin America?*

JIM LEHRER: Well, we're trying very hard on *The NewsHour* to do it. We do it more than anybody. But since September 11, nobody has paid any attention to what's going on in Latin America. But nobody has paid much attention to anywhere other than Afghanistan and the Middle East since the fall.

We did an interview recently with the Mexican foreign minister, and he was complaining about this very thing, that nobody is paying attention to Latin America. It's understandable but it's regrettable, and eventually I think it'll come back. Here again, we see the smallness of the world, and our interdependence with Latin America is obvious. Yet by reading the American press, it's clear we don't cover Latin America very extensively. We do on *The NewsHour*. We try very hard. We've done a lot, but we could do more.

Thank you all very much.

Young Man with Flyrod

RED SMITH

NEW YORK HERALD TRIBUNE

AUGUST 4, 1951

Vacation was almost over when Mr. Sparse Gray Hackle called and said, "How about a weekend of matching wits with the trout that live in the Neversink River?" Frankly, it looked like an overmatch from the beginning, but it had been the sort of vacation that cried aloud for relief.

A task force of three was made up swiftly. It included a young man of twelve, going on thirteen, who had never before attempted to mislead a trout with a tuft of feather and barb of steel. He had, however, shown an encouraging spirit several summers earlier when he was eight or nine and used to accompany his parent on forays against the smallmouth bass of Wisconsin. The pair would angle lazily through the mornings from a rowboat until the noonday sun drove them ashore. Then they'd seek out the nearest crossroads tavern, where each would satisfy his appetite according to his needs.

On one such day the young man stuffed his face with a ham sandwich, slaked down the mess with a Coke, and observed, "Gee, Dad, this is the life, ain't it? Fishing and eating in saloons."

There was to be no eating in saloons on the Neversink expedition. Mr. Hackle had arranged for accommodations with Mrs. George Stailing, a patient and gracious lady whose farmhouse near Claryville offers immaculate lodging and prodigious fodder and commands a tempting stretch of river. Adroitly dodging thunderbolts that came crashing down out of the Catskills, the car crept through the rainy darkness and made bivouac there.

At least one member of the party had a sleepless night and admitted it next morning, shamefaced, because it does seem childish to get so keyed up on the eve of a day in a trout stream. Always happens, though.

The young man and Mr. Hackle had slept soundly, and they set a punishing pace on the mile-and-a-half hike into the water formerly held by Mr. Ed Hewitt. This is open water now, soon to be converted from river to lake when a dam, in construction, creates a new reservoir so that New Yorkers may have water to emasculate their Scotch. It is beautiful water that comes boiling down out of the great, greenish Camp Pool through a long, rocky run; it was still perfectly clear after a night of rain and, said Mr. Hackle, who knows the river, it was low.

Mr. Hackle set one of his company to floating a dry fly into the broken water at the head of the run. The fly was a big White Wulff, and as it rode the wavelets tiny brook trout slapped at it impudently. They came to no harm. Perhaps they only flicked it with their tails, not actually trying to bite the fly. Or maybe they took sample nibbles, said "Pfui," and spat at leisure, properly confident that the dope holding the rod couldn't get his reflexes working in time to sink the barb into their sassy faces.

Meanwhile Sparse had tied a wet fly to the young man's leader and led him to the middle of the run and watched as the first cast was made. The first cast took a fish. Details can be distasteful. If it was a very young and very small and very inexperienced fish, there is no point in mentioning that. The young man was young and inexperienced, too.

The point is, the young man made one cast and got a rise and set the hook and got the trout home and then sent him about his business with a sore lip and, presumably, greater wisdom than he had possessed before.

Mr. Hackle, who realizes that the great teacher is the one who knows when to let well enough alone, retired to the tail of the run, where he caught and released a couple of juveniles. His pair and the young man's singleton were the only fish hooked that day. That didn't matter; there'd be another chance the next day.

"It's sure got it over bass fishing," the young man said. When he was reminded that he had drawn blood on the first cast of his life, he had the grace to smile in deprecation of the size of his catch. He did not remark that there was, really, nothing difficult about this game.

When it was mentioned that he was the only member of his family to catch a trout in 1951, he laughed with pleasure and made no comment. No intelligible comment, anyway. He was down on all fours in a bramble patch at the moment, and his mouth was full of wild raspberries.

A Mighty Angler Before the Lord

RED SMITH
NEW YORK TIMES
AUGUST 8, 1977

CHILLMARK, MASSACHU-SETTS—"Grandpa," the fisherman asked, watching his companion crawl under a barbed-wire fence, "did you grow old, or were you made old?"

The fisherman had a little plastic rod and a spinning reel with a bobber on the line. He had dug worms out of a compost heap, and now he dunked one in Turtle Pond on Ozzie Fischer's farm near Beetlebung Corner here on Martha's Vineyard. He watched the bobber intently, moving his bait here and there beside lily pads. White water lilies rested on the surface, their petals opened fully. Water striders darted about in cheeky defiance of natural laws. The fisherman noticed a wooden structure floating in the middle of the pond. "The dog has to swim to his house," he said. "It does look like a doghouse," he was told, "but Mr. Fischer built that for ducks in case they wanted to make a nest in it and lay their eggs."

Not even a turtle showed interest in the worm. This may explain why you never see anybody fishing Turtle Pond. However, the swan pond in West Tisbury was only a fifteen-minute drive down island, and it is common to see boys fishing there. Probably the proper name is Mill Pond, but in the fisherman's family it is known as the swan pond because a cob and his pen live and love and rear their cygnets there. The couple's only child this year is already half the size of the parents.

The fisherman was thoughtful on the drive. "Do people who don't have a birthday grow older?" he asked.

Yes, he was told, there is one way to avoid that, but the method isn't recommended.

"Some people don't have a birthday," he said. "They have to pick July." After a silence he added an afterthought. "Or December. I'd pick July."

"It's August now," he was reminded.

"Yes, but there'll be another July."

"Oh, you mean next July. Yes, there are always two—last July and next July." He thought that over and smiled as if the idea pleased him, but he made no comment.

The swans were at the far end of their pond. On the water beside the road were a dozen or more mallards. Parking, the fisherman's companion asked, "How old are you now?"

At first there was no answer. Then, tentatively, "Six."

"Oh? When will you be six?"

"Tomorrow." His birthday is in September.

Reddish-brown weeds showed a little below the surface. "Throw it where the ducks are," the fisherman said. He laughed when the bobber, split shot, and hook plopped in near a duck, startling her. "Now hold the rod still and watch the bobber," he was told.

"What's a bobber?"

"That red and white thing."

"That's a floater," he said, but not impatiently.

Drawn by curiosity, two ducks swam slowly toward the bobber, eyeing it.

"I have to go to the bathroom," the fisherman said. He saw some tall shrubs. "I'll go behind there." He went off at a trot.

While he was gone the bobber submerged, but the bait was lifted clear before a fish could strip the hook or, worse, get himself caught in the fisherman's absence.

"A fish pulled the floater underwater," he was told on his return. "Be ready to catch him."

In a few moments the bobber broke into a jig. The fisherman cranked his little tin reel. Except for a tiny nubbin of worm, the hook was bare.

"The worms are in the car," his companion said. "Keep fishing with that and I'll get another." By the time he got back the hook was clean.

"Next time the floater sinks," it was suggested, "jerk your rod up first to set the hook in the fish and then crank." In a moment, "There! Good, now crank. No, I'm afraid you're caught in the weeds. Just keep cranking. No! You have a fish. Keep cranking. See him?"

A pale belly flashed right, left, and right again. His lips set, the fisherman reeled furiously. He dragged a 9-inch bullhead onto the bank and stared at it.

"Is that the first fish you ever caught?"

"Yes." The tone was hushed.

"Come on, then. We'll take it home and then I'll skin it so your mother can cook it."

"My mommy will laugh her head off," he said. He was jubilant now.

"I'm crazy about my family," he said. "My mother and father and my sister and my cousin Kim, they'll laugh their head off."

FRANK McCOURT Frank McCourt's memoir, *Angela's Ashes* (1996), won the Pulitzer Prize for biography, occupied a place on the *New York Times* best-seller list for 117 weeks, and sold more than 4 million copies in twenty-seven countries and seventeen languages. A teacher of writing in New York City public schools for nearly three decades before becoming a full-time author, he continued his autobiographical adventures with *'Tis* (1999) and *Teacher Man* (2005). In 2007, he published *Angela and the Baby Jesus*. He died on July 19, 2009. He delivered this lecture on October 16, 2003.

FRANK McCOURT

From Copybook to Computer: What You Write on and How You Do It

I'm here, ladies and gentlemen, because of Terry Smith, and I'd probably never have met Terry Smith if I hadn't written a book about growing up poor and miserable and dreaming of escape in Ireland. When Terry was at the CBS News program *Sunday Morning*, he came to Ireland with the producer, Jim Houtrides, to do a piece on me and my family and the place I grew up in, Limerick City. He said, "Let's go to the lane you grew up in," and I said, "No, it's gone." He said, "Well, let's go to something like it," and I said, "Sorry, they're all gone. You can't find a decent slum in Ireland anymore."

At first I didn't know I was talking to the Terence Smith I used to read in the *New York Times*. I certainly didn't know he was the son of the Red Smith I used to read in the same paper. The strange thing about my reading Red Smith was that I understood about half of what he wrote, especially when he wrote about baseball and football. Those two sports left me cold because I grew up playing and watching sports that moved, baby, moved. Someone told me that a soccer player might run 15 miles during a game, and when I glanced at baseball and football on television they seemed to be games of stop and start, scratch and stare. Oh, get on with it, I said. And the funny thing is that the fastest and most vibrant nation in the world has the slowest sports. Right up there with cricket. Someone said the English invented cricket to give themselves some idea of eternity.

That's how I felt about these American sports until I met my wife, Ellen, from California, and she explained what a first down is and an RBI. So I became slightly interested in those sports, especially when the game was stopped, and it always seemed to be stopped, and everyone would start to fight. That was action, close to boxing, the Red Smith subject I liked best. Still I wouldn't want to be questioned too closely about any of those sports.

So, you're saying to yourself, "What does this have to do with the process of writing?"

I had to grab you, didn't I? Surely you don't want someone to get up here and launch into a discussion of how he or she writes, where he or she gets inspiration, does he or she write with a pen or a computer?

When I was a high school English teacher trying to help my students write, I told them, "When in doubt, tell a story." It's not a bad piece of advice, and I might as well take it myself.

Writing itself, for most of us, is hard enough, though when I read Red Smith it looked easy. He had a kind of insouciance, an easy way with the language I thought I could emulate. It didn't work. Just try it.

I had the same experience with Mark Twain when I was eleven years old reading *Adventures of Huckleberry Finn*. I was astounded. It was a turning point in my life. I never knew you could write naturally, that you could use everyday language. My Irish schoolmasters would have denounced Red Smith and Mark Twain for their simplicity and clarity. We were warned we had to write grand sentences adorned with all kinds of flourishes and gesticulations and digressions and phrases and clauses flirting with clauses and phrases and dark seductive parentheses encasing everything, a forbidding grammatical structure that said, "Abandon hope all ye who enter here." A complex, inaccessible sentence would earn you a pat on the head. Simple sentences were held up to ridicule and got you kicked into a corner of the classroom until you came to your senses.

You can imagine the trouble I got into when I came back to school after a weekend of *Huckleberry Finn*. That Monday we were told to sit at our desks and write a two-page meditation on one of the wounds of Jesus on the cross. I have to repeat that: At eleven we were to write a two-page meditation on one of the wounds of Jesus on the cross. Wounds were assigned, and I was lucky to get the crown of thorns. I was one of three to get the crown, and we were the envy of the whole class, who had to struggle for something to say about wounds on hands, feet, and side. I went to town with the head. I didn't just say the crown of thorns had been placed on the head or even pushed through the scalp. I meditated on how thorn pierces scalp and how blood gushes, Divine Blood. For a few minutes I was stumped as to how many thorns there might have been in the crown, but symbolism stirred, and I decided there must have been thirty-three, one for each year of Jesus' life. I wanted to dwell on each thorn, but that would have taken days and time was limited. Besides, the master had looked over my shoulder, and when he saw my simple colloquial sentences, à la Mark Twain, he yanked me from my seat and dragged me to the front of the class. He roared at them to put their pens down. "Now, McCourt, read to the class the blather you've just written."

"But, sir . . ."

"Read, or by God I'll have you hanging upside down from now until Advent."

I read—and I remember my opening sentence as easily as I remember anything that ever got me into trouble: "In all the Holy Land that day no one was more uncomfortable than Our Lord up there on the cross with his poor bleeding head."

I was proud of that opening sentence, sure it would satisfy the demands of the master for stating a theme in a sentence that was more than simple. I continued, "It's very hard for us to think of having a crown of thorns on our heads. You'd have to go home and get out all your mother's darning needles, knitting needles, and sewing needles and shove them into your skull all at the same time. Your hair would be full of blood and it would dribble down to your shoulders and destroy your shirt and the next thing is your mother comes home all shocked at the blood on her needles and the blood flowing down your back."

The master stopped me and asked where I learned to write such gibberish. Gibberish. That was a new word, and I tucked it away until I could get the meaning from some reasonable adult.

I told him I had just read *Adventures of Huckleberry Finn* by Mark Twain. He said Mark Twain was an American atheist who wrote like a child, and I was to stop reading him right away and never write like him again.

I never stopped reading Mark Twain, and for years I tried to write like him. I didn't know then you have to find your own way in the world or in writing or in anything, that the Shannon was not the Mississippi.

Earlier tonight I observed that writing is hard. It's even harder when you have nothing to write on. I'm not talking about subject matter: I'm talking about a simple thing like paper. You'll find it hard to believe that in the twentieth century there was a scarcity of paper anywhere. If you had money you could, of course, go out and buy paper and notebooks, whatever you needed. We didn't have money, and paper in our house was as scarce as ham. In school we had composition books to write in, but you dare not use them for anything but assignments from the master. We didn't take them home. They were distributed every day along with the pens we dipped in the inkwells on the desks.

If I found a piece of paper on the street I'd take it home and scribble on it until my mother needed it to start the fire in the morning, and up the chimney went my early writings, my juvenilia, as the academics would put it.

Then there was another turning point in my young life. I was ambling up the main street of Limerick when I saw a truck outside a house that was being renovated. The truck was filled with plaster and bricks broken beyond repair. You never saw any kind of wood in those trucks, as the workers had already set it aside to take home for their own fires or to sell to neighbors. Nothing was wasted. But what made my heart beat was the rolls of wallpaper flung carelessly here and there. I hoisted three rolls to my shoulders, thinking they'd help start the fire in the morning at home, but when I got there I changed my mind and decided to use the rolls for writing.

Many of you have scribbled on the expensive wallpaper of exclusive hotels: phone numbers, stock quotations, bits of information. But you've never tried it on discarded wallpaper still stiff with plaster and whatever glue was applied to make it stick to the wall.

I hid out with my wallpaper in an abandoned house around the corner from ours. It was said to be haunted, but I didn't care. There were rats, but I didn't care about them either as long as they stayed away from my wallpaper.

I went home and sneaked one of my mother's kitchen knives out of the house. She had only three.

Each of the rolls was 5 feet long, and when I started to scrape off the plaster I whimpered with pleasure. Fifteen feet of paper for the new writing enterprise that had just lodged in my head: a history of Ireland from the earliest times to the day I was born. I had convinced myself that all history ended on that day.

But there was another problem: lack of pen or pencil.

Oh, well. Why didn't you just go to the store and get one?

Because I had no money, and the world wasn't drowning in ballpoint pens the way it is now. Even today, if I see a pen lying discarded on the ground I pick it up and take it home like an abandoned puppy. No pen is safe from my thievery.

With no writing implements I would not have been able to write my huge history of Ireland in that old house. I'd have to take my rolls home and borrow the one pen and the bottle of ink my father used for writing letters for neighbors for a small fee. I could hide the rolls in the coalhole under the stairs, where my mother would never see them, because if she did she'd be tempted to start a fire with them.

But it was too nerve-racking to last. I never knew when my brothers would wander into the coalhole after a ball or a rat or when my mother would need coal for the fire or when my father might demand to know the whereabouts of his pen and bottle of ink.

Early one morning, long before school started, I carried the rolls to my classroom and hid them on top of the closet where the master kept his materials: composition books, pens, the great brown vessel he used to fill the inkwells in the desks.

Every afternoon when school finished I pretended to leave like everyone else but doubled back to the classroom when I thought the building was empty. I told the charlady who cleaned the school I was being kept in for punishment, and she said it was good for me and I should behave myself and not put my immortal soul in danger because as far as she could see the young nowadays were a terrible lot altogether and she felt sorry for all the poor mothers. She saw me scraping the plaster from the wallpaper, but as long as I cleaned up after me she wouldn't tell a soul.

For two weeks I was happy in that empty classroom, that silent school. It was hard writing on the wallpaper with an old nib and ink that turned words into blobs. I had to struggle through a landscape of plaster mountains and bits and pieces of whatever had adhered to the paper. I had to leap gaps where the plaster had come off, taking the wallpaper with it. I was often frustrated, but the challenge of the enterprise was greater than all the difficulties.

The history of Ireland called for the spaciousness and grandness of old wallpaper, and if I didn't know the exact details of the history I made them up. I used up nearly a whole roll of wallpaper on the epic Irish hero, Cuchulain himself. Five feet of Cuchulain. His glorious death took up a foot and a half.

Because I was a good Catholic boy I gave St. Patrick half a roll. I described the way he was captured by Irish pirates and sold to a man in the County Antrim and put out on the hills tending sheep. I made up a heartrending story about how he was starving to death and had to kill a lamb to keep himself going. The lamb wasn't even a Christian, but St. Patrick told him it was good to die early and innocent so that he could go right to heaven, and then he slit the lamb's throat while looking into the lamb's big brown eyes while weeping over the lamb's last "maaaaaaah."

I broke down myself at that point, and the charlady heard me crying and wanted to know what was up with me, and when I told her she said that was a sin I just committed, making up things about St. Patrick, who would never kill a lamb. She said she had a good mind to tell my mother, but she'd let me off this one time.

I toiled away at my history of Ireland, making it up as I went along. (I've discovered in recent years that's what some historians do anyway, so I was way ahead of my time.) I got all the way up to the Battle of Clontarf, where Brian Boru, High King of Ireland, beat the hell out of the Vikings, the one time the Irish won decisively on the field of battle. I was describing his death by a sneaky Viking when my teacher walked in, my schoolmaster, Mr. O'Dea, and I nearly died at my desk with my wallpaper unrolled all over the room. I knew why he had returned: a forgotten umbrella.

The charlady stuck her head in the door. "I don't know what he's doing here, Mr. O'Dea," she said. "I don't know in God's name what he's up to."

He went to his chair behind his desk. "Come over here."

I stood before him. "Now what are you doing in this classroom at this time of day?"

"Ah, sir. I'm writing."

"And what is all that stuff lying around the room?"

"That's my wallpaper, sir, for writing on."

"Wallpaper! What are you writing on wallpaper for?"

"That's all I could find, sir, for my history."

"Your history? What history?"

"Ireland, sir. I'm writing the whole history of Ireland from the very start to the day I was born."

He told me to bring him the first roll. He wanted to see how Ireland began and he started to read, pausing when lumps of plaster got in the way of the narrative.

"In the beginning Ireland was nothing but—what's this?—turf, turf with shamrocks growing out of it but then God took pity and put people there with clothes on and all."

He put the wallpaper down. "Who told you all this?"

"It was in my head, sir."

"That's not proper history, you know. You're taking liberties. Do you know what I'm talking about?"

"I don't, sir."

"You can't just go and make up history. It has to be based on facts. Where did you get that wallpaper?"

"It was thrown out in a lorry, sir."

He went to his closet and brought back two composition books. "Here. If you're going to write the whole history of Ireland, you'll run out of wallpaper in no time. When you fill these composition books let me know, and we might have another for you."

He stared at me for a while, and I blushed and felt uncomfortable until he got to his feet and did something extraordinary. I wasn't used to the kind way he was talking now. He patted my head. My mouth went dry and I felt dizzy.

Schoolmasters never patted boys' heads.

Heads were put there to be rapped and punched and banged against the wall.

Mr. O'Dea took his umbrella and walked out and left me with a changed world. I never knew a schoolmaster could be human like that, and it made me want to write the best history of Ireland that was ever written. In a few days I filled the composition books, but a week later he told my class what I was doing. He called me to the front of the room to read the part about Brian Boru and the mean Viking, and I was ashamed because of the way he praised me, and I knew I'd be taunted at lunchtime in the schoolyard. There was tittering when I described how the mean Viking sunk his hatchet in Brian's skull, giving him a moment to say a perfect act of contrition, and Mr. O'Dea pulled the tittering boy from his seat and knocked him around the room. The boy was my enemy ever after. He turned half the class against me, and there was so much teasing and taunting in the schoolyard I was sorry I ever started that history of Ireland.

I took the rolls of wallpaper home to my mother, but she complained they were so slow to burn she'd spend a whole day waiting to boil water for a cup of tea.

I gave up the history, but I never stopped writing. Language was all we had, and it was free. If I'd grown up in Italy I could have become a painter or a sculptor or a musician. They had the materials and the tradition. Our tradition was oral and, later, literary.

But the strange thing was that I, for one, never thought of my own life or the lives of my community as proper material for writing. No schoolmaster ever told us to write about ourselves, never asked us what we thought about anything. There was one valuable exercise, which, I think, came in handy in later years: the examination of conscience before you went to confession. In that activity there was a kind of intellectual rigor. You had already learned the sins and the various shadings of sin. Now you had to scan your life and see where you might have transgressed. You knew also you had to be honest, or the priest would know.

How? How would he know?

He'd know. That's all. He's a priest. Stop asking foolish questions and go on with your examination of conscience.

Little Catholics of my generation examined their consciences but didn't know they were engaged in a powerful autobiographical act. We scrutinized our lives for the good and the bad, especially the bad. You didn't go to confession to report on the good you had done, on your virtues. You went to seek forgiveness for your sins.

And that was a form of writing. That is why so many of my generation remember so much and so vividly. No, it's not therapy nor anything like it. Sigmund Freud is reported to have said, "There is one race of people for whom psychoanalysis is no use at all: the Irish."

Confession was a form of storytelling. So, I suppose, is therapy, but therapy doesn't have the power, baby. Confession offers immediate results: absolution and a return to a state of grace. And it's free. If you made a good honest confession, you knew that if you died then you shot right up to heaven to rejoice forever in the contemplation of the Divine Countenance.

To grow up Irish Catholic was a mixed blessing: pure hell for the habitual sinner, rich material for the future writer.

After I'd abandoned my definitive history of Ireland I turned to writing short plays with religious themes in which I always played some kind of heroic priest. I forced my brothers to act in my plays, though Malachy, the one next to me in age, refused. He said my plays weren't even funny, and he'd rather be out on the street kicking a ball. The other brothers, Michael and Alphie, were young enough to be bullied, though they resisted when the script called for martyrdom by hanging. I tried to explain martyrdom to them and the rewards they'd get in heaven, but they just looked restless and said they had to pee. I think I realized then how hard it was to explain or persuade, and that may have been my first attempt to teach.

Since we had no television or radio, no CDs, no mechanical entertainments at all, we fell back on imagination, fantasy, creation, the dream world. When I taught high school in New York I would listen to my students talking about what they watched last night. We talked about what we did last night. We made up our own games. We talked about what we'd do when we grew up. We bragged about the great feats of our fathers.

Talk, talk, talk. Scribble, scribble, scribble. I saved bits of paper for my new project: a detective novel. The detective's name was the Blue Green. I don't know why I didn't give him a regular name, though he did bear a strong resemblance to me at the age of thirteen: handsome, charming, witty. Also, he spent much of his time rescuing fair maidens from sinister Chinese along the banks of the Thames River right there in the center of London. I thought all detective novels had to be set in London like the novels of my favorite writer then, Edgar Wallace. I never thought there might be detectives in Limerick and even if there were, what use would they be when there were no Chinese in the city threatening the fair maidens?

Why didn't I write about what was under my nose? Why didn't I realize that the lanes of Limerick were pulsing with stories? Seán O'Casey, up there in Dublin, looked around him and felt and wrote. So did Joyce, though I knew nothing about him. You'd hear his name, but it was said he wrote upside down or backwards or something, such a lunatic he wasn't even banned.

We read Dickens. He wrote about what was under his nose, but that was all right. It was London. But who would want to read about Limerick? Who would care a fiddler's fart about people in the lanes of Limerick? No, it was all laid out. You could write about saints in distant places, you could write about Jesus on the cross, you could write about sinister Chinese in London, you could even write about cowboys and Indians, but you yourself were off limits. All the people around you were off limits.

But there was gossip, wonderful, rich, juicy gossip. My mother would sit with the women of the lanes drinking tea and gossiping, and I'd sit in a corner listening. My father would put on his cap and stalk out muttering, "Gossip, gossip, gossip." But he was from the north and a bit odd in his ways.

My mother and her friends didn't know I was hiding in the coalhole under the stairs. They didn't know I was learning more about life from them than I ever learned in any book or college course. And if I didn't know you could write about this, I still tucked it away along with memories of the day the schoolmaster patted my head.

By the time I left Ireland at nineteen it was clear that I wanted to be a writer. I had enough money now to buy notebooks, but I still didn't know you could write about yourself and what you came from. I read Joyce's *Dubliners* and Sherwood Anderson's *Winesburg, Ohio*, but that was Dublin, that was distant Ohio.

I was barely off the boat when the Chinese attacked Korea and America got nervous and turned to me and drafted me. Instead of Korea they sent me to Germany and assigned me to the Canine Corps to train attack dogs. (That was good practice for my future career as teacher.) For some reason they sent me to company clerk school, where I learned to type. I knew that would come in handy and help me become a famous writer. I always liked those stories about tough-guy writers like Hemingway and Steinbeck who banged away on battered old portable typewriters on battlefields or in Greenwich Village attics.

Then I went to college in New York and got in over my head. I tried to write like this one and that one. I tried to write like the charming lyrical Irish. It didn't work because I didn't trust myself to tell my own story.

I kept on scribbling in notebooks, but it was all whining and despair leavened with dark thoughts of suicide. I'd read somewhere no writer is worth his salt who hasn't despaired and thought of suicide.

I have forty years' worth of these notebooks, and I keep them to remind myself of what an ass I was and my potential for continuing asshood.

It may have been the teaching that liberated me as man, as writer, and that took thirty years. In the beginning I put on the teacher mask. I am the teacher. You are the student. I know all the answers.

They were ahead of me. My students had dropped their masks a long time ago, and now they wanted honesty. I had to drop the mask and drop the teacher act in class and on the page. I began to talk to them about simplicity and clarity and writing about what was under their noses. I didn't know it, but all this time I was talking to myself. I was a teacher, but more and more, more and more, oh, God, more and more I wanted to write. Scribbling in notebooks was no longer satisfying. I had to break out. My students asked me about my life. I doled it out in dribs and drabs. They delighted in some of my stories and demanded to hear them again. I obliged. It was better than trying to teach grammar or what in God's name John Donne was talking about.

They said I should write a book.

I did.

And that's why I'm here.

Thank you, Terry Smith, for getting me here and Red Smith for your example.

And thank you, Notre Dame, and on Saturday may you squeeze that California orange to pulp.

Editor's note: Two days after his Red Smith Lecture, Frank McCourt attended his first collegiate football game in America, Notre Dame versus the University of Southern California. USC won 45–15 en route to a 12–1 season and the national championship in the final ranking of the Associated Press.

Jim Thurber

RED SMITH

NEW YORK HERALD TRIBUNE

NOVEMBER 4, 1961

The obituary described James Thurber as "shy, introverted, self-deprecatory." Chances are he wasn't any of these. His public manner was diffident until something caught his interest or stirred him to argument, and something almost always did. Then he spoke freely with force and vigor and wit and no trace of self-consciousness.

If he was an introvert, he did not betray it at a party, where he was almost sure to be the center of attention, controlling the conversation, dominating the discussion. Widely informed, he could smash an adversary in argument on practically any topic, including topics on which he only appeared to be informed.

"You are aware of course," he would say, "that the Throckmorton Report disposed of that point definitely, proving that on the circumstances you describe. . . ." The adversary wouldn't be aware of this at all, partly because no Throckmorton Report ever existed, but inasmuch as he was pretending to some knowledge of the subject he could hardly admit that.

If Jim was self-deprecatory, it was only about his slight physique, his blindness, his not quite splendid grooming. He did not underrate himself professionally. No man of taste could have failed to know how good he was, and he was a man of rare taste.

Because virtually everything moved him to laughter—publishers were an exception; most of them moved him to rage—he poked fun at himself as freely as he might skewer any other target.

"Your drink's here, Jamie," Marc Simont, his artist neighbor in West Cornwall, Connecticut, said one night, setting a highball at his elbow. Jim said thanks, and a little later, groping for the glass as he talked, he knocked it over. He made no more of that than a person would who could see, but when it happened again with a fresh drink he sprang to his feet and delivered an impassioned protest to an imaginary House Rules Committee about the untidy habits of this member, Thurber, who persistently loused up the club premises on the flimsy pretense, the hollow excuse, that he was blind.

His witty eloquence made it funny, and like all his humor it was also bitterly poignant.

As a kid with the sight of only one eye, Jim tried to pitch in sandlot baseball, though he was no athlete. In his newspaper days he never was a member of a sports department, though as a correspondent in France after World War I he did cover events like a tennis match on the Riviera between Suzanne Lenglen and Helen Wills. He remembered and quoted a line written by his brother, who did a hitch in sports in the era when Wee Dickie Kerr was a twenty-game winner with the White Sox: "Little pitchers have big years."

Jim was an avid sports fan with catholic tastes in games. He loved to spin yarns of football days at Ohio State in the time of Chic "Gimme the Ball" Harley, who was more or less the prototype of a character in "The Male Animal." Jim was a member of a little tennis club in West Cornwall. As his sight failed, he turned to the radio to keep him abreast of baseball developments.

In "The Catbird Seat," one of his most inventive and savagely penetrating short stories, he borrowed the title and other cornpone expressions like "tearing up the pea patch" from the mother tongue of Red Barber, then voice of the Dodgers.

Everybody knows, of course, that he invented the midget whom Bill Veeck signed on some years later as a major league player with the St. Louis Browns.

Jim Thurber was the greatest humorist of his time and probably, as the obituary suggested, America's greatest since Mark Twain. He recognized and appreciated his enormous talent but resented the fact that in many minds the definition of humorist was "unserious." Mentioning this rather angrily on a television program recently, he said, "I except Great Britain and Continental Europe," where, apparently, he was accepted as the thoughtful and perceptive critic of humankind that all great humorists are.

KEN AULETTA Ranked as America's premier media critic by *Columbia Journalism Review*, Ken Auletta has written "Annals of Communications" columns and profiles for *The New Yorker* since 1992. In his articles and books, he explains who's behind the messages, what motivates their actions, when new technologies become influential, where consequences occur, why such work is significant, and how the public should understand the new information environment. A former columnist for the *Village Voice* and the *Daily News* in New York, Auletta is the author of many books, including *Three Blind Mice: How the TV Networks Lost Their Way* (1991), *The Highwaymen: Warriors of the Information Super Highway* (1997), and *Backstory: Inside the Business of News* (2003). He delivered this lecture on September 8, 2005.

KEN AULETTA

Whom Do Journalists Work For?

T ed Turner, who pioneered CNN and early programming for the cable industry, visited Germany several years ago to address a prominent audience. His staff prepared his remarks, but the always unpredictable Turner—who was once known as "the mouth from the South"—chose to ignore the draft and wing it.

"You know," he began, "you Germans had a bad century. You lost World War I. You lost World War II. You were losers."

The audience was shocked. Turner's staff wanted to dive under the table. But then Turner reclaimed his audience by declaring, "But I know what it's like. When I bought the Atlanta Braves, we couldn't win either. You guys can turn it around. You can start making the right choices. If the Atlanta Braves could do it, Germany can do it." The audience was now laughing with Turner, not at him.

In the course of preparing a Turner profile, I asked him, "Why did you do that?" He said, "I don't know. I'm like Zorba the Greek. I just get up and dance sometimes."

What if I began today by telling you what I don't like about college students:

- I don't like that you don't read.

- I don't like your movies and Web sites.

- I don't like your docility.

- I don't like that Notre Dame beat Pittsburgh in football last week or that all you students seem to care about is sports.

Now that I've dug a hole, let me dance out by telling you: I don't believe in making sweeping generalizations, except to make a point. My point: Beware of stereotypes.

This point was driven home to a roomful of reporters during the 1980 presidential campaign between President Jimmy Carter and the challenger, Ronald Reagan. President Carter's Soviet affairs adviser, Dr. Marshall Shulman, was briefing the reporters on how complicated relations between the two countries were when suddenly a reporter asked, "Isn't the problem with President Carter's dealings with the Soviet Union that it is too complicated and the public can't understand it?"

"Ridiculous!" sniffed Dr. Shulman.

"So explain to us, Dr. Shulman," shot back the reporter, "how you would simply explain Carter's policy on a bumper sticker."

"You cannot reduce foreign policy to a bumper sticker!" sputtered Dr. Shulman.

"I insist," said the reporter.

"How many words am I allowed?" asked Dr. Shulman.

"Two," answered the reporter.

A devilish smile crossing his face, Dr. Shulman said, "My bumper sticker would read, 'Accept Complexity.'"

Good journalism must accept complexity. Today I'd like to talk about media caricatures, as well as the business—journalism—Red Smith and I share. Although he was a columnist and free to opine, Red Smith never painted his subjects as if they were cartoons. He reported. And when he reported, he did not write to please team owners or athletes. He wrote for the reader. When Cassius Clay changed his name to Muhammad Ali and proclaimed, "I am the greatest," or when he denounced the war in Vietnam, Red Smith had to be offended. But as David Halberstam writes in the introduction to *The Best American Sports Writing of the Century*, Red Smith's "ability to change his mind about Cassius Clay/Muhammad Ali when most men of his generation were so offended by Ali's style, theatrics, and politics that they did not deign to see the brilliance of him as a fighter and the originality of him as a man, is part of his enduring legacy."

Smith was also a great storyteller, which is vital to journalism. Among the best pieces of advice I received as a relatively young journalist came from William Shawn, the legendary editor of *The New Yorker*. The year was 1980 or 1981, and I was proposing a story idea. I told Mr. Shawn—everyone called him Mr. Shawn—that when you rode the subways and saw the hostile faces, when you looked at the murder-by-stranger statistics or long-term welfare dependency or the number of homeless people, something different was happening with poverty in America. People were more cut off, more hostile. They weren't just income poor. "I don't know what to call this group, or even the right questions to ask," I told Mr. Shawn. "But I know it's an important story."

"It sounds like a sociological yack piece," Mr. Shawn responded. "You need a vehicle to tell the story." He gave me weeks, months, to find one.

Mr. Shawn understood, as did Red Smith, that storytelling is critical to hooking readers. He also understood that a journalist needed time to gather facts and to comprehend context. A year and a half later, *The New Yorker* published my three-part series, "The Underclass," which grew into a book. After the first two installments appeared in *The New Yorker*, we were editing the third part, which focused on what might be done to alleviate the underclass. I was told that for space reasons we had to cut it back 40 percent. I protested that this would gut the piece, that we owed it to our readers to pose possible solutions for the grim reality I had spent maybe forty thousand words describing.

Mr. Shawn politely asked me to give him a half hour to reread the third installment. A half hour later he fetched me, and I followed him into the composing room, where he said, "We cannot cut this piece back 40 percent. What are my options?"

He was told he could either cut whole sections of the magazine, like the movie reviews or the arts section. Or he could add eight pages to the magazine at a cost of about $80,000. He added the eight pages.

That will probably never happen again. I'm not sure it should. But it does provoke the question I have chosen as my topic: Whom does a journalist work for?

Shawn believed we worked for our readers, not shareholders. My friend Peter Jennings, who died recently, received a fat weekly check from ABC—as does one of your previous Red Smith Lecturers, Ted Koppel—but at bottom each believed he served the audience, not the corporate parent. They worked their sources, but they did not trim their reporting to please sources. They, like the rest of us, sometimes compromised. Journalists in television too often chase ratings, while print journalists too often juice up headlines. However, day in and day out Jennings, like Koppel, tried to offer citizens the information we need to make decisions in a democracy.

They believed, as do the best journalists—or the best public officials—

that they are public servants. What flows from this assumption are some pretty startling conclusions. If everyone in journalism, including the folks who sign our checks, truly embraced this assumption,

- Media corporations would worry less about Wall Street, profit margins, and the stock price.

- The definition of news would harden. There would be less Michael Jackson and Runaway Bride and more international news.

- There would be more investigative reporting because the press would highlight its watchdog role, the checks-and-balances function that helps prevent the abuse of power.

- The panic within news organizations to locate an audience distracted by so many choices—to make more noise in order to boost circulation or ratings—would sometimes be resisted by editors who remind their bosses that they hold a public trust.

- Journalists would build in more checks and balances to our own abuse of power, welcoming more independent ombudsmen. We would encourage the kind of transparency we demand from government and corporations and would prominently admit our mistakes.

Pretty radical, yes?

And what might the CEOs who sign our checks say to this? They would probably insist that this is a cartoon. They would say that employees in public companies, including its journalists, are also concerned about the stock price because their pensions and stock are linked to it. They would say that without money from Wall Street investors, media companies will not be able to raise the capital that buys expensive printing presses or funds overseas bureaus. They would say that journalism that just gives its audience only what it thinks is important will continue to lose audience. They would say the press must abandon its elitist model and give the public more of what it wants rather than what we think it needs. For the public does not just consume news to be educated, they also wish to be entertained. Serious journalists may rail at Michael Jackson coverage, but there's an audience for it.

The CEO who signs our checks probably believes journalists are unmindful of the real world. In the real world you have to listen to your customers, and we know the customers want Michael Jackson, and shorter stories, and less foreign and government news, more infotainment, and more news they can use. Since fewer readers and viewers are buying newspapers or magazines, or watching network news, we have to try new things, they say. What's wrong with survey research and focus groups that reveal what the public is interested in? Isn't a good business supposed to understand its customers? And if we don't invest in survey research, how are we going to learn why young people are not buying newspapers and magazines or watching television news the way their parents did?

The research already tells us: Spurred by the two-way communication made possible by the Internet, the audience wants less of a Voice-from-God journalism than a conversation. They want shorter stories. They want to lend their voice to restaurant or movie reviews. They want to be able to communicate via e-mail with reviewers.

Further, the people who sign our checks will say, "If journalists are implacably hostile to the business side of their enterprises, they will fail to create the team culture every enterprise needs." After all, the sales force that sells ads or subscriptions does make possible the salaries of journalists.

These two worldviews suggest perhaps the biggest conflict within journalism: the cultural divide between journalists and their corporate owners. It is second nature for corporate executives to extol synergy, profit margins, share price, lowering walls between divisions, extending the brand, and teamwork.

The clash comes because the journalistic culture is so different. Journalists prize independence, not teamwork; more bureaus and spending on news, not profit margins. We want a wall between news and sales, and we often see synergy as shilling. Journalists worry more about their readers and viewers, and businesspeople worry more about Wall Street. Businesspeople abhor waste and usually want to quantify things. Journalists understand waste is inherent to journalism—waiting for calls to be returned, waiting to get a second source, waiting for plane connections, waiting to get someone to talk. And journalists know good reporting and writing are hard to quantify. There are business folks who understand this—the Sulzbergers of the *New York Times* do, as do the Grahams of the *Washington Post*, or Ted Turner.

Turner created CNN on faith, not management studies proving CNN would be a great investment. The studies said the opposite. And though

Turner became a billionaire and pressed for ever higher profits, he is lionized by many journalists who worked for him at CNN because he often made decisions that cost money but built the CNN brand. He created the first world news network. He aired documentaries on weighty subjects at a time when CBS, NBC, and ABC had largely abandoned them. He kept his team in Baghdad to cover the first Gulf War in 1991.

Where do I come out in this debate? Let us concede it is wrong to portray our corporate bosses in cartoon-like fashion as greedy capitalists unconcerned with anything but maximizing profits. Most business executives I've covered do not wake up each morning determined to do something bad. They, like the rest of us, want to be proud of their work, even if they don't always do things to merit that pride. Let us also concede that most journalistic enterprises need to make a profit, and to make a profit they must be like supermarkets, offering a range of choices to their customers—international news, weather, sports, business, gossip, movie reviews, cartoons, the results of planning board meetings, etc. But too often those journalistic supermarkets have become specialty stores. In news, they too often promote one product to the virtual exclusion of others. Look at what's happened to the network documentary units that once probed poverty or the Defense Department or public education. Now NBC devotes entire hours to "exclusive" interviews with the Runaway Bride or Amber Frey. CBS's *48 Hours*, which once vividly took viewers inside hospital emergency rooms and government meetings, is now called *48 Hours Mystery*. ABC's *Primetime* thinks it's got a "scoop" when they snare actor George Clooney for an at-home interview, as they have this fall.

We journalists are baiting our own trap. Today we are threatened by many forces, none more so than our lost trust among the public. According to a recent Pew Poll, 62 percent of Americans believe the press is biased. Two-thirds of the American people don't trust us. This lack of trust is a dagger aimed at journalism's heart.

It is often said that journalism has an ethics problem. Usually when we speak of ethics we refer to some form of dishonesty—like Jayson Blair of the *New York Times* or Jack Kelley of *USA Today*, each of whom made up stories. Lying is, of course, a serious and alarming problem. But lying is not, I believe, at the heart of what ails journalism.

What most ails journalism are vices that can be captured by five bumper sticker words: *Synergy. Brand. Humility. Hubris. Bias.*

Let's start with synergy. We see synergy at work when

- TV networks choose to air shows produced by their own studio factories, and then they get their morning news shows to conduct interviews with the stars, forging a great promotional platform for these shows. This past year, ABC's *Desperate Housewives* was featured on ABC's *Good Morning America* every Friday, giving the audience a taste of what the show would feature Sunday night. And again on Monday morning *GMA* featured outtakes or an interview with one of the stars. NBC used to do the same thing when it had *Friends* on Thursdays, just as *The Early Show* on CBS does with *Survivor*.

- Texas-based Clear Channel Communications, the largest owner of radio stations, pushed on its stations the music performed at the Clear Channel concerts it runs.

- Media companies like News Corporation or Gannett or Tribune—or take your pick—justify their many acquisitions by saying they can achieve "economies of scale." And they do save money by combining finance or human resources or other functions. But they have another synergy in mind as well. News Corp. has as part of its business plan that their Fox News can promote stories from their *New York Post* or *Sky News* or the *Times of London*, just as their book publishing arm can lock up their stars—or give book contracts to powerful figures, like the daughter of China's premier or former House Speaker Newt Gingrich. News Corp. is hardly alone.

  Business executives also believe these synergies can build the corporate brand, which brings us to a second vice: the infatuation with brands. Few business buzzwords are invoked more tiresomely and are less understood.

- Yes, NBC extended its brand by doing an hour-long news special on *Friends*, but at what cost to the credibility of NBC News?

- Yes, *60 Minutes II* attracted a lot of notice for their exclusive last September about George W. Bush and the National Guard. But when it came out that CBS rushed its report during the presidential election and made serious mistakes, what did this do to the credibility or brand of CBS?

- Yes, Clear Channel gained leverage over performers, just as Sinclair Broadcasting used its political muscle last year to air an attack on Democratic candidate John Kerry on all its stations. But this exercise of power alarmed citizens and sparked a movement to curb big media.

- Yes, doing ABC's *Good Morning America* from Disney World promotes the brand and is good corporate synergy. But if ABC News is perceived as shilling for its corporate parent, it loses credibility.

In news—and this is the part business executives often miss—credibility is the brand.

It would be a too-simple bumper sticker to blame all journalistic vices on an imposed business culture. The august *New York Times* printed a long boxed editor's note in May 2004 in which they apologized to readers for not being rigorous enough in reporting on weapons of mass destruction prior to the invasion of Iraq. A major reason, the note declared, was as old as journalism itself. It read, "Editors at several levels who should have been challenging reporters and pressing for more skepticism were perhaps too intent on rushing scoops into the paper."

Scoops.

The brand—the credibility—of the great *New York Times* was tarnished—as was that of CBS and Dan Rather—for chasing scoops.

A synonym for credibility is *trust*. Think of the trust CNN gained when Ted Turner insisted that CNN stay on to report from Baghdad as bombs were falling during the 1991 Gulf War. CNN may have lost money producing an epic twenty-hour series on the origins of the Cold War, but how do you quantify what this Ted Turner decision did for CNN's credibility and trust? Edward R. Murrow lost sponsors when he reported on the demagogic behavior of Senator Joseph McCarthy in the 1950s, but it is one of the reasons CBS came to be called "the Tiffany network."

There are more subtle issues that engender trust. Do we, as reporters, always remember that we work for our audience? Think of White House reporters or others who sometimes pull their punches so as not to antagonize a source. Think of sportswriters who worry too much—as Red Smith did not—about how a general manager might react to a story. Think of reporters who turn too many stories into soap operas populated by cardboard figures.

Journalists only gain trust when we are transparent, which brings us to the third vice: lack of humility. Humility is what CBS lacked for twelve days after it aired its report asserting that it had documents proving that George W. Bush got into the National Guard to avoid military service in Vietnam and did not meet his military obligations. CBS insisted that its documents were real. They were wrong, yet it took them twelve days to acknowledge this.

Humility is the true backstory of good journalism. In many ways, it is the most vital quality possessed by a good journalist. A journalist shines, of course, who can write well, and is accurate, and can think clearly. But before we write a word we must ask questions and listen to the answers. Do the blowhards on cable TV listen? Think of the last time in the weeks prior to an election a talking head was asked, "Who's going to win?" You can count on one hand the number of times you've heard anyone answer, "I don't know."

In journalism today a premium is placed on sharp opinion, on *wow*. It is very easy to get very full of yourself. Appear on TV often and you become a mini-celebrity. Your lecture fees go up. People want to know your opinion, even when your main task as a journalist is supposed to be to gather the opinions of others. I'm always amazed watching some Washington-based shows when they have as a guest the speaker of the house or a Cabinet member, and they have the official wait as pundits opine on what is really happening in the nation's capital. The official was there less as a source of information than as a prop for the pundits.

We reporters enjoy First Amendment protections, but we don't have subpoena power. People don't have to talk to us. They do for many reasons, among them that they trust we are searching for the honest truth. The less we listen, the less they will talk to us.

They also talk to us, sometimes, because we promise them anonymity, which is why the case of Judy Miller of the *New York Times* is so important. By refusing to divulge sources she had promised confidentiality, Miller is standing up for all journalists. Name a scandal—Watergate, insider trading, Enron, political corruption, Abu Ghraib. How many of these would have seen the light of day without anonymous sources? Very few. We protect the public's right to know when we protect sources who want the information out in the public arena but don't want to lose their livelihoods. Yet if those sources believe journalists will not protect their confidentiality, we all lose.

Lack of humility often leads to a fourth vice: hubris. There's a fine line between losing the humility to listen and becoming truly self-important. After she brilliantly exposed Abu Ghraib prison abuses, CBS producer Mary Mapes became so full of herself, I suspect, that she became too convinced of her own infallibility, too zealously determined to prove that

George W. Bush cheated. He may have. But journalism is about proving, not asserting, facts.

Howell Raines lost his job in 2003 as editor of the *New York Times* not because he wasn't a good journalist but because of hubris. Like Caesar, he thought most of those in his employ were inferior. He would abuse and insult them, hold meetings in which the dialogue went one way, be cheap with compliments, and somehow he thought this would raise what he liked to say was "the metabolism" of the paper. Raines helped the paper win a miraculous seven Pulitzer Prizes because of the brilliant job he did as editor after 9/11. But by the time of the Jayson Blair disclosures in 2003, he had wasted all his capital, and the newsroom rose up to demand a less hubristic chief.

Hubris, of course, is common to the business world. The merger in 2000 between AOL and Time Warner failed because of hubris. Executives behind this deal thought they could ignore cultural differences between the companies, thought they could will the two companies to grow by 30 percent per year—and when they couldn't meet this arrogant goal, their stock collapsed. Dennis Kozlowski, the former CEO of Tyco, came to think of himself as an emperor who could charge to the company the cost of an extravagant birthday party for his wife.

Finally, a fifth vice: bias. There is much discussion these days about press bias. And I believe we do see examples of political bias in the press. If you were watching Fox News during the aftermath of Hurricane Katrina, you could not fail to notice that in the early days Fox often rooted for their conservative commander-in-chief. If you read the *New York Times* accounts of abortion or gun control or poverty you will sometimes discern a liberal bias. You would see bias at CNN when Ted Turner was in charge and the network ran pro-environmental stories.

But I don't believe the dominant press bias is political. Deputy White House chief of staff Karl Rove said in a speech in April that "the press is less liberal than it is oppositional." Every president, be he a Democrat or Republican, complains about the press, just as most every mayor and governor does. And what they most often complain about is that we spend unhealthy amounts of time seeking out conflict.

There's another way to describe this bias for conflict. It is often a market-driven bias—for conflict, for sizzle, for wow, for keeping our audience entertained. And, of course, for getting scoops.

Some believe Dan Rather has a liberal bias. But if Rather got a story about John Kerry faking his wounds in Vietnam, he'd have run with it. Just as the so-called "liberal" *New York Times* pounced on stories recounting the quick profits Hillary Clinton once made in the commodities markets.

One sees the bias for conflict in press coverage of the Swift Boat Veterans, or of Bush and the National Guard, or of the endless caravan of polls we conduct, telling readers or viewers who's ahead this week.

At the same time, the press too often downplays vital issues a president must confront. While we gauge who's ahead in the latest poll, we often ignore what Bush's tax cuts will do to the budget deficit, or how much Kerry's promises would have cost. With baby boomers about to retire, we don't sufficiently explore how our Social Security contract will be fulfilled. We did not pay attention when the president and the Congress cut appropriations to secure the levees in New Orleans. The media often find these stories boring. In truth, the public probably does as well.

We see a bias for conflict and sizzle elsewhere, in the World War III–like coverage of the Michael Jackson trial, or of a missing teenager in Aruba.

We see it in a preoccupation with ratings and circulation.

These, too, are ethical issues, for the people who sign our checks want more sizzle, more gotcha stories that attract more customers. They have a market-driven bias that can distort good journalism.

Interestingly, this analysis is shared by many on the left and the right. The left is comfortable talking about market-driven biases, about the excesses of capitalism. In doing a story nearly two years ago on the Bush White House and the press, I was surprised to learn that Bush shared this analysis. Of course, the Bush White House did not condemn capitalism. But they did condemn the press's search for the sensational, for selling more newspapers or finding stories that would boost the ratings.

Believing that the press is interested in the sensational, which is too often true, the Bush White House goes overboard and treats the press as a special interest, not as people who serve the public interest. Of course, if we don't represent the public, they don't have to talk to us. "What about the press's checks-and-balances function?" I asked White House chief of staff Andrew Card. "You don't have a checks-and-balances role," he said. That is the role of Congress and the courts. This is a major reason the Bush administration has held fewer press conferences than any modern president and is often so hostile to the press.

What's the solution? I don't have an easy antidote. I do start with this: In journalism, form dictates content. Tell a reporter he or she has only five hundred words—fewer if it's a TV story—and they need a lead and "a nut graph" that gets to the essence of the story right away, and that form almost surely dictates the content of the story. So what would I do?

1. I would give journalists more time and more space. Too often, journalists are like firefighters. The alarm rings, and we race to cover a story. Many of these are false alarms. They are stories we are reacting to, not thinking about. Or we spend our time at the press briefing asking sharp, conflict-oriented questions. Many of these are mindless questions.

   Live news has some of the same problems. Technology is a great friend of journalism. We can go live from anywhere in the world. Light, handheld cameras allow us to travel quickly. First faxes, then cell phones, then the Internet, allowed citizens in the most repressive countries to communicate with the outside world, to become our eyes and ears. But journalism is about sifting information, finding different voices, trying to get at the complex truth, offering context. It is not just a bird's-eye view. Live television or Webcasts—or blogs—can be like fireworks, dazzling, awesome, but soon the sky is dark again.

   We see the value of time and space with the contextual coverage of Hurricane Katrina days after it struck New Orleans. We see it in Bob Woodward's second book about George W. Bush, *Plan of Attack*, where we learned how the president really made decisions. We see it in Seymour Hersh's accounts of the war in Afghanistan or Abu Ghraib in *The New Yorker*.

2. Journalists and their editors and the people who sign our checks have to be willing to risk boring our audience by reporting on dry but vital subjects like budget deficits or underfunded Social Security. It's not easy, but good storytellers can find ways to make the turgid come alive.

3. "Objectivity" is a false God. We are human beings, and we screw up or have biases that are hidden from us. But fairness is possible; balance is possible; not stereotyping the people we write about is possible; conveying complexity is possible. We can be skeptical without being cynical.

   Journalism need not seek a false balance. We need not say, "It is alleged that the Bush administration claims it is shrinking the deficit." We can find out if that claim is true or false. We are not reporting on a Ping-Pong match, where we report the ping and the pong of the contestants. If we are to serve the public, sometimes the press must referee. We are not there to judge who is right or wrong, but we are there to adjudicate facts.

4. As we need many voices and localism in media, so we need diversity in our newsrooms. Big media tend to homogenize, but so does a newsroom that is not made up of diverse races and religions and political views.

5. There are those who believe a partisan press is an answer. They believe different newspapers and magazines and TV networks openly championing a party or a point of view—as was true in America in the nineteenth century, or is often true in Europe today—will produce a marketplace of ideas. I believe the opposite is true. If you think what I and other journalists report is dictated by partisanship, then we will further polarize American society. Conservatives will seek facts from their outlets and liberals from theirs. There will be no common set of facts. The press will be even more distrusted than it is today. And the consensus on which a democracy is predicated will be harder to achieve.

6. Journalists need to better communicate to the business folks who sign our checks. We have to find a language to help them understand that they will not be able to build a valuable journalistic brand without good journalism, which is expensive. This communication chasm between us will be hard to bridge.

7. If we truly shared the same assumption that journalists were public ser-vants and had a public trust, we would better address the five deadly vices. If journalists were constantly reminded of their public trust, we would be humbler. We would make more effort to combat our biases. We would worry less about synergy and brand and more about trust and credibility.

8. Finally, be prepared to be fired.

I am not alarmed that many of these eight points feed the perception that journalists are elitists. If journalism wants to call itself a profession, and if democracy depends on information, then journalists work for the public interest not by granting the public a vote over what we do. We can't be like a politician who just follows the polls. Our job is not to just shovel at the public what they think they want, because what they want changes. Or is sometimes wrong. Look how it changed after 9/11. Before 9/11, the public was less interested in Islam and international news. After 9/11, they asked why the media hadn't told them more about Osama bin Laden and Islam. The public wants more Angelina and Brad, more Runaway Bride. But does that mean we must give it to them?

A decade ago in Dallas, I interviewed Intel CEO and chairman Andy Grove at the annual meeting of the American Society of Newspaper Editors. The Internet was just taking off, and people were predicting that in the future we would not need middlemen, neither editors nor networks. We would program for ourselves. So I asked Grove, "In the future, what will be the value of the editors in this hall?"

He looked out at the sea of a thousand editors and said, "Zero. In the future we will not need you. We will create our own newspapers online. We will design it ourselves. We will not need an 'intelligent agent.' If I am interested in health news and sports, that is the news I will read. But you will not decide. I will decide. It will be My Newspaper."

Three years later, I was questioning Grove on another public stage and I asked, "You once predicted that newspapers would have little value in the future because the Internet allowed everyone to create My Newspaper. Do you still believe this?"

"No," he said. "I was totally wrong. I did not appreciate the value of serendipity. I could not predict that I would want to know about Sarajevo or Rwanda. I realize that we do need 'intelligent agents' to help us sort out important information."

Ted Koppel said here five years ago that anyone can be a journalist. Bloggers and the Internet and cell phones with digital cameras deputize citizens to act as journalists. This is great, and when the tsunami struck South Asia or Hurricane Katrina struck the American South, the first horrifying pictures came from citizen journalists who turned their digital cameras and e-mails on to describe the giant waves and horrible devastation. But not everyone can be a good journalist. A good journalist is trained to give context, to get all sides of a story, to be fair, to be accurate, to give more than a bird's-eye view of reality.

So whom do we work for? You don't always know it, and sometimes we don't live up to it, but journalists are as much public servants as the people you elect to office.

So the next time you wonder, "How do I square my sense that the press screws up with the argument that the press serves a vital public service? How do I square the sensational and the serious, the way the press got weapons of mass destruction wrong and got right the failure of the Bush administration to respond quickly enough to the devastation of Hurricane Katrina? What's the answer to those paradoxes?"

I think F. Scott Fitzgerald had the correct answer to this riddle when he said that "the test of a first-rate intelligence is the ability to hold two opposed ideas in the mind at the same time and still retain the ability to function."

That, my friends, is a long but pretty accurate bumper sticker.

A Very Pious Story

RED SMITH

NEW YORK HERALD TRIBUNE

MAY 4, 1948

At the Derby, Walter Haight, a well-fed horse author from Washington, told it this way.

There's this horseplayer, and he can't win a bet. He's got patches in his pants from the way even odds-on favorites run up the alley when he's backing them, and the slump goes on until he's utterly desperate. He's ready to listen to any advice when a friend tells him, "No wonder you don't have any luck; you don't live right. Nobody could do any good the way you live. Why, you don't even go to church. Why don't you get yourself straightened out and try to be a decent citizen and just see then if things don't get a lot better for you?"

Now, the guy has never exactly liked to bother heaven with his troubles. Isn't even sure whether they have horse racing up there and would understand his difficulties. But he's reached a state where steps simply have to be taken. So, the next day being Sunday, he does go to church and sits attentively through the whole service and joins in the hymn singing and says "Amen" at the proper times and puts his buck on the collection plate.

All that night he lies awake waiting for a sign that things are going to get better; nothing happens. Next day he gets up and goes to the track, but this time he doesn't buy a racing form or scratch sheet or Jack Green's Card or anything. Just gets his program and sits in the stands studying the field for the first race and waiting for a sign. None comes, so he passes up the race. He waits for the second race and concentrates on the names of the horses for that one, and again there's no inspiration. So again he doesn't bet. Then, when he's looking them over for the third, something seems to tell him to bet on a horse named Number 4.

"Lord, I'll do it," he says, and he goes down and puts the last $50 he'll ever be able to borrow on Number 4 to win. Then he goes back to his seat and waits until the horses come onto the track.

Number 4 is a little fractious in the parade, and the guy says, "Lord, please quiet him down. Don't let him get himself hurt." The horse settles down immediately and walks calmly into the starting gate.

"Thank you, Lord," says the guy. "Now please get him off clean. He don't have to break on top, but get him away safe without getting slammed or anything, please." The gate comes open and Number 4 is off well, close up in fifth place and saving ground going to the first turn. There he begins to move up a trifle on the rail and for an instant it looks as though he might be in close quarters.

"Let him through, Lord," the guy says. "Please make them horses open up a little for him." The horse ahead moves out just enough to let Number 4 through safely.

"Thank you, Lord," says the guy, "but let's not have no more trouble like that. Have the boy take him outside." Sure enough, as they go down the backstretch the jockey steers Number 4 outside, where he's lying fourth.

They're going to the far turn when the guy gets agitated. "Don't let that boy use up the horse," he says. "Don't let the kid get panicky, Lord. Tell him to rate the horse

awhile." The rider reaches down and takes a couple of raps on the horse and keeps him running kind, just cooking on the outside around the turn.

Wheeling into the stretch, Number 4 is still lying fourth. "Now, Lord," the guy says, "Now we move. Tell that kid to go to the stick." The boy outs with his bat and, as Ted Atkinson says, he really "scouges" the horse. Number 4 lays his ears back and gets to running.

He's up to third. He closes the gap ahead, and now he's lapped on the second horse, and now he's at his throat latch, and now he's past him. He's moving on the leader, and everything behind him is good and cooked. He closes ground stride by stride, with the boy working on him for all he's worth and the kid up front putting his horse to a drive.

"Please, Lord," the guy says. "Let him get out in front. Give me one call on the top end, anyway."

Number 4 keeps coming. At the eighth pole he's got the leader collared. He's past him He's got the lead by two lengths.

"Thank you, Lord," the guy says, "I'll take him from here. Come on, you son of a bitch!"

JUDY WOODRUFF Formerly chief White House correspondent for NBC News and an anchor at CNN, Judy Woodruff is a senior correspondent on the *PBS NewsHour* and moderator of the monthly program *Conversations with Judy Woodruff* on Bloomberg Television. From 1983 until 1993, she served as chief Washington correspondent for *The MacNeil/Lehrer NewsHour*. Recipient of an Emmy Award and the Edward R. Murrow Award, she is the author of *This Is Judy Woodruff at the White House* (1982). She delivered this lecture on April 12, 2007.

JUDY WOODRUFF

Are Journalists Obsolete?

I am so pleased to be at Notre Dame, particularly to participate in a lecture series celebrating the remarkable career of Red Smith.

Unlike Walter Wellesley Smith and his son, my good friend Terry, no one in our family attended this distinguished university. We do have some Notre Dame ties, however.

My husband is a trustee at Wake Forest University, which several years ago selected your former provost, Nathan Hatch, to be its president. A Presbyterian becoming a president of a formerly Baptist college with the invocation given by a Catholic priest. (That was Father Theodore Hesburgh. If you can't get God, that's the next best choice.)

It was a scene that would have pleased Jefferson and Madison.

Our oldest son's godfather is Mark Shields, the columnist and commentator and a graduate of the class of 1959. Mark's spiritual impact was clear when Jeffrey's first words were "Beat USC."

I know there has been some anxiety over Notre Dame's football fortunes recently. I can only say, as an alumna of Duke University and an avid Blue Devil basketball fan, that after this past year, I feel your pain.

Among the reasons it's so special to be here is the man who introduced me. Terry Smith and I have been friends and colleagues for more than three decades. He has been a valued associate, a great journalist at the *New York Times*, at CBS, and at *The NewsHour with Jim Lehrer*, and he's now doing longer form pieces and articles.

There is something else that makes Terry special. It cannot always be easy to be the son or daughter of a legend, especially following in the same trade. Consider how few offspring of prominent politicians or business leaders have similarly succeeded.

Terry has—and more. Although he covered foreign and political news, not sports, he continued the great family tradition of which there can be no higher praise.

As the history of twentieth-century American journalism is written, Red Smith has taken his place with the Lippmanns, the Murrows, the Bradlees, and the Ted Turners as one of the towering figures. He once observed that there's "nothing to writing. All you do is sit down at a typewriter and open a vein." If only it were so easy for us mortals.

He has been gone for more than a quarter century, but that grace, that style, those unique insights endure. I just gave my twenty-year-old son, who loves sports, the book *Red Smith on Baseball*.

The title of our conversation this evening—"Are Journalists Obsolete?"—is of more than passing interest to me. Next year my husband, also a journalist, and I expect to have three children in college; whether it makes for the best narrative, my answer thus will be no.

Yet that question no longer seems frivolous.

We, or at least we of the so-called mainstream media, seem perpetually pessimistic these days, and not without cause.

Every year the Project for Excellence in Journalism, sponsored by the Pew Research Center, does a survey on the State of the News Media. The 2007 report is not encouraging. Virtually every media sector—newspapers, network television, local television, cable television, national magazines—is losing readers or viewers. Moreover, most of these venues are investing fewer resources in covering the news.

Newspapers have lost circulation for three consecutive years, down about 7 percent.

One of the country's great journalistic chains, Knight-Ridder, vanished last year, bought by the McClatchey chain, and then major papers (like the *Philadelphia Inquirer*) were sold again. Knight-Ridder was a profitable company with margins that many industries would die for—just not profitable enough for Wall Street and this climate. The bottom line trumped the journalistic line.

The Tribune Company, with its flagship *Chicago Tribune* and crown jewel acquisition, the *Los Angeles Times*, may soon cease to exist as we have known it. Few expect that will produce better journalism. I hope we're wrong.

Dow Jones, the owner of the *Wall Street Journal*, has a market capitalization today that is half what it was seven years ago; the *Journal*, in a cost-saving move, has reduced the physical size of the newspaper.

The *Baltimore Sun* and *Boston Globe*, once two of America's prized regional newspapers, have eliminated all their foreign bureaus. The *Dallas*

Morning News, which in the 1980s and 1990s transformed itself from a mediocre to a superb paper, is retrenching.

Anxiety abounds at even the most successful places. Arthur Sulzberger, Jr., the publisher of the *New York Times*, told an interviewer, "I don't know whether we'll be printing [the print edition of] the *New York Times* in five years, and you know what? I don't care." The central growth and profit center for the Washington Post Company is not its flagship newspaper, the *Washington Post*, or *Newsweek* magazine, but Kaplan Educational Services, a tutoring program.

Any great journalistic venture needs three central elements: integrity, ambition, and resources. And the best guarantor of that is ownership, and the best ownership is a family with values.

Yet the Chandlers of the *Los Angeles Times* and the Binghams of the *Louisville Courier Journal* and the Knights illustrate an irrefutable reality: Journalistic families, like others, grow in geometric proportions, and journalistic values and pride usually erode with generational change.

One salvation, some argue, is private ownership, which is not as subject to the quarterly private passions of publicly traded companies. Yet experiences in Santa Barbara and apparently now in Philadelphia suggest that this is no panacea.

In my business of television news, the picture is no more encouraging. Network news audiences are steadily declining, and fewer and fewer resources are devoted to covering the news. The expendability of a Ted Koppel crystallizes the difference, not just in degree but in kind, from the values of less than a generation ago.

The world, everyone agrees, is far more interdependent today than ten or twenty years ago. What happens in Shanghai or Berlin or Tehran profoundly affects us. Yet there are only half as many foreign correspondents today for CBS, ABC, or NBC as there were two decades ago. After September 11, there were countless stories on why we do not understand each other around the world. But on that day none of the television networks had a correspondent based in a predominantly Muslim country. Not one.

Cable television news, the Excellence in Journalism survey reports, is now facing many of the same concerns of the older media; to adjust it is focusing more of its programming around personality and opinion shows and therefore less on news coverage.

I worked at CNN for twelve years; it was a terrific place, and I consider Ted Turner one of the genuinely influential journalistic leaders in American history. In taking CNN from an idea in his head to the 24/7 global news network that has had a transforming effect on TV news, and arguably on print news as well, he proved all the skeptics—who told him he was crazy—wrong. He didn't care what people thought, or else he never would have taken the chance he did, which lost money for the first several years it was on the air.

I fully expected as cable competition grew and matured that one of those news outlets would calculate—for business reasons—that there is a market for quality journalism: "Let's try to get Jim Lehrer away from public television or provide a new home for Ted Koppel." It has not occurred.

Local television news, most radio news, and magazines offer, if anything, an even bleaker picture.

Moreover, even apart from the dismal economic realities, the press has suffered a series of credibility cataclysms: the Jayson Blair scandal at America's most prestigious newspaper, the failure to report on the government's duplicity *before* the Iraq war, and the Scooter Libby trial, which revealed a seamy underside of Washington journalism, cozy relationships, and promiscuous promises of anonymity that seemed to put the interests of sources and accessibility ahead of that of readers and viewers.

Then there is the blogosphere. There is, of course, much more to this than news. There are single-parenting blogs, Red Sox blogs, celebrity culture blogs, and, unfortunately, a proliferation of pornographic sites.

The overall explosion is stunning. In 1999 there were twenty-three blogs. Today there are almost 30 million, and the blogosphere doubles in size about every six months.

It certainly is playing a large role in the dissemination of news and information; just look at all the attention the 2008 presidential candidates are paying to the Web in all of its forms.

There is much to celebrate. It is participatory, enabling people in Enderlin, North Dakota, or Edenton, North Carolina, to create a virtual community as well as people in Manhattan or Manhattan Beach. It has energized the political interest of many citizens in an outlet less dependent on commercial pressures.

There have been huge triumphs: The stories forcing Trent Lott to step down as Senate majority leader in 2002, the exposé of the CBS report on George W. Bush's alleged draft evasion, and the current controversy over Attorney General Alberto Gonzales's firing of eight U.S. attorneys were all driven by the blogs.

Yet, journalistically, this is a new world, much of which ignores the best of the old-media values. There is little accountability. Matt Drudge continues to flourish, despite a plethora of false stories that he has run time and again that would have cost most good newspaper or broadcast editors their jobs. Stories—from the Swift Boat misrepresentations in the 2004 campaign to the phony story on Barack Obama supposedly having attended a Madrassa school—that have been picked up by the mainstream media and become part of the dialogue.

There will be vast changes in the times ahead, though this reality is unlikely to be altered. With its independent spirit, "ultimately," one smart blogger recently observed, "blogging is not a practice over which you can hope to establish broadly accepted rules of engagement."

Further, however much traditional print and broadcast venues switch to online, there is a genuine worry whether they will have or be willing to expend the resources required for some of the most important journalism.

The *New York Times* worked for more than a year on the exposé about illicit government eavesdropping in the wake of 9/11. That type of story doesn't come from one simple tip from a source or one purloined document.

And one of the most impressive journalistic achievements in my time in Washington was the multipart *Washington Post* series this past winter on the mistreatment of wounded Iraq and Afghanistan veterans at Walter Reed Army Medical Center. Those stories personified everything journalism aspires to be: an impeccably reported story that gave voice to the powerless and resulted in punishment for the arrogantly powerful, producing the promise of real change.

But two top *Washington Post* reporters, Dana Priest and Anne Hull, spent four months, full-time, reporting this story under difficult circumstances. With the research and editing time, the *Post* probably devoted a year's worth of work to a piece for which there was no guarantee of success.

Will the new media or the reconstituted media in two or five or ten years be willing to devote the kind of resources and take the necessary risks that produce seminal stories like that one or like the stories that the *New York Times* did on eavesdropping?

All right, you're asking, back to tonight's topic, and now that I've made Robert Novak seem like the Prince of Lightness, why do I believe the journalism that Terry Smith and I grew up in—or the journalists who practice it—are not obsolete?

There are three compelling, convincing reasons.

One is to look at some of the other journalism being practiced these days. Papers like the *Times* and *Post*—and certainly the *Los Angeles Times* even under harrowing conditions—continue to provide a vital public service.

There are Tim Russert and Bob Schieffer's Sunday interview shows, the *Economist* magazine, Charlie Rose's public broadcasting program, the foundation that owns and operates the *St. Petersburg Times*, and much of C-SPAN.

These disparate outlets share two common elements: They do good journalism, and their reach and influence continue to grow.

Let me cite three others with which I am associated and thus very familiar.

National Public Radio. For the past decade, the audience and public trust for NPR have grown steadily. To be sure, this was aided by the generous gift exceeding $200 million from Joan Kroc, the McDonald's Corporation heiress, who I understand has also been generous to Notre Dame. But it reflects the commitment to serious, high-quality reporting of news, achieved often with an intellectually interesting and appealing narrative. NPR is actually fun to listen to, and you're learning at the same time.

Bloomberg News. I do a monthly interview program for Bloomberg Television, and my husband runs the Washington print and broadcast operations. Seventeen years ago Bloomberg News didn't exist; today it has 2,200 print and broadcast editors and reporters in 134 bureaus around the world. Every day there are hundreds of well-reported stories from around the globe, principally on finance and economics, but also on politics, sports, and culture. It is a different business model, subscription rather than advertising-driven.

And third, *The NewsHour with Jim Lehrer*, my once and now again home.

The NewsHour, some critics have declared, dares to be dull. Five nights a week we offer serious, thoughtful debate and dialogue on issues of relevance to our society. The best response to those critics is to paraphrase Red Smith, who once said that baseball "is dull only to those with dull minds."

And we average 1.2 million adult viewers a night; that's more than Bill O'Reilly, the top-rated cable program on public affairs. It's more than double the audience of CNN at that hour, and almost four times that of the MSNBC audience. We like our dull minds.

This leads to the second reason that I am optimistic that journalism, as practiced by the Terry and the Red Smiths, is not obsolete. There is a demand for good content. When you aggregate these audiences for all the programs cited above, it is not small.

What good journalists provide is good content, not just information; good content is not just content. It is content where there has been thought, consideration, research. People have sat around a room and discussed, "What is it that we should be covering? What are we hearing from our viewers and our readers that they want us to be covering?"

There is much discussion today about the conflict between the old media and the new media.

That obscures the fact that most of the old media are desperately seeking to adapt to the new world; imagine a newspaper or broadcast journalist who doesn't Google. And most of the new media is derivative; how many stories on blogs can you recall that cannot be traced to newspapers or broadcasts?

And most top news organizations are adapting to a hybrid news model, with a Web staff. Some of the best newspapers—the *Washington Post* and *New York Times*—are competing to develop the most innovative and attractive approach to their Web sites; many are integrating their print and Web operations. They are trying to figure out how to get the Web people and the print people to work together. Similar innovations are taking place in broadcasting at both the national and local levels.

As for the best business model, this remains elusive. Whether it will primarily be subscription- or advertising-driven, or something in between, or altogether different, will be determined by the market.

But whatever the problems, whatever the growing pains, whatever creative destruction the market system produces, the demand and the need for high-quality content will persist. I believe it will not only persist, it will grow. And it will not be satiated by Drudge or Daily Kos or even two of my favorites, Jon Stewart or Stephen Colbert.

I became more convinced this demand for good content will grow—with a more educated and involved citizenry—after spending most of last year on the multimedia documentary project on the group we call "Generation Next"—the students at Notre Dame and their counterparts, in and out of college, ages sixteen to twenty-five.

We talked with them about their hopes, dreams, and aspirations; their views on everything from politics to religion, America's role in the world, family, the values that matter to them, the role of technology in their world—the Internet, cell phones, and iPods—and much more.

We discovered that they—you—are the most diverse generation in American history: 17 percent Hispanic, 14 percent African American, 4 percent Asian, and another significant percentage mixed race. One in every five of them has a parent born outside the United States; one in every eight of them was himself or herself born outside the United States; no wonder they are surprisingly comfortable with people who look and sound different from them. They've grown up with, lived down the street from, or gone to school with young people of many different races, ethnic backgrounds, religions, and cultural values.

Their political attitudes tend to be more liberal. They're more likely than their elders to say that immigration has been good for the country and more likely than those over twenty-six to favor gay rights and even marriage for homosexuals.

What was most clear is that their political attitudes often defy stereotype; in our research, and through the young people we met, we found them frequently carving out their own unique views of the role of government and of the responsibility of citizens.

We found them surprisingly well informed. More than people give them credit for, they were up on national and international events and skeptical of politics (based on what they've seen coming out of Washington the last few years). They're not great readers of newspapers, but they follow news on the Internet and, to some extent, on television. You won't be surprised to know that *The Daily Show with Jon Stewart* was the favorite by far for this generation.

As we learned, something out there is piquing their interest and perhaps creating a thirst to be better informed about the war in Iraq, the cost of college education, the state of the environment, and the economy, as it impacts their ability to find jobs and earn a good living. These were things they told us time and again were on their minds.

Just as interesting, and just as important, we also learned through research that they are more interested in the community around them—in doing something for their fellow man and woman—where they can see tangible results.

More of Generation Next is volunteering to join Teach for America, the Peace Corps, and programs like them. More are giving of their time to tutor underprivileged kids, to volunteer in soup kitchens, or to start neighborhood programs—in the United States or overseas—around poverty, hunger, lack of opportunity, and the environment. This younger generation, in fact, is doing as much volunteer work—is as civically engaged—as any other generation of our time. The political scientists are wondering whether this will lead one day to greater political involvement by this generation.

A generation that is civic-minded, is looking for a better politics, and is more inclusive is a generation that, I think, will be more receptive to good journalism. The form may vary or evolve, and the technology may be quite different, but to meet those demands and to satisfy those minds requires good content. There is one way that will be provided, and that's with good journalism.

And let's hope there is always an appreciation for the excellence in writing personified by none other than the Notre Dame class of 1927 graduate Red Smith.

For people who are caring and curious, the question is relevance.

If anyone asks if Red Smith would be relevant today, I'd call his or her attention to the column he wrote after the October 1951 National League playoff contest between the New York Giants and the Brooklyn Dodgers. That was the famous game in which Bobby Thomson hit a home run in the bottom of the ninth to beat the Dodgers.

Titled "Miracle of Coogan's Bluff," Red Smith's column the next morning began, "Now it is done. Now the story ends. And there is no way to tell it. The art of fiction is dead. Reality has strangled invention. Only the utterly impossible, the inexpressibly fantastic, can ever be plausible again."

What makes that column and so many others stand out is that it was so beautifully written. This was such a huge event in the world of baseball, America's pastime, that by the next morning, practically everyone in the country knew about it. That wasn't true of all sporting news back then; even with the greater readership of newspapers, television was still in its infancy.

There will always be a demand for the sort of brilliant insight Red Smith provided on that morning in October of 1951—like shining a bright light on a story, showing it in a way no one ever thought to see it. We need that even more today than we did then.

I'm honored to be with you this evening.

Thank you very much.

Questions and Answers

QUESTION: *How much independence and security do you have at* The NewsHour with Jim Lehrer?

JUDY WOODRUFF: How much independence and security? Well, we've got a lot of independence because ever since Jim Lehrer and Robert MacNeil started the program—they started a half-hour show back in 1975 and then expanded it to an hour in 1983—they've had autonomy. They've been able to put the program they wanted on the air. They both came to the program with years of experience as journalists in their own right.

Robert MacNeil had been a television journalist for NBC. He had traveled the world and had covered stories everywhere. Jim Lehrer came out of print journalism—he had a distinguished career as a newspaperman—and had begun to work in public television. Together they created something different, something unique. It remains unique today, twenty-four years after they began the half-hour MacNeil/Lehrer program, and it remains independent.

Financially, the program is on good, sound financial footing, but like every other news program and every other public affairs program in public television, it's harder to raise money these days for good news programming. Corporations used to want to be associated with a program like *Meet the Press* or Ted Koppel's *Nightline*, just to name a few. Today, advertising agencies have more sway. There is much more concern about the bottom line every quarter. Wall Street is looking at whether the books are balanced and if companies are not only making money every quarter but making more money than they made in the last quarter. There's intense pressure on all the profit-making companies, and those are the people or the organizations that have been more likely to give money.

Now, if you watch *The NewsHour*, you'll see it also gets money from foundations, and that has continued to be the case. *The NewsHour* is in good shape financially, but it is harder to bring that money in.

We have a wonderful team of people, led by our former executive producer Les Crystal, who is out there talking to a lot of current contributors and potential contributors. If any of you would like to sponsor *The NewsHour*, we will be glad to talk to you after the lecture tonight.

QUESTION: *I've noticed that CNN in recent years has been phasing out a lot of their older anchors, especially the women, and I've also noticed that they've been moving to more showbiz coverage. They have the entertainment segment at night, and they have strong characters, like Nancy Grace and Glenn Beck, who have one-hour shows, so there are time periods in the evening when you cannot have headline news. I know that they are trying to attract a younger audience, but I don't know if they are really succeeding in doing that, and I am wondering if you think they will ever go back to a more traditional approach to attracting audiences.*

JUDY WOODRUFF: Well, the truth is, and I think that I suggested this earlier, the cable networks are in a very different environment today from the environment when Ted Turner founded CNN in 1980. Back then it was CNN all to itself: CNN covering the world 24/7 with a heavy emphasis on news. As the years have gone by, competition has arisen from Fox News and from MSNBC and the Internet and so many other local or regional cable news outlets out there. Virtually every day you wake up and there is more competition. So, with more choices, the audience for each outlet is shrinking.

It's not entirely clear where people are getting their news. We know that the audience for broadcast television has shrunk, and we are now looking at a leveling off of the cable news audience. You've got three channels, plus everything else I mentioned competing for that audience. What does that mean? It means that they are going to do whatever they can—within the boundaries of what they think they can get away with—to attract an audience.

That means a lot of coverage of Anna Nicole Smith; the Runaway Bride was one of my favorites a few years ago; Michael Jackson. I remember we spent hours when I was at CNN following Michael Jackson, waiting to see when he was going to show up at the courthouse. The day he showed up in his pajamas, I think we were on the courthouse picture for about an hour and a half.

The other day CNN devoted—and I think the other cable channels did, too—a little over an hour to the coverage of the Rutgers women's basketball team's news conference focusing on the controversy surrounding Don Imus. So they are covering those types of developing stories, and I would say, of course, when there's breaking news, they gravitate to that. It's in those periods—when there is not an obvious story—that you find them, in effect, falling all over themselves trying to find ways to keep the audience.

The fact is, they're a business, and if they don't keep the audience, if they don't keep the eyeballs, then they can't keep going as a business. So, do I think it's going to turn around? I hate to tell you no, but I don't think so.

I think we are going to be looking to some of the venues I mentioned earlier as good examples: some of the Sunday shows on the networks; what Ted Koppel used to do at ABC and is now doing periodically for the Discovery Channel; NPR. There will be other venues that will come up, and I think the Internet offers some good prospects for programming. But I think we've passed the time when we can expect to see wall-to-wall coverage of serious news.

QUESTION: *Do you write your own material and decide what you're going to talk about?*

JUDY WOODRUFF: On *The NewsHour*? Yes, I do. Now, we have a staff of writers and producers, and we work as a team in putting the program together. For example, there will be a team of people who may do a first draft, but whoever is anchoring the program—and it's usually Jim Lehrer—will then go in and rewrite everything.

For instance, last night I did an interview with two reporters on the John McCain campaign, because John McCain made an announcement yesterday about his position on the Iraq war, hoping to relaunch his campaign. He's had a lot of problems recently. I had the assistance of two or three off-air reporters who did the research for me, and I made additional phone calls and put it together.

Television is very much a team effort. We write as much as we possibly can. Sometimes, if we are doing three or four things simultaneously, we may have to depend on somebody else, but we certainly edit everything that we do on the air. Ultimately it is the product of the person who is speaking it.

QUESTION: *You implied that journalists are going to have to evolve in the future. I wonder if you could give us a little more detail about what a journalist in ten or twenty years is going to have to retain, going to have to lose, and going to have to develop from the journalist of today. Is that going to be possible, and will good writing be enough?*

JUDY WOODRUFF: A very, very good question, and I'm glad that you asked it. I think good writing is at the very core of what we do as journalists. In fact, when young people ask me, "What should I major in? Should I major in broadcast journalism or something else?" I say it doesn't much matter what your major is, but my strong recommendation is that you get the best liberal arts education that you can.

Study history, study economics, learn a little bit about psychology, philosophy, religion. Learn about all of these things, and write as much as you can, because whether you go into print journalism, television, or certainly now the Internet, you've got to be able to write. Whether you're writing long form, where you have a day or weeks to write a piece, or whether you've got minutes to write, writing is a skill that's always going to be essential. So I would say that's the bottom line.

Beyond that, I would say be prepared to be flexible. We don't know into what form journalism will evolve. Television isn't about to go away. So if you're interested in television journalism, writing is still important. You will need all the reporting skills that you would pick up whether you're working for a newspaper or working for the Internet.

I think what's very important is that these new forms of journalism retain some of the core values we prize today in our great journalistic institutions and that they begin to develop accountability and transparency. There is going to have to be, I think, a system of accountability, and we in the media are only as good as our credibility.

If we're giving you information that you can rely on, that you can trust, it seems to me that's worth its weight in gold. There were plenty of times, for example on CNN, when we didn't have the whole story yet but still were on the air; I always tried to say, "This is all we know, this is what we have heard up to this moment." Transparency will become increasingly important because viewers and readers are smarter today than ever about the media. They follow where you get your information. They're comparing sources with other sources, so we are all going to need to be more open, and when I say transparent that's what I mean: We need to be clearer about how we get our information, including what we left out.

We only have a minute or two minutes to do a typical story, if it is television. We can offer more on our Web site. If you're doing a story for a newspaper, there will be guidance to readers to look at the Web site.

I think writing and flexibility are important. Just be prepared, because it's like getting on a wild ride at the amusement park: You don't know where you're going to come out. Most people I know who are very smart about journalism aren't really sure today what it's going to look like in ten years. Those of you who inherit journalism, who are the next generation of reporters and editors and producers, it's really going to be in your hands.

QUESTION: *Have you written a book?*

JUDY WOODRUFF: I wrote a book with help right after I had my first child in 1981. I'll tell you the story very quickly. I was covering the White House for NBC, and the *Washington Post* had asked me to keep a journal for the first month or month and a half of the Reagan presidency about what it's like being a television reporter in the White House, and I did. I kept a daily journal and transformed it into an article for the *Post* Sunday magazine in the spring of 1981, right after Ronald Reagan went into office.

Some publishers called and said, "We liked it. We'd like you to turn it into a book." Coincidentally, I was pregnant with my first child, and I foolishly agreed. In retrospect, I wish I hadn't, because in order to get it done and get it done by the deadline, I had to work with a writer who came in and basically just interviewed me nonstop for about three months and then helped me turn that into a book. But it was not perfect. It came out after my son was born, and it was a time when I was paying more attention to my son.

But that's the book that I've written. I'm not sure that I'm ever going to write another one. I am surrounded by writers. My boss at *The NewsHour*, Jim Lehrer, seems to turn out a book a year, and they're all successful. Robert MacNeil has written books, so I probably will eventually write a book. The idea that at thirty-four you would write about your career is a little, well, full of yourself.

QUESTION: *What is the title of it?*

JUDY WOODRUFF: It's out of print. It's *This Is Judy Woodruff at the White House*. When it came out, the picture they put on the cover, the dust jacket of the book, was my White House press pass, because it was all about being at the White House. Well, it turns out there is a law against reproducing the press pass, and the Secret Service literally came and impounded the covers of the book. They went into the plant where the books were printed and took out all the covers. They went to bookstores and pulled them out. The cover became a collector's item, because the Secret Service took them and shredded them or something. We had to quickly come up with another cover.

QUESTION: *It seems to me that people are not taught the value of information itself. Who should do that? Should journalists be in charge of doing that?*

JUDY WOODRUFF: I think that's a big question. I think that has to do with everything from families to our education system to public schools to our great universities, like Notre Dame, and the news media in this country. All of it is like a big stew. It's all mixed together, and somehow people, wherever they come from, have a different idea, as you put it, of the value of information.

I would hope that as we pay attention to the world we live in that more and more of us see that we can't ignore what's going on in the world around us. I mean, certainly since 9/11 it's critical. We went through a period in this country when foreign news—international news—was in a decline. The television networks were doing public opinion polls, and the answers they were getting back to the question "What are you interested in?" were, "I'm interested in the economy, I'm interested in education and what's going on in my neighborhood." Foreign news was down at the bottom, and that was the reason that many news bureaus were closed for the television networks and then ultimately for newspapers as well.

I would hope that we now see the importance of knowing the world around us, because for all the reasons that you're all very well aware of, the United States is far more interconnected to the rest of the world than we've ever been.

But that's only one part of the story. There are important stories right in our own neighborhoods and in our own communities that I believe too often are not being covered by our own local television and radio stations and newspapers. There is more formula coverage that I see coming out of many local television stations, where they have so-called show doctors come in, consultants, who might say, "Emphasize traffic accidents and crime, and maybe you can squeeze in a minute or so about what happened at city hall or what happened in the school system." You've heard the phrase, "If it bleeds, it leads." Is that really a formula for informing the public?

I think we are so fortunate to live in one of the freest countries in the world when it comes to the information we can get. But many people don't take advantage of that. We have the opportunity to vote, and only about half of us who are eligible go to the polls. Some of the responsibility for this is on citizens themselves. People have to want to go get information. They have to buy a newspaper, go to the Web, read the Indianapolis newspaper Web site, read the *Chicago Tribune* Web site, and so on. People do that, but not enough.

QUESTION: *What will the three leading issues be in the upcoming presidential election of 2008, and which party will have the advantage on each of those three issues?*

JUDY WOODRUFF: I think the war in Iraq is far and away the main issue. It may be number one, number two, and number three unless there is some resolution or some dramatic change in the war. I think that all of the candidates know that. That's why they are struggling mightily to come up with the right position. Some of them have a position. Barack Obama likes to point out that he was against the war before it started, and you have gradation of opinion all the way to the other end, with John McCain lashing himself to the Bush administration's position on the war.

Beyond that, I would say immigration is going to be an issue in the minds of many people. There is no clear sign to me right now that any action is going to come out of Congress on that because the parties are so divided. The Republican Party is very divided, but so are the Democrats.

I think the issue that should be discussed, and I'm not sure it will be, is health care. I think it's a crisis in this country; it's been ignored for way too long since the early days of the Clinton administration, when President and Mrs. Clinton made a flawed proposal. They hadn't put it together in the most politically smart way, but it was an attempt that could have provided a stepping-off point to come up with a solution, and ever since then health care has been seen as practically the third rail.

QUESTION: *What about global warming?*

JUDY WOODRUFF: I think the environment and climate change or global warming is an issue, but I don't know that it's going to be in the top three. I think for some people it's going to be very important. It's like so many other things. You hear about how people vote their pocketbook. If people have lost their jobs or are in danger of losing their jobs, they're going to vote the economy.

If they see a tangible change, something tangible happening in the environment that worries them, that they think is going to affect their lives, then they're going to vote that, and you've got very different opinions on that in this country. You've got the auto industry in the Detroit area very much worried about these new regulations that some folks, both Democrats and Republicans, are trying to push through—fuel efficiency standards, for example. So I think there will be some version of that that will be debated. I think that all of these things will be discussed. But I do think the war in Iraq will be number one, far and away.

QUESTION: *When you have an opinion on an issue and you're trying to do a down-the-middle show, like* Inside Politics *or* The NewsHour, *how do you make yourself seem as fair and balanced as you possibly can be?*

JUDY WOODRUFF: I've been covering politics and covering the news for so long, I've developed what I think is an ingrained ability to keep my views to myself. I don't believe, by the way, in any such thing as objectivity. You can't have pure objectivity. Journalists are people; we're human beings; we have opinions, so the best we can do is try to be fair and learn to keep our views to ourselves and really work hard to do that.

If I sense in myself that I have a view, I bend over backward to make sure that I'm asking questions of both sides. But I do think that after time you develop an ability to keep it under wraps.

Almost every time I go out and speak in public, people want to know if the press is biased. Sure, there are reporters who have opinions, and some of them have stepped over the line, and some of them have influenced coverage in ways that they shouldn't have. But, by and large, the reporters I know for the mainstream media, the national newspapers, television, certainly at *The NewsHour* and when I was at CNN, kept their opinions to themselves. You just learn how to do it.

QUESTION: *It seems that it's more difficult to have a successful career in journalism. What advice would you give to students who want to be journalists?*

JUDY WOODRUFF: I want to tell you that if you think you want to be a journalist, you can be a journalist. Whatever you have set your sights on, whether it's working for a newspaper, for television, for the Internet, for radio, if you want it, go after it. Even if it means creating your own news organization—and, by the way, your generation is doing that. You're much more entrepreneurial than any generation that I'm aware of. That's what we found in our reporting last year.

Taking everything I've said—and I meant everything I've said—these are tough times for the mainstream media, who've been around a long time, but we're evolving. This is a time of change. Some of what we have today will survive, some of it won't, but something else will come along. And when I say good content will be needed, there will be an audience and an appetite for that. You can be part of creating that good content, whether it's a newspaper you publish or online.

I wouldn't take no for an answer. When I went into the business, people said, "You've never taken a course in journalism," "You've never written for a school paper," and I hadn't. But I had decided I was interested in politics, and I really wanted to find out what it was like to cover politics, and so I tagged along. I was a newsroom secretary at an Atlanta television station. That was my job right out of college, and I was determined I was going to learn, and I believe you can do that, and I don't think that's wishful thinking.

If you're determined and you don't take no for an answer, you can do it, whether you end up working for a big company or a medium-size newspaper or a television or radio outlet or create your own new news organization. Your generation is going to get news differently in many respects than the way we do now. But don't be discouraged.

Thank you all so much.

Miracle of Coogan's Bluff

RED SMITH

NEW YORK HERALD TRIBUNE

OCTOBER 4, 1951

Now it is done. Now the story ends. And there is no way to tell it. The art of fiction is dead. Reality has strangled invention. Only the utterly impossible, the inexpressibly fantastic, can ever be plausible again.

Down on the green and white and earth-brown geometry of the playing field, a drunk tries to break through the ranks of ushers marshaled along the foul lines to keep profane feet off the diamond. The ushers thrust him back, and he lunges at them, struggling in the clutch of two or three men. He breaks free, and four or five tackle him. He shakes them off, bursts through the line, runs head-on into a special park cop, who brings him down with a flying tackle.

Here comes a whole platoon of ushers. They lift the man and haul him, twisting and kicking, back across the first-base line. Again he shakes loose and crashes the line. He is through. He is away, weaving out toward center field, where cheering thousands are jammed beneath the windows of the Giants' clubhouse.

At heart, our man is a Giant, too. He never gave up.

From center field comes burst upon burst of cheering. Pennants are waving, uplifted fists are brandished, hats are flying. Again and again the dark clubhouse windows blaze with the light of photographers' flash bulbs. Here comes that same drunk out of the mob, back across the green turf to the infield. Coattails flying, he runs the bases, slides into third. Nobody bothers him now.

And the story remains to be told, the story of how the Giants won the 1951 pennant in the National League. The tale of their barreling run through August and September and into October. . . . Of the final day of the season, when they won the championship and started home with it from Boston, to hear on the train how the dead, defeated Dodgers had risen from the ashes in the Philadelphia twilight. . . . Of the three-game playoff in which they won, and lost, and were losing again with one out in the ninth inning yesterday when—oh, why bother?

Maybe this is the way to tell it: Bobby Thomson, a young Scot from Staten Island, delivered a timely hit yesterday in the ninth inning of an enjoyable game of baseball before 34,320 witnesses in the Polo Grounds. . . . Or perhaps this is better:

"Well!" said Whitey Lockman, standing on second base in the second inning of yesterday's playoff game between the Giants and Dodgers.

"Ah, there," said Bobby Thomson, pulling into the same station after hitting a ball to left field. "How've you been?"

"Fancy," Lockman said, "meeting you here!"

"Ooops!" Thomson said. "Sorry."

And the Giants' first chance for a big inning against Don Newcombe disappeared as they tagged Thomson out. Up in the press section, the voice of Willie Goodrich came over the amplifiers announcing a macabre statistic: "Thomson has now hit safely in fifteen consecutive games." Just then the floodlights were turned on, enabling the Giants to see and count their runners on each base.

It wasn't funny, though, because it seemed for so long that the Giants weren't going to get another chance like the one Thomson squandered by trying to take second base with

a playmate already there. They couldn't hit Newcombe, and the Dodgers couldn't do anything wrong. Sal Maglie's most splendrous pitching would avail nothing unless New York could match the run Brooklyn had scored in the first inning.

The story was winding up, and it wasn't the happy ending that such a tale demands. Poetic justice was a phrase without meaning.

Now it was the seventh inning and Thomson was up, with runners on first and third base, none out. Pitching a shutout in Philadelphia last Saturday night, pitching again in Philadelphia on Sunday, holding the Giants scoreless this far, Newcombe had now gone twenty-one innings without allowing a run.

He threw four strikes to Thomson. Two were fouled off out of play. Then he threw a fifth. Thomson's fly scored Monte Irvin. The score was tied. It was a new ball game.

Wait a moment, though. Here's Pee Wee Reese hitting safely in the eighth. Here's Duke Snider singling Reese to third. Here's Maglie wild-pitching a run home. Here's Andy Pafko slashing a hit through Thomson for another score. Here's Billy Cox batting still another home. Where does his hit go? Where else? Through Thomson at third.

So it was the Dodgers' ball game, 4 to 1, and the Dodgers' pennant.

So all right. Better get started and beat the crowd home. That stuff in the ninth inning? That didn't mean anything.

A single by Al Dark. A single by Don Mueller. Irvin's pop-up, Lockman's one-run double. Now the corniest possible sort of Hollywood schmaltz: stretcher-bearers plodding away with an injured Mueller between them, symbolic of the Giants themselves.

There went Newcombe and here came Ralph Branca. Who's at bat? Thomson again? He beat Branca with a home run the other day. Would Charlie Dressen order him walked, putting the winning run on base, to pitch to the dead-end kids at the bottom of the batting order? No, Branca's first pitch was a called strike.

The second pitch—well, when Thomson reached first base he turned and looked toward the left-field stands. Then he started jumping straight up in the air, again and again. Then he trotted around the bases, taking his time.

Ralph Branca turned and started for the clubhouse. The number on his uniform looked huge. Thirteen.

TIM RUSSERT After several years in politics and government, Tim Russert joined NBC News in 1984 as senior vice president. He was named Washington bureau chief in 1988 and moderator of *Meet the Press* in 1991. Over the next sixteen years, Russert became the longest-serving moderator of the longest-running network program in television history, with *Meet the Press* developing into the most-quoted news broadcast in America and abroad. Winner of an Emmy Award and an Edward R. Murrow Award, he was named by *Time* magazine in 2008 as one of the most influential people in the world. Laureate of fatherhood, he was the author of *Big Russ and Me* (2004) and *Wisdom of Our Fathers* (2006). He died on June 13, 2008. He delivered this lecture on April 14, 2008.

TIM RUSSERT

When Politicians Meet the Press

The world of politics may have the Kennedys, the Bushes, and the Clintons, but we journalists can proudly lay claim to the Smiths, Red and Terry, father and son, whose clear, cogent, thoughtful, and engaging prose informed, inspired, sometimes even provoked an appreciative reader—and so too, I hope, when politicians "Meet the Press."

This is the sixtieth year of *Meet the Press*. People often ask about my favorite interview. I've read all of them or watched the video that is available, but my own personal favorite happened in the middle of a presidential campaign in May of 1992.

George Herbert Walker Bush was running for reelection. He was in second place in the polls. In third place was the presumptive Democratic nominee, William Jefferson Clinton, and leading the polls was Ross Perot.

He walked into the studios in May of 1992, sat down, and the program began. I said, "Mr. Perot, welcome to *Meet the Press*, your first appearance. You are an announced candidate for president. You have said the deficit is the most important problem confronting our nation. What is your solution?" He said, "What?"

I said, "This is the way it works. You announce you're running for president. You identify the problem, and then you offer a solution."

He said, "Now, then, if I knew you were going to ask me these trick questions, I wouldn't have come on your program."

And so our exchange began, and he was rather feisty. The program ended, and he left, and so did I.

I caught a shuttle flight from Washington to New York. The flight attendant ran down the aisle, and she said, "That interview with Ross Perot was unbelievable. What do you think of him?"

I said, "Ma'am, unlike a lot of places on talk radio or on cable news and now the Internet, I really don't offer my personal opinions. I try very hard to offer objective questioning, so that you, the viewer, the voter, can listen and come to your own judgment. But I am endlessly curious—as a viewer, as a voter, as a flight attendant, what did you think of Ross Perot?"

She paused, put her head down, looked up, and said, "He strikes me as the kind of guy who would never return his tray table to the upright position."

And so it began. *Meet the Press* started on television in 1947, co-founded by Lawrence Spivak, and, yes, a woman, Martha Rountree. I had the opportunity to meet with Mr. Spivak before he died and talked to him about *Meet the Press*, and what he saw as the mission when he started the program. He said, "It's simple. I learn as much as I can about my guests and their positions on the issues, and then I take the other side, and I do it in a persistent way, but a civil way."

I knew then that it was a mission that I wanted to accept and adopt. Now, times have changed. The candidates or politicians who come on *Meet the Press* have far more handlers and pollsters and spin doctors than they used to.

There are some legendary interviews with Senator Mike Mansfield of Montana, who became the majority leader of the Democrats in the Senate. At one particular time, the questioners actually ran out of questions because Senator Mansfield would say, "Yep," "Nope," "Maybe."

No more. I now am forced to put things on the screen. How did that happen? I will say to a guest, "I'm sorry, Congressman or Senator or Governor, but what you just said is much different from what you promised people when you were running for reelection."

"Oh, no, Tim, you're taking that out of context. You're misquoting my words."

"No, no, Senator, I have it right here."

"Tim, I'm sorry, your viewers would be very disappointed at the way you're treating me this morning."

It got to a point where one well-known congressman from Texas came on and he said, "No, you're misquoting me," and I said, "Sir, I have a press release from your office right here." His response, "Oh, I said it in writing, okay."

I realized then that precision of thought and words was necessary, and so now we show the guest's own words. Think of the vocabulary of Washington we have lived through. Tax increases became "revenue enhancement." Misleading someone became "that statement is no longer operative."

These are challenges to us, and there are vehicles or tools we can use to frame an issue for the viewer by saying, "Senator, this is exactly what you said, in your own words. Let me play the video." It's not as a form of "gotcha," but as a way to demonstrate that "says here" is an opportunity to show us your intellectual journey or, if in fact you've changed your mind, explain it to us.

I am continually surprised that more politicians do not say, "I have changed my mind. I did say that four years ago, but let me explain what I have learned since then, and why I will vote differently next week." I believe the country would salute such an opportunity to be open-minded and a willingness not to be a slave to this notion of consistency.

I also had the opportunity to interview the philosopher-king of the English language, my boyhood idol, Yogi Berra. He had written a book on baseball and on the things that he had said. So my first question is, "Yogi, did you really say the things they say you said?"

We all know the most obvious ones—"When you come to a fork in the road, take it," or "No one goes to that restaurant anymore because it's too crowded."

So I asked his son, Larry, Jr., "Is this real? I need to know in terms of preparation for my interview." He said ask him about the pizzeria.

I said, "Yogi, I am told you went into a pizzeria and ordered a mushroom and pepperoni pizza." The waiter said, "Would you like that cut in six or eight slices?" Whereupon Yogi said, "Six. I can't eat eight." A precision of language, yes, but a logic the Holy Cross fathers would, I think, find lacking.

Much has changed in the sixty years of *Meet the Press* or the twenty-five years since James Reston of the *New York Times* gave the first Red Smith Lecture in Journalism here at Notre Dame. Ninety percent of us no longer watch the evening news at 6:30. Back then it was Uncle Walter, Walter Cronkite, or Huntley–Brinkley, Chet and David, and yet I am convinced that viewers are now getting more information.

C-SPAN is different from *Larry King Live*. The information spectrum is broad and vast. There are blogs on the left, blogs on the right, and yet they're different from the editorial pages of the *New York Times* or the *Wall Street Journal* in terms of their tone and many times their civility. But, I believe, there is still a deep and abiding recognition in the value of the so-called mainstream media.

It's not enough to simply confirm your political views by only watching or accessing outlets that reinforce your views and do not challenge them. That is what I believe is a simple but important premise. Why?

Because all my discussions with presidents, both while in office and after they left, and their advisers, while in office and after they left, and in my reading of history, particularly presidential history, I am ever more convinced that a leader cannot make tough decisions unless he or she is asked tough questions. It is the only vehicle that brings them to closure, that forces any sense of intellectual rigor, that forces them to find a way to reconcile the political advice or the political pressures brought to bear.

It will not be enough in a democratic society to simply have those on the left or right who are the pamphleteers and unwilling to challenge the views of people they support. Tough questions need not be the loudest or the most sensational or the most theatrical, but rather probing and, hopefully, incisive.

A case in point is the war in Iraq. There's been much discussion about the lead-up to the war and whether the appropriate questions were asked of our leaders.

I've had the opportunity to go back and read all the transcripts of the interviews on *Meet the Press* and many of the other programs. It is interesting to note that in October of 2002, when the vote was cast to authorize President Bush to go to war with Iraq, 80 percent of the American people supported that effort; two-thirds of both houses of Congress voted in favor of that resolution. Why?

There was a consensus that Saddam Hussein had weapons of mass destruction, and that was not only put forward by George Bush, Dick Cheney, Condoleezza Rice, Donald Rumsfeld, and Colin Powell, but it was also accepted and adopted by Bill Clinton, Hillary Clinton, John Kerry, Chris Dodd, Joe Biden, and practically the entire leadership of the Democratic Party.

We now have learned there was a National Intelligence Estimate that was made available to members of Congress that contains some caveats, particularly from the State Department and some from the Energy Department, which questioned whether or not the case was a slam dunk—in George Tenet's phrase—that Saddam had weapons of mass destruction. But that document was classified and not shared with the public or the press.

During the lead-up to the war, I thought it was imperative to ask our guests to explain as clearly as they could their judgments in wanting to go to war with Iraq. The Sunday before the war began, Vice President Cheney came on *Meet the Press*, and there were a variety of assumptions that he was laying out.

The first was that we would be greeted as liberators, a phrase that became infamous. At that time, I said, "Mr. Vice President, what if you're wrong?" I asked about General Eric Shinseki, the Army chief of staff, who said it would take several hundred thousand troops to maintain security in Iraq. He said, "I disagree; that is an overstatement."

I asked about the cost of the war, then estimated to be about $100 billion. He said that would not be the case, that oil revenues would be available to pay for a significant part and cost of the war. Lastly, I asked about the Shiites, the Sunnis, and the Kurds—and whether they would be able to come together in a democracy. And he said of all the places in the world facing a similar situation, he was convinced that Iraq was uniquely situated to do this.

At that time, there were no right or wrong answers. In hindsight, many people say, "Why didn't we say, 'You are wrong, Mr. Vice President'? Why didn't you challenge him and say, 'Of course we're not going to be greeted as liberators'?" Why?

Because that's not my job. As a member of the mainstream media, as the moderator of *Meet the Press*, my job is to find out, to draw from my guests their thinking: What are we doing about Iraq and why?

Liberators, the size of the force, the cost of war, whether or not there would be ethnic reconciliation or strife. Those were the issues then. E. J. Dionne, Jr., of the *Washington Post* now says that this exchange is probably the most revealing document that exists about the mind-set of the Bush administration in going to war. The easy thing for me to do at that time would have been to be bombastic and theatrical and say, "What are you doing? Why are you doing this to our nation?"

Again, it is the line that I think is so important to observe for those of us who are in the mainstream media. We need to do as much preparation as possible in order to ask challenging questions, so that we can have an opportunity to go back and make a judgment as to whether the judgments of our leaders, our policy makers, were accurate.

You can raise questions as to whether or not the Democratic Party should have been more in opposition, but that's a political question and not a journalistic one. I had people in opposition to the war on *Meet the Press*. They were not the leaders of the Democratic Party, because they had chosen to support the war.

This is the first time since 1952 that an incumbent president or vice president will not lead the ticket of one of the major parties in a general election. It's the first time in eighty years that an incumbent president or vice president is not seeking to lead one of those tickets. That's why there were so many candidates running. That's why there is such intense interest in this race, and it is only intensified by the fact that there is an opportunity for the nation to elect its first woman or its first African American as president.

But it is not enough to simply cover the history or cover the drama or, I dare say, cover the faux pas, although they are a necessary part and ingredient of our coverage, because it gives us an insight into the way a candidate reacts and withstands pressure and adversity.

I do believe, however, that issues in 2008 are so important to cover, just as they were leading up to the war in Iraq, and they are enormously significant as we sit here tonight. Think about the big differences on the big issues that we in the mainstream media have a firm obligation to cover.

Take the war in Iraq. John McCain says that we will stay until we achieve victory or success, and we will have a presence, perhaps diplomatic, but a presence in Iraq for fifty to one hundred years. Barack Obama and Hillary Clinton say that we must get out by calendar year 2009 in a significant way and done in an orderly way, but in an emphatic way.

Both of those candidates must be asked, "What happens if a full-scale civil war erupts, and there is a complete breakdown in Iraq with significant bloodshed and atrocities? Would you then maintain the right to reinsert American troops?"

Or, to John McCain, we need to know, "How long will you wait for victory and success, and how do you define victory and success?"

There is no right or wrong answer. The question may be even more important than the answer, but it must be asked, so that you the voter, you the viewer, have an understanding as to what is at stake in this election.

In my dad's words, you want to be able to take the measure of the candidates, to size them up, and then come to some conclusion, some judgment, as to whether or not you want to entrust them with the enormous power of sitting in the Oval Office and making a judgment about war and peace.

There's the issue of health care—over 45 million people without it today. How do we get health care to our people so as to avoid the enormously difficult and, dare I say, expensive proposition for tens of millions of Americans of using emergency rooms as the health care provider of first resort?

Immigration—15 million immigrants are here illegally. What happens? What should be their status? Should they be able to stay, and what about their children who were born here and who are American citizens? Would we break up or separate families? What do we do? These are questions that demand answers.

Or take energy independence, where a nation is so concerned about a war on terror and our national security—and justifiably so in light of what happened to us at 8:46 A.M. on September 11, 2001—and yet reliant on oil from Saudi Arabia, Venezuela, Iran, and Iraq. We all know what could happen overnight. We all know that Brazil decided to fuel its entire automobile fleet on sugar cane because they were concerned about reliance on imported oil.

We are the United States of America, and we must meet and talk about this challenge and what role alternative energy sources would play in that, not just wind and solar, but what about coal? What about nuclear? France, a nation that is perceived as liberal and progressive in its outlook, is getting around 80 percent of its power from nuclear. Is that applicable to our nation?

These are questions that I think define this race. Take Social Security and Medicare. Forty million of us now receive those programs. The baby boom generation is getting old and reluctantly admitting it, but there will be 80 million of us in the next fifteen years. Forty million to 80 million on Social Security and Medicare.

When Franklin Roosevelt started Social Security, he was a genius. Why? He set the age of eligibility at sixty-five. Why? That was life expectancy then. So you made it to the program for a month or two—and thank you very much for applying.

But now life expectancy is seventy-eight, seventy-nine, eighty years old. Double the number of people on Social Security, and they'll be there for fifteen years, and I've asked each of these candidates, "What are you going do? How do we deal with that program now, so that people can plan for the next fifteen years?" It was a Democratic president, Bill Clinton, at Georgetown University in 1998, who said if we do nothing, we will have to double the payroll tax or reduce benefits by a third.

Both options are unacceptable, both to politicians and to the body politic. But there are a whole variety of other measures that can be taken. Democrats, Republicans, liberals, and conservatives all know it, but they are reluctant to talk about it because they are afraid of being punished by the voters, and many journalists are reluctant to ask it because the subject "makes the eyes glaze over."

They asked Willie Sutton why he robbed banks. He said, "Because that's where the money is." There is no possible way that we can arrive at a balanced budget in Washington without dealing with the problems of Social Security and Medicare, and everyone knows it.

How do you prepare for this presidential race as a journalist or as moderator of *Meet the Press*? It is essential that I do what I didn't do when I was in college. I had been taught that if I would read my lesson before class, show up at class on time or perhaps early, get a good seat, pay close attention, take copious notes, review my notes after class, the exam would be easy. I know they were right. I did not do it.

But it is what I do now each and every day. Newspapers are central to what I do, another form of mainstream media. They are invaluable in the work product because of the number of people gathering the news and the resources they generally have. I read the *New York Times* and the *Washington Times*. I read *The New Republic* and *The National Review*. I read *The Nation* and *Human Events*.

I read left, right, and center. Many of my friends say that I now have confused myself, and they might be right. But I think it is imperative for an independent journalist, someone who is trying to ascertain to the very best of his or her ability what is the truth of the candidates' positions. What is their consistency? What is their intellectual grasp and understanding of the issues confronting us?

We need to accept another premise, and that is neither party nor any ideology has a monopoly on good ideas or the truth. It is essential that we come to grips with that, whether the president is Ronald Reagan or Bill Clinton or John McCain or Hillary Clinton or Barack Obama. Our mission does not change.

I spoke to David Brinkley, an icon on Sunday morning public affairs television for some two decades before I took over on *Meet the Press*. I said, "David, how do you take everything you learn in the course of a week and distill it into one hour on a Sunday morning?" He said, "It's impossible. You have to understand the limits of your medium, but recognize that most interviews on the weekday morning shows are six or seven minutes and on the cable news shows perhaps five or six minutes. So you have an oasis when we think of an hour on Sunday morning. But always understand the limits."

You are introducing subjects to people or presenting candidates or governors or senators or policy makers in the hope that people will become more interested and more curious and want to know more about them and their positions on the issues. And this is where the Internet has been a blessing, because we can now link on our own Web site on *Meet the Press* to all the various writings and position papers of the candidates that appear on *Meet the Press*.

But Brinkley went on, "Recognize that there are limits and never forget it." I said, "Well, give me an example, David." He said, "All right, fine. If Moses came down from the mountaintop with the Ten Commandments today, how would television news cover that?"

I said, "I don't know."

He said, "Moses came down from the mountaintop today with the Ten Commandments. Here's Sam Donaldson with the three most important."

I understand the limits of our profession, but it does not in any way deter us from trying to do our level best to draw out each and every politician or policy maker so that you, the viewer and the voter, can make an intelligent decision.

The criticism of the mainstream media is heated and many times warranted and will only increase in the future. But it should not in any way be suggested that therefore the mainstream media are irrelevant or should not exist. We are the equivalent of a referee, and the pamphleteers on the left and right are working us for a call. If they challenge our reports or challenge our analysis, they're hoping the next one goes their way.

I do not see any of these outlets or parts of the information spectrum as competitors. I believe they complement what we do. I am absolutely overjoyed that young people are watching Stephen Colbert or Jon Stewart, programs that I've had an opportunity to go on.

If people who would not be watching *Meet the Press* or reading the *New York Times* are instead deciding they want to engage in a political dialogue or conversation at 11:00 or 11:30 at night, I think that's constructive. I also have a deep enough appreciation and understanding of life and demographics that a Colbert or Stewart viewer today will be a *Meet the Press* viewer with a baby on his or her lap ten years from now.

It is something I believe is imperative, that all journalists understand that it is not in our interest to be critical of one another's work simply for competitive reasons. If someone from ABC or CBS has an interview with the president or the presidential candidates and does a good job, it is imperative that those of us in the same profession applaud and salute that, and not to deride it out of competitive jealousy. It is essential that the politicians understand and the pamphleteers understand that we hold our mission, protected by the First Amendment, as near and dear as they hold their mission to elect their candidate.

People often ask how difficult all this is. Compared to walking backwards in the snow and the wind to grammar school when I was in south Buffalo, this is easy. I often think about the lessons I learned growing up with my dad, my mom, and my three sisters.

I lost my mom a few years ago, but my dad and three sisters are still here. They are to me the cheapest and most accurate focus group a journalist could have because their thinking is undiluted by official Washington. They look at things from a very commonsense perspective and are very willing to share their candor with me.

My dad is someone who is extraordinary in my life. He went to war when he was just eighteen years old, World War II, and was terribly hurt when his B-24 Liberator crashed. He spent six months in a military hospital, and then he came home and met my mom and started a second mission— and that was to raise and educate their four kids.

My dad worked two full-time jobs for thirty years as a sanitation man and as a truck driver for the *Buffalo News*. He introduced me to a newspaper at the youngest of all ages. My memory of my dad, taking just an hour break between his jobs, is him sitting in his chair reading a newspaper cover to cover.

And my mom would bring us to the kitchen table to do our homework. We never had play days back then. We would go out in the street and play until 4:45, and then we knew we had to be home, and we had to do our homework while she cooked supper.

We couldn't trade our pencil for a fork until she had signed our homework every night, underscoring the emphasis she placed on scholarship and achievement and finishing our assignments.

All those lessons that are so central to what I do today were reinforced at the earliest ages in school, and so when a politician gets to "Meet the Press," he is also meeting Sister Mary Lucille, who summoned me to the front of the room in seventh grade with one of these suggestions: "Timothy, we need to find an alternative vehicle to channel your excessive energy."

So she started a school newspaper and made me the editor and the chief writer and the stapler and the collator and the mimeographer. But I fell in love with it, and I became a much better student because of it, and when President Kennedy was assassinated we sent off a special edition to Washington and received a standard reply, I'm sure, from President Johnson, Jacqueline Kennedy, and Robert Kennedy, which I still have today.

It was for me the first time there was a nexus between the written word of a little boy from Buffalo and official Washington, and because of my work on that paper, I was awarded a scholarship to Canisius High School, a Jesuit high school, where I encountered the likes of Father John Sturm, the prefect of discipline, and when you "Meet the Press," you are also meeting Father Sturm, because he threw me against the lockers for some perceived indiscretion my first few days at class. I said, "Father, please, I'm new here. I'm still trying to master all the various requirements of a Canisius student. Don't you have any mercy?" He said, "Russert, mercy's for God. I deliver justice."

And so the creativity is Sister Lucille, the accountability is Father Sturm, the hard work and the discipline are instilled by Mom and Dad.

I have no doubt that the SAT scores of the incoming class at Notre Dame and probably most people in this room are far beyond my reach, but the one thing that I do know is that the preparation that is necessary, and that we are all capable of, is the absolutely true essential to being a good journalist, particularly when a politician is going to "Meet the Press."

I want to know more about issues than they do, so if they attempt to suggest to the viewer, the voter, that there's an easy path or a way that doesn't quite add up or something that sounds so easy and convenient and simplistic because it is, I'm in a position to call them out and try to bring them back to a point where they're giving an honest answer to an honest question.

As long as I have a microphone, I will endeavor to do that—to question our leaders aggressively and persistently but always in a civil tone, to try to explain our politics and policy in a meaningful, understandable, and, I hope, even an interesting way.

I believe that is the ultimate affirmation of the legacy of Red Smith, and I also believe an affirmation of the values of this wonderful place that we call Notre Dame.

Thank you.

Writing Less— and Better?

RED SMITH

NEW YORK HERALD TRIBUNE

JANUARY 11, 1982

U p to now, the pieces under my byline have run on Sunday, Monday, Wednesday, and Friday. Starting this week, it will be Sunday, Monday, and Thursday—three columns instead of four. We shall have to wait and see whether the quality improves.

Visiting our freshman daughter (freshwoman or freshperson would be preferred by feminists, though heaven knows she was fresh), we sat chatting with perhaps a dozen of her classmates. Somehow my job got into the discussion. A lovely blonde was appalled.

"A theme a day!" she murmured.

The figure was not altogether accurate. At the time it was six themes a week. It had been seven, and when it dropped to six that looked like the roller coaster's end. However, it finally went to five, to three, and back to four, where it has remained for years.

First time I ever encountered John S. Knight, the publisher, we were bellying up to Marje Everett's bar at Arlington Park. He did not acknowledge the introduction. Instead, he said, "Nobody can write six good columns a week. Why don't you write three? Want me to fix it up?"

"Look, Mr Knight," I said. "Suppose I wrote three stinkers. I wouldn't have the rest of the week to recover." One of the beauties of this job is that there's always tomorrow. Tomorrow things will be better.

Now that the quota is back to three, will things be better day after tomorrow?

The comely college freshman wasn't told of the years when a daily column meant seven a week. Between those jousts with the mother tongue, there was always a fight or football match or ball game or horse race that had to be covered after the column was done. I loved it.

The seven-a-week routine was in Philadelphia, which reminds me of the late heavyweight champion, Sonny Liston. Before his second bout with Muhammad Ali was run out of Boston, Liston trained in a hotel in Dedham.

I was chatting about old Philadelphia days with the trainer,

Willie Reddish, remembered from his time as a heavyweight boxer in Philadelphia.

"Oh," Willie said apropos of some event in the past, "were you there then?"

"Willie," I said, "I did ten years hard in Philadelphia."

There had been no sign that Liston was listening, but at this he swung around. "Hard?" he said. "No good time?"

From that moment on, Sonny and I were buddies, though it wasn't easy accepting him as a sterling citizen of lofty moral standards.

On this job two questions are inevitably asked: "Of all those you have met, who was the best athlete?" and "Which one did you like best?"

Both questions are unanswerable, but on either count Bill Shoemaker, the jockey, would have to stand high.

This little guy weighed 96 pounds as an apprentice rider thirty-two years ago. He still weighs 96 pounds, and he will beat your pants off at golf, tennis, and any other game where you're foolish enough to challenge him.

There were, of course, many others, not necessarily great. Indeed, there was a longish period when my rapport with some who were less than great made me nervous. Maybe I was stuck on bad ballplayers. I told myself not to worry.

Someday there would be another Joe DiMaggio.

ACKNOWLEDGMENTS

A book with many authors is a work of many kindnesses. Red Smith Lecturers are not only invited to deliver a public talk at the University of Notre Dame but also asked to shape their spoken words for a wider reading audience. We're sincerely grateful that some of America's busiest people agreed to participate in this series.

For the first dozen years, the sponsor of the Red Smith Lecture was the Coca-Cola Company. Several executives were involved in guiding the project; however, Donald R. Keough, president and chief operating officer at Coca-Cola from 1981 to 1993, deserves special recognition and thanks. Longtime chairman of Notre Dame's Board of Trustees, he constantly sees new possibilities to improve the university—and he then acts to make them realities.

Since 1998, John and Susan McMeel and Universal Press Syndicate (now Universal Uclick) have generously supported the Smith Lectureship. John McMeel, a 1957 graduate of Notre Dame, is chairman of Andrews McMeel Universal, the parent company of Universal Uclick and Andrews McMeel Publishing. In addition to this lecture series, John and Susan are making certain the written word flourishes in perpetuity at Notre Dame through their endowment of the McMeel Family Chair in Shakespeare Studies. Literate expression has neither better nor more beneficent friends.

Initiator of the Red Smith Writing Scholarship at Notre Dame and colleague in creating and sustaining this lecture series, Terence Smith has done as much as any son could do to honor a father. A 1960 alumnus of Notre Dame and an award-winning journalist for the *New York Times*, CBS News, and *The NewsHour with Jim Lehrer*, he has spoken movingly about Red Smith at several of the lectures. The prologue he wrote for this book is yet another substantive and much-appreciated contribution.

As Notre Dame's president, Rev. Theodore M. Hesburgh, C.S.C., conferred an honorary doctorate on Red Smith in 1968, and fifteen years later he spoke at the first Smith Lecture to inaugurate the series. A frequent participant in activities related to this lectureship, he also took a personal interest in the development of the Smith Writing Scholarship as it came into being. Dedicating this book to Father Hesburgh is a small way of thanking him for all that he's done to advance the study of journalism, writing, and every other subject at Notre Dame since 1952.

At the beginning of this project, Professor Donald P. Costello, the chairman of the Department of American Studies at Notre Dame, and Roger O. Valdiserri, the university's sports information director, proved invaluable for the guidance they provided a callow faculty member with limited knowledge of how Notre Dame and the wider world operate. Their involvement and that of Robert L. Dilenschneider helped establish the foundation for the lecture series at a critical time in its history, and Mr. Dilenschneider continued to offer wise counsel for a quarter century, despite his obligations with the Dilenschneider Group in New York City and his own career as a respected and prolific author.

George Rugg, the curator of the Red Smith Collection in the Department of Special Collections at Notre Dame's Hesburgh Library, answered many questions and located needed materials as this book's introduction was being written. As he collected requested documents, he also revealed that Smith didn't save several years' worth of newspaper columns and most of his magazine articles. It seems that the careful craftsman was more focused on the next assignment than on cataloging what he'd already composed.

However, Smith's work appears in many book-length collections, including nine volumes exclusively devoted to his journalism. Ira Berkow's *Red: A Biography of Red Smith* (1986) is invaluable in recounting "the life and times of a great American writer," as the dust-jacket phrase under the title promises.

Cheryl Reed worked her word-processing magic to get the lectures and articles ready for the publisher. Matt Storin, former editor of the *Boston Globe* and currently a faculty member in the John W. Gallivan Program in Journalism, Ethics & Democracy at Notre Dame, offered shrewd suggestions for the introduction and for the volume as a whole. In addition, Indiana's most revered sportswriter, Bob Hammel, provided several insights on his craft that greatly helped in writing the introduction.

Throughout the first twenty-five years of the Smith Lecture series, Judy and Mike Schmuhl have contributed, as only they can, to making academic and writing life more delightfully possible. This book, too, owes much to their kindness and love.